# Vathek &
# The Escape from Time

## Bicentenary Revaluations

William Beckford aged twenty-one, by George Romney.
Reproduced by courtesy of the National Trust.

# Vathek &
# The Escape from Time

## Bicentenary Revaluations

edited by
**KENNETH W. GRAHAM**

**AMS PRESS**
**NEW YORK**

Library of Congress Cataloging-in-Publication Data


Vathek and the escape from time : bicentenary revaluations / edited by
Kenneth W. Graham.
          p.      cm. -- (AMS studies in the eighteenth century : no. 15)
    Bibliography:  p.
    Includes index.
    ISBN 0-404-63515-6
    1.  Beckford, William, 1760-1844.  Vathek.  2. Time in literature.
I. Graham, Kenneth W. (Kenneth Wayne)  II.  Series.
PQ1957.B39V338    1990
843'.5--dc19                                                                89-6471
                                                                              CIP

All AMS books are printed on acid-free paper that meets the
guidelines for performance and durability of the Committee on
Production Guidelines for Book Longevity of the Council on
Library Resources.

AMS PRESS
56 East 13th Street
New York, N.Y. 10003, U.S.A.

Manufactured in the United States of America

This volume is dedicated in grateful
memory to two Beckfordians

André Parreaux
1906 – 1979

Boyd Alexander
1913 – 1980

AMS Studies in the
Eighteenth Century, No. 15
ISSN: 0196-6561

*Other titles in this series:*

1. Paul J. Korshin, ed. *Proceedings of the Modern Language Association Neoclassicism Conferences, 1967—1968.* 1970.

2. Francesco Cordasco. *Tobias George Smollett: A Bibliographical Guide.* 1978.

3. Paula R. Backscheider, ed. *Probability, Time, and Space in Eighteenth-Century Literature.* 1979.

4. Ruth Perry. *Women, Letters, and the Novel.* 1980.

5. Paul J. Korshin, ed. *The American Revolution and Eighteenth-Century Culture.* 1985.

6. G.S. Rousseau, ed. *The Letters and Papers of Sir John Hill, 1714—1775.* 1982.

7. Paula R. Backscheider. *A Being More Intense: A Study of the Prose Works of Bunyan, Swift, and Defoe.* 1984.

8. Christopher Fox, ed. *Psychology and Literature in the Eighteenth Century.* 1988.

9. John F. Sena. *The Best-Natured Man: Sir Samuel Garth, Physician and Poet.* 1986.

10. Robert A. Erickson. *Mother Midnight: Birth, Sex, and Fate in the Eighteenth-Century Novel—Defoe, Richardson and Sterne.* 1986.

13. Richard J. Dircks, ed. *The Letters of Richard Cumberland.* 1988.

14. John Irwin Fischer et al., eds. *Swift and His Contexts.* 1989.

# Contents

**INFLUENCES**

# ACKNOWLEDGMENTS

Several of these essays developed from papers presented at the Conference of the American Society for Eighteenth-Century Studies held in Williamsburg, Virginia in 1986 and in the *Vathek* Round Table of the meeting of the International Society for Eighteenth-Century studies held in Budapest in 1987. The editors and contributors are grateful to the organizers of those conferences. We are particularly grateful to Domokos Kosary and the organizing committee of the Budapest conference for agreeing to devote a Round Table to as singular and exotic a subject as Beckford's *Vathek*. Their imaginative leadership permitted an exciting and fruitful meeting of Beckfordians from at least seven different countries.

This project received financial support from the Social Sciences and Humanities Research Council of Canada. Assisting in various computer processes were the patient, cooperative and invaluable secretarial staff of the Department of English at the University of Guelph, Jan Walker, Gail McGinnis, and Olga Griffin.

For the frontispiece, Romney's portrait of a confident William Beckford at the age of 21, I would like to thank the National Trust.

The editor and publishers wish also to thank the following, who have kindly given permission for the use of previously published material:

Orbis Litterarum: *International Review of Literary Studies* for authority to publish "*Vathek;* The Inversion of Romance" by Randall Craig,

Wissenschaftliche Buchgesellschaft in Darmstadt for permission to publish a translation of chapter 2.2.2 of Jürgen Klein's *Der gotische Roman und die Ästhetic des Bösen*,

*Research Studies* for permission to publish "*Vathek*, Heaven and Hell" by Peter Hyland.

# CONTRIBUTORS

**MICHEL BARIDON** has published *Gibbon et le Mythe de Rome*, a study of the genesis of the *Decline and Fall* (Paris, 1977) and articles on Defoe, Johnson, Montesquieu, the Gothic imagination, and the English garden. He is now working on a book, *l'Esthétique de la Sensibilité*, exploring the relation of the scientific movement to artistic and literary creation.

**RANDALL CRAIG** has published a number of articles on British fiction and the theory of the novel. His book, *The Tragicomic Novel: Studies in a Fictional Mode from Meredith to Joyce* is forthcoming from the University of Delaware Press.

**BRIAN FOTHERGILL** is the author of *Beckford of Fonthill* (1979) and has written other biographical studies of eighteenth-century figures including Sir William Hamilton, the Earl-Bishop of Derry, and Horace Walpole. He is Vice-President and Chairman of Council of the Royal Society of Literature and a Fellow of the Society of Antiquaries of London.

**FREDERICK S. FRANK** has published several books and articles on Gothic fiction and Gothic bibliographical study. Among these are: "The Gothic Romance: 1762–1824" in *Horror Literature: A Core Collection and Reference Guide* (1981); *Guide to the Gothic* (1984); *The First Gothics: A Critical Guide to the English Gothic Novel* (1987); *Gothic Fiction: A Master list of Twentieth-Century Criticism and Research* (1988); *and Montague Summers: A Bibliographical*

*Portrait* (1988).

**R. B. GILL** has published articles on Renaissance and eighteenth-century satire, as well as on the theory of tragedy and comedy. His latest effort on Beckford is "The Selves of Beckford: Biography and *Vathek*," delivered at the VIIth Congress on Enlightenment in Budapest.

**KENNETH GRAHAM** has published on William Beckford, William Godwin, Ann Radcliffe, Frances Burney, and Robert Kroetsch. He is a past president of the Canadian Society for Eighteenth-Century Studies; for whom he edited volume six of *Man and Nature/L'Homme et la Nature*. He is editor of the recent collection, *Gothic Fictions: Prohibition/Transgression,* published by AMS Press.

**PETER HYLAND** has published *Disguise and Role-Playing in Ben Jonson's Drama* (1977) and edited *Discharging the Canon: Cross-Cultural Readings in Literature* (1986). His study of Shakespeare's *Troilus and Cressida* is forthcoming from Penguin.

**JÜRGEN KLEIN** has published on the history of English literature, theory of literature, aesthetics, and epistemological problems of the humanities. His books include *Der Gotische Roman und die Ästhetik des Bösen* (1975), *Byrons romantischer Nihilismus* (1979), *Theoriengeschichte als Wissenschaftskritik* (1980), *England zwischen Aufklärung und Romantik* (1983), *Radikales Denken in England: Neuzeit* (1984), *Virginia Woolf: Genie - Tragik - Emanzipation* (1984), *Beyond Hermeneutics* (1985), *Astronomie und Anthropozentrik*

(1986), *Anfänge der englischen Romantik* (1986), *Francis Bacon oder die Modernisierung Englands* (1987). He is now working on a book entitled *Englische Literatur: eine Sozialgeschichte.*

**TEMPLE J. MAYNARD** has articles published or forthcoming on William Beckford and Robert Jephson. His edition of *The Plays of Robert Jephson* was published by Garland in 1980. He is now working on a book that will comprise a critical re-evaluation of Jephson's dramatic and satiric writing.

**MARIA LAURA BETTENCOURT PIRES** has published *Walter Scott and Portuguese Romanticism* (1979), *Portugal Seen by the English* (1981), *A History of Children's Books in Portugal* (1982), and *William Beckford and Portugal* (1987) as well as essays and articles on English and American literature now forthcoming in book form.

**J. E. SVILPIS** teaches seventeenth- and eighteenth-century literature, stylistics, and popular literature. He has published on neo-Latin bibliography, Samuel Johnson, the Gothic novel, and science-fiction magazine illustration, and is currently working on eighteenth-century oriental tales and on the mad scientist in science fiction.

**DEVENDRA VARMA**'s contributions to scholarship include *The Gothic Flame, The Evergreen Tree of Diabolical Knowledge* and the life-long service of making Gothic novels available to the general reader. Frederick S. Frank's bibliography, *Guide to the Gothic*, contains 26 references to Professor Varma, a signal recognition of his impact on the field of study.

# INTRODUCTION

When Lady Margaret Beckford died on May 26th, 1786 from complications arising from the birth of her second child, it was the second of two blows that transformed her husband, William Beckford, from a creative and confident man of the world into a bitter exile. The first blow occurred in 1784, when Lord Loughborough circulated the scandal that Beckford had been caught in a homosexual relationship with the adolescent William Courtenay while Beckford and his wife were staying with the Courtenay family at Powderham Castle. When the scandal reached the newspapers, the helpless Beckford was condemned on the basis of innuendo to a social ostracism far more intense than that felt by Byron a generation later.[1]

It is not clear what future Beckford projected for himself in 1784 on the eve of the scandal. Connected by birth and marriage to the highest reaches of British political and social life, controlling two important seats and occupying a third in an unstable Parliament, Beckford could look forward to the early achievement of an initial goal of a barony. With peerage attained he could devote his considerable talents for languages and music, his creative imagination, and his majestic income founded on Jamaican sugar, to a future of his choice. Already he had given evidence of talents that pointed in directions both social and solitary. His musicianship and wit made him a lively and welcome guest in social gatherings, yet he had also demonstrated the passion and the drive to be a writer. His social standing and wealth, combined with his talents, made likely the ultimate achievement of a high post in British diplomacy. Certainly in October 1784 with a draft of *Vathek* completed and the newspapers confidently announcing his forthcoming elevation, a golden future seemed within his grasp.

The Romney portrait in the frontispiece captures the self-confidence of the twenty-one year old Beckford. The casual carelessness of his posture and the face that expresses assurance and even arrogance demonstrate the painter's insight into his subject. It is the face of a man sure of himself and confident of his future, a man who was taking control of his life and was willing to live it with a degree of audacity. Audacity was reflected in the atmospheric Christmas party that followed upon his twenty-first birthday, and in the inspiration for *Vathek* that he reported to have arisen from that party.

Lady Margaret's death closed the most fruitful period of Beckford's young life. He wrote much in the busy years leading to 1786, but his crowning achievement was *Vathek*. Between 1781 and 1786, he wrote his oriental tale in the French language, collaborated in the preparation of an English version, and initiated a larger creative concept that would have seen *Vathek* as the frame tale to a suite of four stories of evil acts and criminal passions, all set in the Orient. *Vathek* and the *Episodes* were to end together in the Hall of Eblis with the collective damnation of Vathek and his companions in evil. In 1783 he was completing the first draft of *Vathek* in French, and enjoying exciting and dangerous relationships with Louisa Beckford (the wife of his cousin Peter) and the boy William Courtenay, when he agreed to the wise wishes of his family and married Lady Margaret Gordon. He had given his draft of *Vathek* to the Reverend Samuel Henley to translate into English when the Powderham scandal drove him and his wife out of England. His letters to Henley in 1785 and 1786 show him continuing with the *Episodes*, revising Henley's translation, and making plans for the publication of a combined edition of *Vathek* and the *Episodes,* first in French and then in English. With the death of Lady Margaret he seems to have lost the will to go on with the project. The journal he kept the following year during his stay in Portugal shows that an acute and even debilitating sense of loss continued to affect him.

[T]he recollection of my agonies last year, when I lost the very Being I ever truly loved, poured in so thick upon me that the tears started in my eyes, and the swelling of my heart almost deprived me of respiration ... I think of the peaceful hours we passed together at Vevey. I know they are gone without return, and that no power can recover them.[2]

Considering that these lines were written in 1787, it is not hard to imagine how much more severely he must have felt the loss a year earlier.

While the strain of Lady Margaret's death induced debility, an independent event awakened Beckford briefly from his lassitude. It was probably early in 1786 that Henley grew aware of Beckford's design for a combined edition. One can postulate a number of factors that influenced his decision to exclude himself from participation in that design. Immediate publication would mean an immediate return on a work of three years' duration, and Henley seemed regularly short of money. Perhaps, in addition, Henley wished to sever a connection, unseemly for a clergyman, with a notorious object of scandal. In any case, he sold the rights to his translation to Joseph Johnson and its publication in June 1786 initiated the collapse of Beckford's plan for a combined edition in English but set in motion a sequence of events that would result eventually in authoritative versions of *Vathek,* in both languages published under Beckford's supervision.[3] Henley's decision to publish his translation independently and without Beckford's permission forced Beckford to rush his French manuscript into print, first at

Lausanne in an edition dated 1787 and then in a corrected version at Paris in the summer of the same year. In 1815 and 1816 Beckford had the time and inclination to thoroughly revise and publish both the French and the English versions of *Vathek*. In Beckford's lifetime the *Episodes* were never published; had it not been for the provocation of Henley's publication, perhaps Beckford would never have permitted even *Vathek* to appear. It is an irony of Beckford studies that while his love for Lady Margaret cost the world the combined version that Beckford's imagination had projected, Henley's betrayal ensured the publication of *Vathek*.

*"Vathek" and the Escape from Time* is about the past, present, and future of a literary text. The last collection of essays on Beckford came out in 1960 on the occasion of the bicentenary of Beckford's birth. Edited by F. Moussa Mahmoud and published in Cairo, *William Beckford of Fonthill 1760-1844, Bicentenary Essays* ranges widely through Beckford's experience as a traveller, builder, landscape gardener, and collector. It includes essays by the two foremost Beckfordians of the time, André Parreaux and Boyd Alexander, to whose memories the present collection of essays is dedicated.[4] Like the Mahmoud volume, this collection enjoys the breadth of perspective afforded by a multiple authorship. It offers, in addition, a unity of focus. It confronts, not Beckford generally, but his most important work, *Vathek*, a work that holds keys to most facets of Beckford's creativity.

Conceived in confidence and revised in sorrow, *Vathek* is bizarre and enigmatic; it is also probably the most influential oriental tale of the eighteenth century. The source of its *bizarrerie* may be traced to the circumstances of the generation and production of its text, the enigma it poses may be explored in the many ways it can be read; and its influence can be seen in works of art and scholarship from the eighteenth century to the present. The essays of this collection engage in their different ways these three areas of source, significance, and influence.

As appropriate to bicentenary revaluations, *Beckford's "Vathek" and the Escape from Time* is organized around the theme of *Vathek* and time. The keynote essay is Professor Temple Maynard's "The Escape from Time and the Movement Underground," which examines the importance of time and timelessness as central concepts in *Vathek* and recurring motifs in other of Beckford's works of fiction. The other essays in the volume pick up on this time motif. This introduction has recounted the events behind the preparation of *Vathek* in two languages and the separate and independent publications in 1786 and 1787. Brian Fothergill's essay relates aspects of Beckford's life and travels to the landscape and structures of *Vathek*. The essays of Devendra Varma and Janis Svilpis place *Vathek* in another aspect of the past—the oriental tradition: for Svilpis *Vathek* subverts the English oriental apologue and to Varma it echoes the doom and sensuality in the writings of the Persian Sufi poets. Michel Baridon relates *Vathek* to its own time as an *avant-garde* work: its aesthetic immoderation is a response to the most modern artistic and scientific challenges of its age.

The middle part of the volume examines *Vathek* in the eternal present of interpretation. The essays choose different ways of engaging the enigma of *Vathek*. Frederick Frank and Randall Craig explore *Vathek* in the context of romanticism—as a Gothic romance or as a subversion of traditional romantic patterns. Jürgen Klein has translated and adapted a chapter of his monumental study, *Der Gotische Roman und die Ästhetik des Bösen*, to reflect on the implications of *Vathek*'s decadent orientalism. Peter Hyland approaches the work through ideas of journey and landscape and Russell Gill through narrative technique.

The third division of the volume deals with *Vathek*'s fate as a literary text. Two essays trace influences in countries removed from Beckford's England. Professor Laura Bettencourt Pires discusses the history and influence of *Vathek* in Portugal, Beckford's spiritual homeland. My essay speculates on the impact of *Vathek* and Fonthill on America's Edgar Allen Poe. The final entry in the volume is an up-to-date checklist of modern *Vathek* scholarship by Frederick S. Frank, the foremost contemporary bibliographer of the Gothic and fantastic.

To escape from time, a work of art must challenge the conventions of its form and the ideologies of its era. *Vathek* does so in a multitude of ways: in the characters it presents, in its narrative voice, in its closure, in its orientalism, its decadence, and its *avant-gardisme*. In the terminology of Roland Barthes, *Vathek* is a *scriptible* text, productive not merely of *plaisir* but of bliss — of *jouissance*. André Gide's experience of Hogg's *Justified Sinner* echoes the response of many after reading *Vathek*: "It is long since I can remember being so taken hold of, so voluptuously tormented by any book."[5] The rich variety of perspective in this volume attests to the creative torment that *Vathek* still generates.

A new collection on Beckford is past due, and the bicentenary of *Vathek* was an appropriate occasion to gather the findings of a new generation of scholars who have fallen under the spell of Vathek's compelling eye. *Beckford's "Vathek" and the Escape from Time* reflects significant discoveries in Beckford scholarship and employs both traditional and contemporary critical approaches to deepen understanding of Beckford's narrative.

Kenneth W. Graham

REFERENCES

[1]The full story is told vividly in Brian Fothergill's *Beckford of Fonthill* (London: Faber and Faber, 1979), pp. 141–175.

[2]Boyd Alexander, ed., *The Journal of William Beckford in Portugal and Spain 1787–1788* (London: Rupert Hart-Davis, 1954), p. 227. Scattered through the journal are six other references expressing his sense of loss.

[3]Kenneth W. Graham, "*Vathek* in English and French," *Studies in Bibliography* 23 (1975), 153–166.

[4]Fatma Moussa Mahmoud, ed., *William Beckford of Fonthill 1760-1844 Bicentenary Essays* (Cairo, 1960; rpt. Kennikat Press, 1972).

[5]André Gide, Introduction to James Hogg's *The Private Memoirs and Confessions of a Justified Sinner*. (London: The Cresset Press, 1947), x.

# THE MOVEMENT UNDERGROUND AND THE ESCAPE FROM TIME IN BECKFORD'S FICTION

Temple J. Maynard

One has only to compare the tempo of a novel by Richardson with one by Fielding, or to consider the fluctuating rhythms of a narrative by Defoe, to realize that the perception of time is of major importance in the eighteenth-century novel. The world which the characters inhabit is coloured, indeed characterized, by action and movement in time. The mortal condition is a temporal progression, and man's perception of flux and decay conditions his behaviour throughout his conscious life. Naturally, this perception is reflected in literature, frequently by the depiction of states of existence where the wasting process is less apparent, is retarded, or denied. Of this nature are some myths of a golden age, some aspects of the pastoral scene, some forms of religious prose, and some depictions of paradise. In eighteenth-century England two *genres* particularly rich in the presentation of an altered temporal perception were the oriental and the gothic. In each, the reader is most obviously taken from the real world, and events occur in a temporal stream far different from that of our every day experience. In the work of William Beckford these two *genres* come together, and the result is a sharp disorientation from the normal. In Beckford's early and unfinished tale, *The Vision*,[1] and in both the frame-tale of *Vathek*[2] and in the *Episodes*,[3] the perception of time and place is largely responsible for the intense atmosphere and the curious tensions which are generated.

Because of its publishing history, *Vathek* is commonly read without the *Episodes* that were an integral part of the original conception. The reader is even less likely to compare it with the long story, *The Vision*, though that early work is closely related to *Vathek* in a number of interesting ways. When *Vathek* is read in isolation, the concern with time may seem an insignificant or accidental aspect, while the journey to the underworld may appear as no more than a superficially orientalized analogue of the Christian hell, necessitated by Beckford's apparently conventional moral ending. But when they are examined together, these works reveal a preoccupation with time and mortality. In all of them a perception of the fleeting nature of youth and love is associated with a retreat into enclosed spaces which are frequently subterranean. They thus reiterate an association found in Beckford's letters and rhapsodies from a very early date. But this linking of the descent into subterranean precincts with the indulgence of a forbidden or illicit passion is common in the oriental mode, and a glance at its incidence in that *genre* may further clarify Beckford's intent. Incidentally, similar situations occur in the gothic, though most of the more fully developed examples are subsequent to the publication of *Vathek*.[4] But especially in those oriental tales which came to England *via* France—in Galland's edition of the *Arabian Nights*, in the *Persian Tales* of Petis de la Croix, and in the effusions of T. S. Gueullette such as the *Chinese Tales*, the *Tartarian Tales*, and the *Mogul Tales*[5]—Beckford would have found stories where a descent beneath the surface of the earth was linked with an escape from mundane commitment, the indulgence of forbidden love, or an apparent stay in the flux of time.

In the *Arabian Nights* and the *Persian Tales*, the movement underground opens the way to enchanted realms where the usual constraints
of terrestrial existence may be put aside. Gardens of edenic beauty,
caves of treasure, fields of flowers, or trees of jewelled fruit attract the
sight, while entire subterranean landscapes replete with their own light
and water may welcome the intrepid adventurer or seduce the unwary.
Such a subterranean garden of jewels, complete with halls of treasure,
prefigures untold riches for Aladdin in the *Arabian Nights*,[6] while an
underground palace offers a sanctuary of love in the story of the
Second Callendar.[7] A complete landscape of this kind occurs in the
*Persian Tales* :

... arrived at the Foot of the Mountain ... I soon perceived a large Opening, the
dreadful Darkness of which was no Invitation to enter it ... I went without Hesitation ... tho' there was not a glimpse of Light to direct me; I found the Ground was
a Descent; and marching still forward for fifteen or twenty Hours, I doubted not
but I was descending to the Genies of the Earth. At last the Darkness was dissipated, and I beheld the Light of Day, which I began to think I had lost for ever.
The Light led me into a flowery Meadow, the most beautiful I ever saw. The trees
in it were loaden with the fairest fruit.[8]

Regions like this abound in the *genre*, and seem to offer security, freedom from responsibility, riches, or a time for love.[9]  They can be
treacherous, but for a time the wanderer may enjoy the delights that
are offered. However, such places belong to the genii, and a mortal is
in dangerous company in these realms, as a passage from George
Sale's Preliminary Discourse to his edition of the Koran makes clear:

The *Orientals* pretend that these Genii inhabited the world for many ages before
*Adam* was created, under the government of several successive princes, who all

bore the name of *Solomon*: but falling at length into an almost general corruption, *Eblis* was sent to drive them into a remote part of the earth there to be confined.[10]

Apparently they were not very securely confined. Throughout the oriental *genre* adventurous men descend to the regions inhabited by the genii, or stumble on their caves and palaces, some of which are near the surface and the habitations of mankind. Some of these genii are well-disposed towards men and are helpful. Others are inherently evil, and always looking for ways to do harm. The trick is to tell which kind of genie one is dealing with. Frequently they extract a severe price for their help or guidance. Nevertheless, the pangs of a hopeless passion may lead a despairing lover to hazard his present life and eternal welfare for a few hours or days of consummation.[11] But there is a sense in these tales that the asylum or the assistance received from the genii may be worth the price, however fleeting the enjoyment may be. Certainly the protagonists of Beckford's fiction are journeying down paths blazed by earlier travellers. His mages, giaours, afrits, dives and peris are variations of the genii, and can be expected to mislead mankind, even if they are not totally malicious.

The conflict between the consciousness of social responsibility and the desire to escape with a loved one inevitably suggests to Beckford a movement underground. The situation is complex. On the one hand, subterranean precincts seem to promise a secure retreat where one can escape the constraints of society for a time. On the other hand, the spartan rigor of the accommodation in some of the scenes Beckford depicts would seem to represent the price paid for such indulgence. Something must be given up for love. A dream-vision or rhapsody written by Beckford circa 1779, will illustrate the point:

I seemed stretched in a dreary cave—across which ran several bubbling streams—no termination of the Grot was visible—its roof was lost in obscurity—heaps of cocoa-nuts were piled—to all appearance around me—so immense that whole nations I think could never have consumed them ... I had not long surveyed this Realm of Darkness and silence before an Angelic Shadow issued suddenly from the depth of the cavern leading in its hand the one I love—he flew to me. I sprang forwards to catch him in my arms. Rest happy said a thrilling voice—no one shall disturb you for ages. The great power—source of all felicity—has abstracted you from both [sic] the multitude of his creatures—as examples of perpetual tenderness—and has alloted this cave—sunk deep in the center of the Earth, for your abode. Those piles of nuts are destined for your nourishment—if ye freely renounce the lustre of the Sun for each other.[12]

A diet consisting entirely of coconuts might occasion the first notable tensions in such a seclusion, but one feels that the bargain would soon seem altogether mistaken. However, just such a retreat recurs in *The Vision*, while variations on the same theme appear in the *Episodes of Vathek*. In another guise the same imagery can be found in Beckford's mature recollections of the notorious Christmas celebration at Fonthill. Reminiscing about this event, Beckford reinvokes the key elements of this topos:

Immured we were "au pied de la lettre" for three days following—doors and windows so strictly closed that neither common day light nor common place visitors could get in or even peep in—care worn visages were ordered to keep aloof ... Our société was extremely youthful and lovely to look upon ... The solid Egyptian Hall looked as if hewn out of a living rock ... an interminable stair case ... appeared as deep as the well in the pyramid ... delightful the straying about this little interior world of exclusive happiness surrounded by lovely beings ... what absolutely appeared ... a Demon Temple deep beneath the earth set apart for tremendous mysteries ... Whilst the wretched world without lay dark, and bleak, and howling, whilst the storm was raging against our massive walls ... the very air of summer seemed playing around us ... [13]

These few phrases, culled from several pages which would support the same interpretation, further illustrate the prevalence of this imagery in Beckford's thought. The exclusion of all save his youthful companions would re-inforce the concept of timelessness which is consistent with such a setting. The word "immured" which begins the preceding quotation, though it may mean "walled up," carries a common connotation of "entombed," a meaning especially fitting in this context.

As has been frequently pointed out, Beckford's sense of oppression, and the need to escape from it, led him early to the oriental tale; the long story, part of which was published by Chapman as *The Vision*, may date from as early as 1777.[14] What is especially notable about it is that the bulk of the action takes place underground. The vast majority of earlier oriental tales are set on or above the surface of the earth. From the first, Beckford's impulses led him to choose for inspiration those stories where the action takes place subterraneously. It is precisely in these stories that the tyranny of time seems most often compromised.

*The Vision*, as it stands, is patently an unfinished work. Those fragments of its continuation in rough draft which were apparently unknown to Chapman seem never to have been integrated with the rest of the tale.[15] The main body of the material as we have it is comprised of a series of enclosed gardens, caverns, grottoes and valleys through which the main character travels as he ventures further and further into a subterranean realm. Each enclosure takes the narrator further from his mundane past into a subjective and romantically realized inner realm. The reader will speedily recognize the materials from which *Vathek* was later to be cast; even the female figure is similarly named Nouronihar. His journey, and the incidental ordeals he must undergo, both purify him and make him worthy of the love of the Persian maiden. Reunited in the innermost edenic landscape, the young William and his Nouronihar take refuge from the coming season of storms in a cave. Attendant dwarfs roll a huge stone over the entrance that twelve mortals could not shift. All sound fades away. The cave is provisioned, illuminated, and they are alone. The young protagonist declares that he has all he wants: let the storms rage outside, alone with Nouronihar he asks for no more, "No! my fondest wishes never rose to such a measure of happiness!"[16] Surely, the significant fact about *The Vision* is not that it was never finished, but that it does end at just this point. The additional segments were destined never to be incorporated with this introductory material. In the light of Beckford's later writing, fiction and non-fiction, one may assert that what we are witnessing is not a mere breakdown in the narrative or a failure of inspiration. Rather, the elaborate plans for the continuation were never fully realized, and the fragment ends here, because this is precisely the point at which Beckford needed to arrive.[17] He has his main characters at a point farthest from the real world, where no power on earth can reach them, and where they are permitted to remain by some special dispensation. All the princes in *Vathek* and the *Episodes* seek just such a sanctuary, one which we may presume had a powerful appeal for the author himself.

In the frame-tale of *Vathek* the preoccupation with time and mortality, while not overtly emphasized, is prevalent. Seen in the context of Beckford's other fiction it becomes even more obvious. Time is a

major motivating force for Vathek. His hankering for the treasures of
the pre-Adamite sultans, and the gems and gold in the palace of subterranean fire, is largely due to his longing for a more lasting influence and power, for the extension of his hegemony through time. The
battle within him, such as it is, is fought between the indulgence of
immediate sensual pleasure, and an implied promise of release from
mortality.

Vathek is already "Ruler of the World," of the Moslem world at
least, and within his sphere he possesses almost unlimited power. He
can exercise his whims without regard to any retributive action. He
has inherited fabulous wealth and can afford to spend lavishly on
structures like his palaces and his tower, and the people constantly
supply more at his command. How can he desire anything that he
doesn't already possess? What is there in the treasures promised by
the Giaour more wonderful than what he already has, or could
acquire? Can we believe he would give up his considerable wealth
and his royal position for a pair of marvelous sabres and their like, or
even the carbuncle of Giamschid? He can hardly add significantly to
his vast collections nor extend much further his current enjoyment of
luxury. No, what Vathek seeks at Istakar is the eternal continuance of
his power. His goal is the extension of his influence and his mortal
existence through time which he believes could be granted by the
associates of the Giaour.

That Vathek wants more from life than other men we already
know, hence his addition of the five new wings to the palace of Alkoremi in which each of the senses may be indulged to excess. But it is
significant that the collection of rarities from every corner of the earth
could not satisfy Vathek himself who was, "of all men ... the most

curious."[18]  Vathek's wish, "to know every thing; even sciences that
did not exist,"[19] is a clue to his character. He is not content with the
lot of mortal man. But while Mahomet opines that Vathek's tower is
built, "from the insolent curiosity of penetrating the secrets of
heaven,"[20] what Vathek really seeks in the astrological studies in
which he engages on its summit is a favorable prediction of his own
future. He seeks to wrest secrets from the stars in order to control his
destiny, to avert the effects of time, and to postpone or avoid a personal mortality.

It is the antiquity of Istakar, and the legendary nature of the riches
stored up in the halls of Eblis, that wins Vathek's adherence to the
quest. In the very name of the treasures of the pre-Adamite sultans
there is an inference of longevity that could be coexistent with the
creation.[21] Vathek expects to take his place beside the pre-Adamite
kings, or even to usurp their position. The Giaour speaks to him of,
"the treasures which the stars have promised thee,"[22] and intimates
that they will be "conferred" upon him.[23]  Vathek is further intrigued
by reading in the parchment, "that is the region of wonders: there shalt
thou receive the diadem of Gian Ben Gian; the talismans of Soliman;
and the treasures of the pre-adamite sultans: there shalt thou be sol-
aced with all kinds of delight."[24]  The language is ambiguous, or
intentionally misleading, when the Giaour implies the alert corporeal
existence and consciousness of the pre-Adamite kings. He tells
Vathek, "it is there that Soliman Ben Daoud reposes, surrounded by
the talismans that control the world."[25]  Repose is unknown in these
regions, as all who come there soon learn. But Vathek could hardly
avoid accepting this picture, since it is in complete accord with leg-
ends of the early sultans, pre-Adamite and post-Adamite, which are

prevalent in the oriental *genre*, and which Beckford can suppose both Vathek and his readers will recollect.[26] Carathis also understands the situation in this way. She expects Vathek to reign in the halls of Eblis as, with a notable instance of maternal solicitude, she declares, "either I will perish, or Vathek shall enter the palace of fire. Let me expire in flames, provided he may reign on the throne of Soliman!"[27]

The means of attaining access to the palace of subterranean fire and acquiring these treasures also suggests something of their nature. They are to be won by propitiating the Giaour and the other agents of Eblis with human sacrifice. Vathek expects to ascend the throne of Soliman without a personal demise. It is the shedding of blood, the offering of human lives, that will pay for his release from mortality. The death of his victims will avert his own death. His transference to the underworld is, to that extent, successfully accomplished, though the eternity he has bought is not the expected boon. The fifty children thrust into the chasm, the immolation of countless citizens on the tower, and the burning of the mummies that are themselves representative of a battle fought against death; these are the talismans which Vathek hopes will gain for him an eternity of infernal dominion. Curiosity enters into his motivation, it is true; greed is not totally divorced from his impulse; but the vital, impelling force lies deeper than that. Vathek seeks in his way, what Gulchenrouz is given in another, the perpetuated enjoyment of a mortal, sensual existence.

The *Episodes of Vathek*, as we have them, are comprised of two complete tales and a portion of a third, though more may have been written.[28] In each, the escape from time or from social constraint is associated with the retreat into enclosed spaces. Ultimately and ironically, as is the case in the frame-tale of *Vathek*, each protagonist seeks sanctuary in the halls of Eblis, mistakenly believing that in those sub-terranean precincts he can realize his desires. Meanwhile, each charac-ter, again like Vathek, tries to ignore or deny the social mores in a series of intermediate retreats into gardens, caverns, or palaces. Each tale conveys a sense of withdrawal, often hasty and ill-considered, from duty and from life. Each story in its own way illustrates an intense and altered perception of time, leading the characters finally and precipitously to the underworld.

In the first Episode, "The Story of Prince Alasi and the Princess Firouzkah," the Prince accepts with reluctance the tasks of a ruler. But as he tells his own tale he emphasizes that he did not abuse his position:

I fulfilled all my duties exactly, and only from time to time indulged in the delights of solitude. A tent, disposed after the Persian manner, and situated in a dense forest, was the place where I spent these moments of retirement, moments that always seemed to pass too quickly.[29]

But Alasi's exact adherence to duty doesn't survive the arrival of Firouz/Firouzkah, the princess masquerading as a non-existent twin brother, who instantly wins his love. Although he had "already extended beyond its customary term" his indulgence in "seclusion and solitude,"[30] he lingers still longer. After their return to his court, Alasi is content for awhile to see Firouz shine in company, but as he becomes more helplessly under the spell of this self-indulgent figure, this changes. He soon recognizes the "essential badness" of Firouz's heart, but seems powerless to resist the appeal. Alasi comes to share the sentiments of so many of Beckford's characters who would say, as Firouz soon does, "Why are we two not alone in the world?"[31] Thus

Alasi's existing impatience with his public responsibilities is augmented. It is in accordance with their desire to be alone together that Firouz induces Alasi to alienate his betrothed, the Princess Rondaba, and embroil the country in war.

The love of Alasi for Firouz is apparently not of the kind that inspires and sustains royal judgment or heroic valor. Inevitably, when Firouz is wounded and subsequently revealed as Firouzkah, Alasi is only too content to be carried off by magic to the subterranean palace of the Mage. Here for a time Alasi and Firouzkah enjoy what each of Beckford's protagonists longs for, the indulgence of passion in a protected subterranean environment. It is enough for Alasi; seeing the enchanted landscape, replete with, "the most beautiful and delicious products of the earth," Alasi exclaims, "what is it to us if we have been carried into Cheheristan itself? The true realms of bliss are in thine arms!"[32] He thus articulates the sentiments of all the lovers in Beckford's fiction. No more self-sufficient stance could be adduced.

But if love is all in all to Alasi and Firouzkah, time is still their enemy. The Mage sanctions and facilitates their union, and Alasi, like Vathek, is enabled to enjoy his love for awhile, indulged in amorous dalliance and magical entertainments by the attentive Firouzkah and the Mage's dives. Almost, they seem already to have escaped temporal constraint. Alasi confesses, "Her assiduous care, her ingenuity of tenderness, made my every moment hurry by in such voluptuous enjoyment that I was in no case to measure the flight of time; and the present had so far obliterated the past that I never once thought of my kingdom."[33] This is the nearest that any of the princes in these tales will attain to freedom from time and mortal care; it most closely approximates the similar situation of the young narrator of *The Vision*.

But this is not really a place removed from temporal sway, and the idyl must end. The Mage announces his imminent departure for the palace of subterranean fire, which he describes in terms reminiscent of Vathek's understanding of the place:

I am expected in the Palace of Subterranean Fire, where I shall bathe in joys untold, and possess treasures passing man's imagination. Ah! why has this moment of supreme felicity been so long delayed? The inexorable hand of death would not then have torn from my side my dear Soudabé, whose charms had never suffered from the ravages of Time! We should then have partaken together of that perfect happiness which neither accident, nor the vicissitudes of life, can ever mar in the place to which I am bound.[34]

The Mage believes, as do others, that time can have no effect there, and that death will have no power. The vocabulary is reminiscent of language usually used to describe heaven, rather than the underworld, and Alasi responds in a similar vein, "where is that divine sojourn in which a happy eternity of mutual love and tenderness may be enjoyed? Let us follow you thither."[35]

Alasi is undismayed when the Mage tells him he must do homage to the infernal powers in order to attain this boon, "I will worship any god you like ... if he will suffer me to live for ever with Firouzkah, and free from the horrible fear of seeing pale disease or bloody steel threaten her beauteous life."[36]   Even the sacrifice of human hair required to propitiate these powers no more daunts Alasi than the sacrifice of the fifty children to the Giaour had daunted Vathek. He is prepared to behead any number of his faithful subjects in order to collect it. The Mage is himself a deluded victim of the infernal powers, and believes he has won an eternal reward. He exults, "see all these locks of hair that ornament my Hall of Fire—dear evidences that I am about to enter the gates of the only place where lasting joys are to be found."[37]  The unscrupulous Firouzkah is likewise convinced, and motivated, like Alasi and the Mage, by her desire for release from mortality, "You will agree, my dear Alasi, that the sacrifice of a whole tribe of crazy wretches who will not accept our belief, is as nothing if we can obtain thereby the supreme felicity of loving each other to all time."[38]  Alasi, fearful of losing Firouzkah, is easily persuaded to return to his own country and, by declaring the religion of fire and scalping all who oppose it, to collect such quantities of hair as will win him an eternity of voluptuous indolence with Firouzkah in a fiery afterlife. They put the plan into practice and with the strength of the army to back them collect the necessary hair for the ritual. However, despite their readiness to confront eternity, some doubts remain, and Alasi and Firouzkah linger *en route*, "we could not bring ourselves to finally abandon our present pleasures for those we had been led to anticipate."[39]  But the journey to Istakar is finally accomplished, and they burn ten camel-loads of hair in order to gain entrance *via* the ebony portal. Like all the characters who win their way into the halls of Eblis, they are amazed at their reception. They have avoided the uncertainties of a normal span on earth, it is true; but they have gained an eternity, not of seclusion and safety, but of agony and despair.

In the second of the *Episodes of Vathek* the concern with time, though prevalent, is presented somewhat differently in that much of this theme is carried by the interpolated history of Homaiouna who is, by her very nature as a peri, free from mortal considerations. By a curious twist, however, her period of expiation on earth subjects her for a time to some of the inconveniences of human nature, though she is not subject to death. Her history, in which she recounts a series of happenings in the magical country of Ginnistan, augments the reader's perception of what it would mean to be free from the fears of mortality. This awareness is extended in the main narrative of this Episode by Prince Barkiarokh as he makes pretense of a similar magical nature in his wooing of the Princess Gazahidé. Barkiarokh is well aware of the ubiquitous human concern with time and mortality. He wins the hand of his Princess by feigning that through the powerful Jinn, Asfendarmod, whom he claims as his father, he can grant her a stay in the aging process and postpone her death. He falsely reports Asfendarmod as saying, "tell her that, for wedding gift, I allow her to retain, unimpaired, her beauty and her youth, during the hundred years she will live with thee!"[40] It is clear that this promise influences her decision to marry Barkiarokh, because the King, her father, abdicates in favour of Barkiarokh and allows the marriage, saying, "I ask for no greater boon than to see my daughter always fair, young and happy— unless, indeed, you should be willing to add to your favours by prolonging my days so that I may behold the lovely children to be born of your union."[41] No clearer indication could be desired to show the ever-present concern with aging and death in these tales.

The whole course of indulgence and crime in which Barkiarokh engages once he assumes the throne involves a perpetual perception of time in that he lives constantly anticipating the effects of the rod of vengeance wielded by his true wife, the Peri Homaiouna. Otherwise, he continues to live as though he were free from mortal restraints and could do as he wished with impunity. Once he sees his daughter, Leila, however, and conceives his overpoweringly lustful passion for her, he must restrain his appetites, for the first time, until he can get her to some place not subject to the Peri's influence. It is thus that he brings her to Istakar, and the brink of destruction, in the hope of possessing her unmolested in the palace of subterranean fire. What he seeks in that place is freedom to indulge a criminal passion, rather than freedom from mortality. In this way his case differs from those of the other princes, but only at the last. The concern with time has been a constant theme throughout this Episode, and it brings him surely to the palace of subterranean fire.

In the fragment of the third Episode we have a further and more oppressive use of time perception, together with a movement into subterranean enclosures. The twin children, Zulkais and Kalilah, love each other in a fashion more intense than is usual between siblings. Beckford is not here moving far from the common themes of the oriental tale. Critics are inclined to see here a quasi-autobiographical reference to Beckford's illicit affection for his cousin's wife. Such may indeed have been part of the inspiration for the story, but it is not without precedent in the *genre*. In the *Mogul Tales*, for example, the History of Canzade, Princess of Ormuz is based upon an incestuous attachment.[42] The children's father, like Vathek, is subject to, "an inordinate desire to control the future," and sought, "to forestall Providence, and to direct the course of events in despite of the decrees of Heaven."[43] Like Alasi and Firouzkah, the twins seek only to escape from society and enjoy each other's company alone. Although their father seems largely responsible for the intensity of their feelings, since he immersed them in the cabalistic lavers which over-heated their blood, he believes that their passion interferes with his son's education. Therefore, the old Emir decides to separate the twins, and so he arranges for Zulkais to be carried a thirty-day trip up the Nile. Here she is rather encouraged in her passion by the unlikely tutor chosen for her by her father. He confesses to similar feelings for his sisters, and indicates that Omoultakos, the Jinn of the Great Pyramid, would enter into her feelings, having in his time been similarly disposed towards his own sister. Under these circumstances there is no chance of Zulkais forgetting her love for her brother; instead she is further incited in her feelings. She is easily persuaded to seek a way back to Kalilah by propitiating the infernal powers. Like Alasi and Firouzkah in the first Episode, all she has ever wanted is time to be alone with Kalilah. It is in order to return to the intimacy of their early childhood together that she attempts to contrive their reunion.

Zulkais agrees to undergo the terrifying initiatory ritual. Time and space close in upon her as she prepares for the ordeal. She waits impatiently for night to begin the procedure which she has been led to believe will bring her to her beloved Kalilah. The movement underground is here more than usually sinister, and quite obviously unsafe. She follows her teacher, the Palm-tree Climber, into a narrow passage leading underground, "not more than four feet high, so that I was compelled to walk half doubled up." The scene continues in a claustrophobic journey:

The air I breathed was damp and stifling. At every step I caught my feet in viscous plants that issued from certain cracks and crevices in the gallery. Through these cracks the feeble light of the moon's rays found an entrance, shedding light, every here and there, upon little wells that had been dug to right and left of our path. Through the black waters in these wells I seemed to see reptiles with human faces. I turned away my eyes in horror.[44]

Not for Zulkais the garden landscapes enjoyed by the narrator of *The Vision*, nor the magical settings that soothe Alasi in his erotic interlude with Firouzkah. Here Zulkais has to confront the subterranean landscape in all its horror, and in something like its true colors. It is a mark of the distance Beckford has come that this young girl can still go on, that her courage survives this onslaught and she can seek love in these purlieus. The low, stone-built passage, the foetid air, the feeble light, serve to emphasize the nature of this setting and this quest. This is patently not a journey toward freedom and love, but the road toward death and the desolation of the tomb.

In leaving her, the Climber tells Zulkais to choose between five staircases leading out of a vast subterranean hall, "One only leads to the treasury of Omoultakos. From the others, which go losing them-selves in cavernous depths, you would never return. Where they lead you would find nothing but hunger, and the bones of those whom famine has aforetime destroyed."[45]   Zulkais is terrified, as she recounts to the princes in the halls of Eblis:

> Judge of my terror, you who have heard the ebony portals, which confine us for ever in this place of torment, grind upon their hinges! Indeed I dare to say that my position was, if possible, even more terrible than yours, for I was alone. I fell to the earth at the base of the block of marble.[46]

In a dream-vision Zulkais is inspired, or deluded, by a figure she takes to be her brother, "Suddenly a voice, clear, sweet, insinuating like the voice of Kalilah, flattered my ears ... 'Allah forbids our union. But Eblis, whom you see here, extends to us his protection. Implore his aid, and follow the path to which he points you.'"[47]  Emboldened and determined, Zulkais begins to ascend the stairway upon which the figure of Kalilah seemed to stand; incidentally, not necessarily the one to which Eblis would have pointed her.

The steps seemed to multiply beneath my feet; but my resolution never faltered; and, at last, I reached a chamber, square and immensely spacious, and paved with a marble that was of flesh colour, and marked as with the veins and arteries of the human body. The walls of this place of terror were hidden by huge piles of carpets of a thousand kinds, and a thousand hues, and these moved slowly to and fro, as if painfully stirred by human creatures stifling beneath their weight. All around were ranged black chests, whose steel padlocks seemed encrusted with blood.[48]

As the tale breaks off here, we have no way of knowing what might happen in this strange environment. Does this chamber in some way represent the womb to which Zulkais and Kalilah are striving to return—the only place where the twins were allowed to be alone together? Is it rather another form for the chamber of death? The padlocked chests might stand for coffins in this unpleasant hall. What is clear is that again the quest for freedom from the temporal condition has led to a dead end. Time itself seems slowed as this claustrophobic vignette usurps the reader's attention. The concerns of the real world fall away for Zulkais as she, like Prince Alasi in the first *Episode*, like Vathek in the frame tale, and like the hero of *The Vision*, seek a world of their own choosing divorced from time and place. In these tales, as so often in the oriental *genre*, such a rejection of the real world carries with it a terrible penalty.

Every reader must notice the tensions generated by *Vathek*, tensions noticeable throughout these tales. In part, the fiction is indulgent as we witness each character thrill and salivate over the most self-centred longings and desires. At times the author is uncritical of these impulses, and it is really only with the shift of tone towards the end that a moral stance is assumed. Beckford's use of the oriental mode was not merely a fortuitous outcome of early reading in the *genre*, or the influence of Lettice, Cozens, Chambers, and Henley; rather, he found in the oriental tales which were his inspiration a preoccupation with a series of related themes, and a certain uncritical detachment from moral condemnation, which must have had a lasting appeal. To some extent, the apparent moral ending of *Vathek* and the *Episodes* may be conventional. Backford would have been influenced by the decided trend, apparent especially in English oriental tales from Addison to Johnson, used to justify and excuse such ephemeral material. He was obviously conscious, also, of the expectations of his readers, and sought to disarm some of the criticism that the subject matter of his fiction was sure to raise. But the sheer weight of repetition of the theme, as each character seeks to escape from the destructive forces of time and the constraints of society in order to remove with a loved object into a subterranean seclusion, carries with it a certain impetus. There is a nostalgia, noticeable especially in *The Vision* and in the history of the Peri Homaiouna in the second *Episode*, but perceptible also in the other tales, for the plight and longings of each of the protagonists. However evil they may be, their hope for immortality, if not their criminal excess, is allowed in the context of the stories to evoke a sympathetic response. In the fiction of William Beckford no final escape from time is possible for any of his human characters, but in the subterranean fantasies of these tales we are invited to share their longing that such a respite were available to mankind.

Simon Fraser University

## REFERENCES

[1]*The Vision; Manuscript of a Romance*, ed., Guy Chapman (Cambridge: Cambridge University Press, 1930).

[2]*Vathek*, ed., Roger Lonsdale (Oxford: Oxford University Press, 1970).

[3]*The Episodes of Vathek*, trans. Sir Frank T. Marzials, ed. Lewis Melville (London: Stephen Swift, 1912).

[4]See especially Lewis's *The Monk* and Maturin's *Melmoth the Wanderer*.

[5]These tales are far less faithful to the spirit of any Arabic or Persian originals than is the work of Galland in *The Arabian Nights* or of Petis de la Croix in *The Persian Tales* or *The Turkish Tales*.

[6]*The Arabian Nights Entertainments*, ed. A. Galland, 6th ed. (London: J. Osborn, 1725) IX, 104.

[7]*Arabian Nights*, II, 44.

[8]*The Thousand and One Days; Persian Tales*, ed. Petis de la Croix, 3 vols., 3rd ed. (London: J. Tonson, 1722).

[9]See The Story of Prince Cameralzaman in *Arabian Nights*, VI, 115 ff. and The Story of the Great Traveller, Aboulfaouaris, in *Persian Tales*, III, 155 ff.

[10]George Sale, *The Koran, Commonly Called The Alcoran of Mohammed* ... (London: J. Wilcox, 1734) p. 73.

[11]The striving for an extension of life, of the years of enjoyment, and the exclusion of apparent danger is a common theme in literature; comparisons may be drawn with Faust and with Melmoth. But the forces that grant such privileges to aspiring seekers commonly deceive them.

[12]Guy Chapman, *Beckford* (New York: Scribners, 1937) p. 57.

[13]J. W. Oliver, *The Life of William Beckford* (London: Oxford U. Press, 1932) pp. 89–91.

[14]The dating of those sections of the manuscript not published by Chapman may be later. I have not seen the manuscript.

[15]The forty-four pages of the rough draft were first printed by André Parreaux in his *William Beckford, Auteur de Vathek: Étude de la Création Littéraire* (Paris: Nizet, 1960), and mentioned by Robert Gemmett in *William Beckford* (Boston: Twaine, 1977) p. 45 ff.

[16]*The Vision*, p. 86.

[17]It is toward such a seclusion as this that each of the stories seems to hurry its protagonists.

[18]*Vathek* p. 2.

[19]*Vathek*, p. 3.

[20]*Vathek*, p. 4.

[21]See George Sale, Preliminary Discourse to his edition of the *Koran* (London, 1734) passim. and John Richardson, *Dissertation on the Languages, Literature, and Manners of the Eastern Nations*, 2nd ed. (Oxford, 1778).

[22]*Vathek*, p. 22.

[23]*Vathek*, p. 22.

[24]*Vathek*, p. 36.

[25]*Vathek*, p. 22.

[26]See the *Persian Tales*, the *Turkish Tales*, and George Sale, ed. *Koran*.

[27]*Vathek*, p. 89.

[28]Robert Gemmett cites a reference from the unpublished notebooks of John Mitford to the effect that a Beckford story concerned a prince who, "had carnal connection with his sister, in the center of the great Pyramid;" cited by Robert Gemmett, *William Beckford* (Boston: Twayne, 1977) p. 116. However, this is hardly conclusive evidence. The sentence could merely refer to the material we have, imperfectly recollected.

[29]*Episodes of Vathek*, p. 4.

[30]*Episodes*, p. 7.

[31]*Episodes*, p. 13.

[32]*Episodes*, p. 30.

[33]*Episodes*, p. 38.

[34]*Episodes*, p. 38.

[35]*Episodes*, pp. 38-39.

[36]*Episodes*, p. 39.

[37]*Episodes*, p. 39.

[38]*Episodes*, p. 39.

[39]*Episodes*, p. 44.

[40]*Episodes*, p. 114.

[41]*Episodes*, p. 116.

[42]See also the story of the First Callendar in the *Arabian Nights*.

[43]*Episodes*, p. 165.

[44]*Episodes*, p. 205.

[45]*Episodes*, p. 206.

[46]*Episodes*, p. 206.

[47]*Episodes*, p. 206.

[48]*Episodes*, pp. 206–207.

# THE INFLUENCE OF LANDSCAPE AND ARCHITECTURE ON THE COMPOSITION OF *VATHEK*

Brian Fothergill

Writing in another context on some of the influences bearing on the "gothic" element in mid and late eighteenth-century architecture and literature I ventured to suggest that "it is a curious fact that Strawberry Hill, Fonthill Abbey, *The Castle of Otranto* and *Vathek* all owe a debt to the Grande Chartreuse,"[1] a list in which I might well have included with equal validity Gray's *Elegy Written in a Country Churchyard*. Certainly this remote and mountainous retreat had a profound effect upon sensitive young minds nurtured in the principles of the Age of Reason in its English Whig manifestation. To such minds, set against the background of a Protestant culture, the very existence of a community of monks, voluntarily secluded from the world, was a curious and unusual spectacle, one of the more quaint encounters to be experienced in the course of the Grand Tour by young men who came from a country that had not known such a phenomenon since before the Reformation. No wonder, perhaps, that it stimulated a reaction against the classical traditions in which they had been educated. But it was the rugged Alpine scenery in particular that excited the most enthusiastic exclamation of both Horace Walpole and Thomas Gray, a scenery that would evoke a similarly ecstatic response from William Beckford when he followed the same path a generation later.

When Walpole first set eyes on the Alps late in 1739 he was not so very far removed in time from the days when travellers had regarded mountains and crags as "strange, horrid and fearful" and men of sensibility had drawn down the blinds of their carriages to protect their eyes from so uncouth a sight as a precipice or a ravine. For John Evelyn, travelling about a hundred years before, it seemed as though "Nature had here swept up the rubbish of the earth in the Alps, to form and clear the plains of Lombardy."[2] To him, and to those who for some considerable time afterwards regarded nature from a similar viewpoint, plains were tranquil and civilized; mountains wild and barbarian. Walpole's aesthetic appreciation (and preparing the way for Beckford after him) reflects no such inhibitions. With a perception already schooled by his father's great collection of old masters at Houghton Hall in Norfolk, his reaction to the dramatic panorama unfolding before him was positive and enthusiastic. "Precipices, mountains, torrents, wolves, rumblings, Salvator Rosa ..." he wrote to his friend Richard West, "Here we are, the lonely lords of glorious, desolate prospects."[3] The descriptive words he assembled together were all later to become recognized ingredients of the gothic novel.

Walpole's initial leanings towards the gothic had been inspired much more by his response to wild scenery, prospects that moved him and his companion so that they "wished for a painter, wished to be poets," rather than from the inspection of mediaeval architectural remains. In two letters to Richard West from Rheims[4] he does not mention the cathedral at all, but the letter describing the visit to the Grande Chartreuse is a panegyric on the theme of "prodigious mountains ... hanging woods, obscured with pines, or lost in clouds ... sheets

of cascades forcing their silver speed down channelled precipices ..."
ending in an authentic "gothic" setpiece of "an old foot-bridge, with a
broken rail, a leaning cross, a cottage, or the ruins of an hermitage," a
picture that in visual terms looks forward to the paintings of Karl Friedrich Schinkel or Caspar David Friedrich in the nineteenth century. It
was scenes such as this, also calling to mind the wildly romantic
images of Salvator Rosa, that fused with Walpole's fascination with
the past to provide a gothic turn to his imagination. It was only later,
when faced with the problems of creating a gothic villa at Twicken-
ham near London, that he began a serious study of actual architectural
forms, and even then it was not so much the architecture in itself as
the "sensations of romantic devotion" it evoked, and feelings of
"superstition" it infused, that captured his fancy.[5]

When Beckford visited the Grande Chartreuse in 1778 he was, of
course, unaware of what was contained in Walpole's letters to West.
He had possibly read *The Castle of Otranto*,[6] he would appear to have
studied Gray's Ode "O tu, severi religio loci" with its early indications
of thoughts that would later be developed in the Churchyard Elegy;
and his reactions to the atmosphere of the place were not dissimilar to
those of his predecessor. Indeed he brought to bear upon the experience he was undergoing a temperament and social background not
altogether so very different from Walpole's. Both were given to fantasy and whim, both were a shade over-civilized, both shared a certain
sexual ambivalence. Each was mother-dominated, each had forceful
and power-loving fathers from whose influence they had early in life
been separated, one by the exigence of high office, the other by death,
and each descended from bourgeois stock on one side to balance an
aristocratic lineage on the other, though in Walpole's case the connec-

tion with trade was further removed and could be accepted with more complacency.[7] They were both acutely aware of their position in the social hierarchy, though Walpole's more relaxed assurance enabled him to avoid the slight taint of the *arriviste* from which Beckford never completely escaped. And finally, whether in the form of letters, journals, occasional verse, or imaginative jottings of one sort or another, both were impelled to commit their thoughts to writing, belonging to that literary species that goes by the name of the "born" writer. It is hardly surprising therefore that, when they came to fictionalize their fantasies in works written in the initial stages of composition with a speed and compulsion that has been likened to automatic writing, they should both in due course draw on the vivid memories impressed on their youthful imaginations by the scenery of the Grande Chartreuse.

For Walpole, the visit to the Grande Chartreuse did little more than initiate in his mind certain subjective trends that would lead him on to an appreciation of what he called "the true Gothic taste". As a result it did not altogether surprise him, when he came to write *The Castle of Otranto,* that such a story should have sprung from "a head filled like mine with Gothic story."[8] Thomas Gray's more original and more profound response to the stimulation of the same scenery, "Not a precipice, not a torrent, not a cliff, but is pregnant with religion and poetry,"[9] would be echoed thirty-nine years later by Beckford in his *Excursion to the Grande Chartreuse* when he wrote, with a similarly introspective sensitivity, that "it was here first, that I felt myself seized by the Genius of the place, and penetrated with veneration of its religious gloom ..."[10] The sight of a peak known as the Throne of Moses evoked another religious reflection: "If that prophet had received his revelations in this desert," he noted, "no voice need have declared it holy ground; for every part of it is stamped with such a sublimity of character as would, alone, be sufficient to impress the idea." But Beckford would not have been Beckford had these pious impressions been left to stand alone and without a hint of the esoteric. Just before he had come to the "great portal" that admits the visitor into the actual domain of the monastery, he declared, he felt at his heart a certain awe that brought to mind "the sacred terror of those, in ancient days, going to be admitted into the Eleusinian mysteries."[11] Here, in the conscious or unconscious link in his mind between the great portal and magic or mysterious cults, we get a first glimpse of ideas that would later be developed in *Vathek*.

Various other themes, indeed, were already present in the mind of this impressionable seventeen-year-old which he would later exploit when he came to write his Arabian tale some four years later. The very frame of mind in which he began his ascent to the monastery had a note of oriental fatalism about it: "We could now distinguish the roar of torrents, and a confusion of strange sounds, issuing from dark forests of pine. I confess at this moment I was somewhat startled; I experienced some disagreeable sensations, and it was not without a degree of unwillingness that I left the gay pastures and enlivening sunshine, to throw myself into this gloomy and disturbed region. How dreadful, thought I, must be the despair of those, who enter it, never to return!"[12]   This sense of fate and despair (that seemed to envisage entrance to the cloister more in terms of a sentence of death than as the answer to a religious vocation) is introduced by a passage describing his approach to the "desert" surrounding the Chartreuse by way of "two pinnacles of rock far above us, beyond which, a melancholy twi-

light prevailed." It is a scene that, not only in its melancholy associations but also in its physical appearance, at once calls to mind the
Caliph and Nouronihar at the close of their adventure approaching by
moonlight the "two towering rocks that formed a kind of portal to the
valley at the extremity of which rose the vast ruins of Istakar." Even
the connection between the portal through which Vathek passed and
the consuming flame that awaited him beyond it, is not entirely lacking in the earlier experience, for after passing the entrance to the
valley marked by the two pinnacles of rock Beckford found his way
stopped by a venerable gateway beyond which he saw a forge resem-
bling an altar and "what added greatly to the grandeur of the object
was, a livid flame continually palpitating upon it, which the gloom of
the valley rendered perfectly discernible."[13]

Beckford came to the Grande Chartreuse at the end of his stay in
Switzerland in the years 1777–8, a period that had seen the composition of his first sustained literary effort *The Long Story* (or *The Vision*,
as Professor Guy Chapman called it in his published edition of 1930),
a work that is now generally acknowledged as a forerunner of *Vathek*.
Chapman himself pointed out how the narrative displayed "evidence
of the burning imagination that devised the Halls of Eblis"[14] and Dr.
Robert J. Gemmett has recently shown its more detailed foreshadow-
ing of *Vathek*, especially in fragments of the story discovered since
Chapman's edition was published.[15]  From this we know that Beckford's mind was already full of Eastern themes at the time he visited
the Chartreuse, though his interest was then more centered upon
Indian history and philosophy than Arabian. He had also started to
show a marked interest in secret or occult ceremonial, as is shown by
the initiation scene in *The Long Story*, a mental preoccupation that no

doubt made him associate the "great portal" on route to the monastery with the ancient mysteries of Eleusinia, just as in *Vathek* the portal of ebony guards the hidden treasures and magic talismans of the pre-Ademite sultans. So, too, as he listened to the monks chanting their office he could imagine them engaged in "mysterious rites that shun the day"[16] a thought that would surely have startled the hospitable sons of St. Bruno whose devotions gave rise to it. But if *The Long Story* sowed some of the seeds that would grow into exotic flower in *Vathek*, the visit to the Grande Chartreuse, which had so moved Walpole and Gray before him, carried the process a shade further in providing some of the visual properties and atmospheric effects that were tò reappear in sinister form in his Arabian fantasy.

When Beckford returned to England he recorded, on 4 December 1778, a long daydream or reverie which in its form and structure has reminded one critic "less of Coleridge's verse than of De Quincey's opium-dreams" and prompted him to ask "did he, like them, take the drug, but without forming a fatal habit?"[17] It would seem, from what we know of Beckford's life, that he was able to induce these almost self-hypnotic moods without the help of any drug or stimulant. The passage is long, over two thousand five hundred words.[18] In the course of it we are taken on a dream journey through strange lands and visit the Fortunate Mountains of Paradise, but it is a mental journey only, conceived while Beckford rests "like Orientals, on cushions of Brocade" seated before the fire in the "vast hall paved with Marble" of Fonthill Splendens. Lulled by this sense of oriental luxury the spirit which accompanies Beckford in his trance guides him to a cavern where "suddenly the spirit of Father *Ureta* rose like a mist from the Chasm and seizing me with its influence, discovered the interior of the

Cave, ascended thro' the mountain, and brought me swiftly to a Castle with many towers of grotesque Architecture. There I saw huge treasures and crowds of unknown Mortals walking in vaulted Halls whose stately arches impressed veneration. Here are deposited ancient records and Histories of which the rest of man are ignorant ..." Again vague hints of *Vathek* drift into the narrative, hints of what are to become the mountain of the four fountains with its summit "overspread with so delightful a plain, that it might have been taken for the Paradise destined for the faithful," as well as the Caliph's tower and the Halls of Eblis where the lost souls wander and where the treasures and talismans repose. In composing such fantasies Beckford tells us "you see my Reason or my fancy is continually employed, when abandoned by the one I obey the other. These two powers are my Sun and Moon. The first dispels the vapours and cleans up the face of things, the other throws over all Nature a dim Haze and may be styled the Dream of Delusions." In this dream-like state the experiences and impressions of his travels, the "waking thoughts and incidents" stored up in his mind, are wrought into narrative prose to give form to his mental fantasies.

It is not without significance that this reverie which begins with the phrase "The Dusk approaches. I am musing on the Plain before the House which my Father reared" should take the form of a long mental soliloquy before a blazing fire in the great hall of Splendens, for architectural influences had as strong a bearing on the composition of *Vathek* as did impressions drawn from the "gothic" grandeur of the Alps. Here indeed is another link with Horace Walpole, for both writers acknowledged in retrospect how their imaginations had been fired by impressions of the houses in which they were living at the time of writing. Walpole's dream of a gigantic hand in armor on the upper bannister of the stairs and his confession to William Cole that he would recognize a picture from the gallery at Strawberry Hill in his story, prompted him to comment in the published description of his villa that the house was "a very proper habitation of, as it was the scene that inspired, the author of the Castle of Otranto."[19] Beckford also, recalling in 1838 the youthful gathering behind the shuttered windows of Fonthill Splendens just before Christmas 1781, declared that he began to write *Vathek* immediately afterwards "thoroughly embued [sic] with all that passed at Fonthill during this voluptuous festival."[20]

Three architectural symbols appear in *Vathek,* the tower, the dome, and the subterranean hall. They mark the progress of the Caliph from his position as tyrant of dubious orthodoxy, through an episode of sensual dalliance, to his final loss of hope as the prisoner of the eternally consuming flame. The tower was, of course, a potent symbol for Beckford during the greater part of his life. He derived a curious satisfaction from placing himself high above the world and looking down with a sense of detachment upon the creatures below, much as the Caliph directed his glance from the top of his tower and saw "men not larger than pismires; mountains, than shells; and cities, than beehives." As early as 1777 Beckford wrote to Alexander Cozens from "the Summit of the Mountain of Salève" describing how he could observe through the thinning vapor "a boundless scene ... the creation of an instant. Objects crowd too swiftly for me to continue, I must abandon my pen and gaze,"[21] while on another occasion he recorded his desire to have an apartment in the highest story of a tower from where he could observe the course of the planets and indulge in astrological fancies.[22]

Equally significant in its relation to *Vathek* is the episode in Letter II of *Dreams, Waking Thoughts and Incidents* dated from Antwerp, 21 June 1780. His mind is actually absorbed in Arabian reflections—"I might, without being thought very romantic, have imagined myself in the city of petrified people, which Arabian fabulists are so fond of describing"—when he discovers the "stupendous" tower of the cathedral. "I longed to ascend it that instant," he writes, "to stretch myself out upon its very summit, and calculate, from so sublime an elevation, the influence of the planets."[23] Two years later he was to write of the Caliph Vathek how "the inquisitive Prince passed most of his nights on the summit of his tower, till becoming an adept in the mysteries of astrology, he imagined that the planets had disclosed to him the most marvellous adventures, which were to be accomplished by an extraordinary personage, from a country altogether unknown." It is at this point, indeed, that the Caliph's own adventures begin with the appearance of the Giaour whose arrival the stars foretold and who is the agent of Eblis sent to tempt Vathek to his doom.

The tower represents Vathek's potency as a sovereign; it is also the secret retreat where he can indulge in heterodox speculation in defiance of the laws of Islam. In addition to this it has a magic significance, for it is from here that the Caliph's mother works her evil spells. This association of the tower with occult rites can be traced as far back as Beckford's adolescence, when in a fragment he called *The Fountain of Merlin* there is a reference to "some gloomy cave or wilderness visible alone by the glare of necromantic towers."[24] The dome, on the other hand, is a more peaceful symbol, representing Beckford's sensuousness as well as his sensibility.

In another literary fragment written in Switzerland and dated Geneva, 22 May 1778, Beckford conceived the idea of a great dome situated "upon some sequestered hill" open on the west side to receive the rays of the declining sun and commanding a view "confined to Woods and Waters, where the ancient Persians meet to pay their adoration to the departing God." This "Dome of the Setting Sun" would contain painting and sculpture to reflect his moods and recall scenes from "'Afric and Ind' those countries most favoured by the Sun." Into this "consecrated dome" Beckford imagined himself retiring to repose, and "in luxurious leisure describe the Scenes which it presents all round me as if my artist had already executed them."[25] When he came to write *Vathek* he reverted to the idea of the dome in the passage describing the Caliph's visit to the Emir Fakreddin, where Vathek delayed his journey in disobedience to his mother's commands and where he was destined to meet Nouronihar and Gulchenrouz, and a voluptuous interlude interrupts his progress to the ruins of Istakhar. In the emir's domain, the "happy valley of Fakreddin," the Caliph soon found himself "beneath a vast dome, illuminated by a thousand lamps of rock crystal: as many vases of the same material, filled with excellent sherbet, sparkled on a large table, where a profusion of viands were spread."

Associated with the same symbol, Nouronihar and Gulchenrouz (who in fact represent Beckford's two "forbidden" lovers, Louisa Beckford and William Courtenay) when we are first introduced to them together, are found just as the sun is about to set, and having lively and inventive fancies, "imagined they beheld, in the gorgeous clouds of the west, the domes of Shaddukian and Ambreabad, where the Peries have fixed their abode." The dome is lacking in the ominous associations that gather round the symbols of the tower and the subterranean hall. It stands for luxury, lovemaking, and the languorous sensations suitable to the hour of twilight and approaching night. It is linked not with demons but with peris, who are good and beautiful spirits existing somewhere between men and angels in Persian mythology, and who were sent into banishment by the command of Eblis himself.

Beckford, in a retrospective moment towards the close of his life, explained very clearly the origin of the idea of the Halls of Eblis where Vathek was to complete the pilgrimage which began with such arrogance and bravado and was to end in the loss, for himself and his companion, of "the most precious gift of heaven— HOPE." "Old Fonthill," Beckford told the journalist Cyrus Redding, "had a very ample, lofty, loud echoing hall, one of the largest in the kingdom. Numerous doors led from it into different parts of the house, through dim, winding passages. It was from that I introduced the hall—the idea of the 'Hall of Eblis' being generated by my own. My imagination magnified and coloured it with Eastern character."[26] There is also some resemblance between Beckford's description in *Vathek* of "various perspectives of halls and of galleries that opened on the right hand and the left; which were all illuminated by torches and braziers, whose flames rose in pyramids to the centre of the vault" and the subterranean passages in *The Castle of Otranto* which were "hollowed into several intricate cloisters," and where "an aweful silence reigned." But here, as Mario Praz has pointed out, the common source was probably the *Carceri* of Piranesi, an artist whose sombre compositions of intricately vaulted halls and passages were familiar to both authors.[27] Beckford, indeed, also associated Piranesi's designs with his own tower fantasies, describing how on his journey to Bonn in July 1780 his imagination had "built castles in the style of Piranesi ... The magnificance and variety of my aerial towers, hindered my thinking the way long."[28]

It might at first seem strange that the young Beckford should have chosen to set the most frightening moment of his story in surroundings suggested by his own home, the scene of his childhood and adolescence. Yet there is much in his life to suggest that he had no very great fondness for Fonthill Splendens, much as he adored the parkland and woods that surrounded it; indeed, it was into these silvan retreats that he so often escaped from the oppressive atmosphere of the house that represented for him his father's bursts of violent temper and terrifying glance (like the Caliph's) and his mother's possessive, cloying affection and narrow Calvinistic creed that taught a damnation as final and as catastrophic as that which destroyed Vathek in his tale. Beckford seems to have abandoned Splendens without much regret, and when he came to create his own tower in the vast abbey he erected nearby he had no qualms in making use of the stones of Splendens as a quarry to transform his gothic vision into reality. But the student of William Beckford's life and writings who regrets the disappearance of Fonthill Abbey (which itself owes a debt to memories of the site and architecture of the Grande Chartreuse) must also lament the destruction of Fonthill Splendens, for a visit today to its "ample, lofty, loud echoing hall" would teach us something about the mind of the author of *Vathek* just as a visit to the still standing Strawberry Hill, which Beckford derided as "a miserable child's box—a species of gothic mousetrap" gives us an added insight into the mind and imagination of the author of *The Castle of Otranto*. While the story of the Caliph Vathek still manages to retain so much of its power and fascination after the passage of two hundred years, it can only be deplored that the same hand that created it should have been responsible for the destruction of the great building that inspired the setting of its grim denouement.

London, England

## REFERENCES

[1]Brian Fothergill. *The Strawberry Hill Set: Horace Walpole and his Circle* (Bridgeport: Faber and Faber, 1983), p. 163.

[2]C. Hussey. *The Picturesque* (London: F. Cass, 1967), pp. 84–6.

[3]Walpole to West, "From a Hamlet among the Mountains of Savoy," 28 Sept. (NS) 1739.

[4]West, "From Rheims" 18 and 20 June (NS) 1739.

[5]H. Walpole. *Anecdotes of Painting in England* (London: Dodsley, 1828), I, 198–200.

[6]In 1834, ten years before Beckford's death, Bentley published *The Castle of Otranto* bound up with *Vathek* and *The Bravo of Venice*.

[7]Beckford was the son of a Lord Mayor of London, while Walpole's maternal great grandfather had held the same office. Walpole's grandfather on the same side had been a timber merchant trading with the Baltic.

[8]"To Reverend Cole", 9 March 1765, *Horace Walpole Correspondence to Reverend William Cole*, ed. W. Lewis (London: Oxford University Press, 1937).

[9]Gray, "To West" 16 November 1739.

[10]R. J. Gemmett, ed., *Dreams, Waking Thoughts and Incidents* (London: Johnson, 1783), p. 265.

[11]Gemmett, *Dreams*, p. 266.

[12]Gemmett, *Dreams*, pp. 264–5.

[13]Gemmett, *Dreams*, p. 265.

[14]G. Chapman, *The Vision and Liber Veritatis* (London: Constable and Company Limited, 1930), p. xiii.

[15]R. Gemmett, *William Beckford* (Boston: Hall, 1977), pp. 49–52.

[16]Gemmett, *Dreams*, p. 279.

[17]G. Bullough, "Beckford's Early Travels and his Dream of Delusion" in *William Beckford of Fonthill, Bicentenary Essays*, ed. F. Moussa Mahmoud (Port Washington: Kennikat Press, 1972), pp. 48–9.

[18]L. Melville, *The Life and Letters of William Beckford* (London: William Heinemann, 1910), pp. 60–6.

[19]Horace Walpole, *A Description of the Villa of Mr. Horace Walpole* (Strawberry Hill, 1784), p. iv.

[20]J. W. Oliver, *The Life of William Beckford* (London: Oxford University Press, 1932), pp. 89–91.

[21]L. Melville, *The Life and Letters*, p. 31.

[22]B. Alexander, *England's Wealthiest Son* (London: Centaur Press, 1962), p. 92.

[23]R. Gemmett, *Dreams*, pp. 58–9.

[24]B. Fothergill, *Beckford of Fonthill* (London: Faber and Faber, 1979), p. 45.

[25]B. Fothergill, *Beckford*, pp. 225–6.

[26]Cyrus Redding, "Recollections of the Author of *Vathek*," *The New Monthly Magazine*, 71 (June 1844), p. 150; quoted in Gemmett, *William Beckford*, p. 98.

[27]M. Praz, *Three Gothic Novels* (London: Penguin Books, 1968) pp. 18–20.

[28]Gemmett, *Dreams*, p. 83.

# ORIENTALISM, FANTASY, AND
# *VATHEK*

## J. E. Svilpis

Eighteenth-century English literary orientalism is a complicated field because it is the site at which a received vision of the Orient absorbed the very different images in *The Arabian Nights*, other translations, and their imitations. Virtuous pagans from Saladin to Aureng-Zebe and vicious infidels like Spenser's Sansfoy, Sansloy, and Sansjoy all belong to a well established discursive system whose object is the construction of an Orient with a European meaning. The influx of genuine oriental tales translated by Antoine Galland, Petis de la Croix, and others in the early eighteenth century disrupted this system, for Sinbad, Ali Baba, and their cronies are unrelated to the Western discourse of vices and virtues. The Occident responded by rewriting the oriental tale in order to cover the disruption, transforming its moral discourse in the process and leaving the scar of a discontinuity as part of the oriental tale's heritage. The most remarkable such tale, William Beckford's *Vathek* (1786), illustrates this by its disquieting use of both traditions, oriental and occidental.

*Vathek*'s relations to its sources and analogues have been studied by a number of careful scholars, André Parreaux foremost among them, and these issues are well if not exhaustively understood.[1] The results of this scholarly project are, however, flawed by a conception of orientalism that must be revised in the light of Edward W. Said's work. To illustrate: Mahmoud Manzalaoui rightly criticizes the classificatory logic of Martha Pike Conant's *The Oriental Tale in England in the Eighteenth Century* (1908), but the grounds of his criticism— that by her classification Conant has misrepresented the "creative orientalism" of the Romantics, "squeezing it in tightly between eighteenth-century pseudo-orientalism and modern, accurate oriental studies"—reveal a progressivist bias, and a similar bias is expressed by Robert J. Gemmett.[2] It is worth emphasizing that the history of orientalism is *not* the record of a straightforward progress through three phases, pseudo-oriental, creative, and accurate. As Said argues, orientalism is a discourse with important political and ideological functions in Western culture, and it has never been nor is it now accurate, though it has always been creative, even in the eighteenth century. In his words, "the Orient is not only adjacent to Europe; it is also the place of Europe's greatest and richest and oldest colonies, the source of its civilizations and languages, its cultural contestant, and one of its deepest and most recurring images of the Other."[3] The history of orientalism has been much more a continually varied tension than an even progress.

The oriental tale in eighteenth-century England was a literature of the Other, and the position that it occupied in the generic system of the time reproduces the colonial paradox that Said identifies: on the one hand, "the Orient ... was culturally, intellectually, spiritually *outside* Europe and European civilization," but on the other, "the Orient and Islam are always represented as outsiders having a special role to play *inside* Europe."[4] Similarly, the oriental tale was by definition an alien genre, but it was widely adopted and subjected to English taste. The original translators themselves tamed the exoticism of their sources.[5] They were followed by writers like Joseph Addison, Richard Steele,

Samuel Johnson, and John Hawkesworth, who produced oriental tales shaped by English morality, imposing native categories of thought even when their intent was satire of the West. Nevertheless, the genre retained the difference from other genres caused by its origins, its settings, and its characters, and this created possibilities for literary subversion and rebellion which were most thoroughly explored by Beckford in *Vathek*.

The precise generic positions of the oriental tale and of *Vathek* are not easy to determine, but Clara Reeve's *The Progress of Romance* (1785) provides a contemporary guide which enables us to place them approximately. Reeve traces the history of narrative fiction and presents the latest development, novelistic realism, as the best and didactically most useful:

The Novel gives a familiar relation of such things, as pass every day before our eyes, such as may happen to our friend, or to ourselves; and the perfection of it, is to represent every scene, in so easy and natural a manner, and to make them appear so probable, as to deceive us into a persuasion (at least while we are reading) that all is real, until we are affected by the joys or distresses, of the persons in the story, as if they were our own (I, lll).[6]

Of course, romances, too, when composed by moral writers of genius, can touch our emotions—" ... they speak to all the noblest feelings of the human heart, and excite to such actions as they describe ... " (I, 97)—but, given her affective emphasis, Reeve must elevate *trompe l'oeil* storytelling above other kinds, and so she does: " ... perhaps there is not a better Criterion of the merit of a book, than our losing sight of the Author" (II, 25).

Her organization validates this criterion: fantastic and non-realistic forms are presented either as precursors of realism, or are lumped together in the dialogue of Evening XI, which deals with a miscellaneous list of "Novels and Stories Original and uncommon" (II, 53). Although Reeve never states it, the natural corollary of her reasoning and her presentation is that non-realism teaches in a different way, and the distinction is that we feel non-realism differently because we do not believe in it. It may excite the reader to emulation, but the further it departs from familiar things, the more it interposes an author's imagination between the reader and the fiction and the more it demands interpretation, an activity that interferes with pure affective response. George Granville, in a note to "An Essay upon Unnatural Flights in Poetry" (1701), gives a rule for reading fictions based on classical mythology: "The Poetic World is nothing but Fiction; Parnassus, Pegasus, and the Muses, pure imagination and Chimaera. But being, however, a system universally agreed on, all that shall be contriv'd or invented upon this Foundation according to Nature shall be reputed as truth."[7] That Granville has something like allegorical reading in mind is shown by his poem—"Important Truths still let your Fables hold, / And moral misteries with art unfold"—and this is a tendency of the greatest importance in eighteenth-century thinking about non-realism and fantasy.

When Joseph Addison, for instance, faces the problem of "the fairy way of writing" (*The Spectator*, No. 419),[8] he rises to his climax with a comment on allegorical personification: "Thus we see how many ways Poetry addresses it self to the Imagination, as it has not only the whole Circle of Nature for its Province, but makes new Worlds of its own, shews us Persons who are not to be found in Being, and represents even the Faculties of the Soul, with her several Virtues and

Vices, in a sensible Shape and Character." The fallacy underlying this conclusion appears when we consider that most of the essay has dealt with specifically fantastic topics: witches, fairies, and the supernatural. Although in this kind of writing "the Poet quite loses sight of Nature," Shakespeare created characters such "that we cannot forbear thinking them natural, tho' we have no Rule by which to judge of them, and must confess, if there are such Beings in the World it looks highly probable they should talk and act as he has represented them," a judgement echoed by Johnson. These are clearly not allegorical persons, and Addison's slide from fantasy to allegory in his discussion mirrors a general difficulty in eighteenth-century views of fantasy. Indeed, Addison exhibits an attitude that may be the cause of this difficulty: despite the example of Shakespeare, he regards fantastic non-realism as low and disreputable, associating it with "an Imagination naturally fruitful and superstitious," with "the traditions of Nurses and old Women," and with "the Darkness and Superstition" of the Middle Ages. Addison's uneasy shuffling of categories illustrates the eighteenth-century impulse to assimilate empirically unjustifiable stories to didactically justifiable allegory.[9]

If critics like Addison found it hard to give a coherent account of fantasy with native roots, they had a yet harder task in the oriental tale. Reeve compares *The Odyssey* to the story of Sinbad the Sailor, concluding that the two are comparable in quality and that " ... there is frequently a striking resemblance between works of high and low estimation, which prejudice only, hinders us from discerning, and which when seen, we do not care to acknowledge ... " (I, 24). She praises *The Arabian Nights* as "a Work of Originality and Authenticity, and let me add of amusement," but almost immediately she turns and dismisses western imitations as "wild and extravagant to the highest degree; they are indeed so far out of the bounds of Nature and probability, that it is difficult to judge of them by rules drawn from those sources," even if "some of them are amusing" (II, 58). This is her own Addisonian lapse, for her criterion of "authenticity" allows her to accept orientalism as a product of the East at the same time as she rejects it when it is produced in the West, and the gap in her logic seems to be related to an ambiguity in her view of amusement.

She tells an anecdote about "the Turkish method of calming the mind," a pleasant story read aloud, in which a Turk comments on the difference between Orient and Occident:

You see my friend, that we are not such Barbarians as many of the Franks believe us,—your people are extremely vain and conceited of their own customs, and yet provoked to see others tenacious of theirs; they laugh at our Turkish stories, and at this method of soothing our cares; yet I conceive that it is as natural and as innocent as gaming, or drinking great quantities of wine, which are your common diversions (II, 63).

This passage, in a discussion of the universal taste for tales and stories, illustrates further paradoxes in English orientalism. Reeve takes an indirect, satirical look at the West, but she also associates entertainment with intoxication, reducing the Orient to something childlike, if not childish, by attributing to it an unsophisticated taste. She allows the Orient to voice its position, but she reasserts the primacy of didacticism, arguing that only those amusing stories which are also moral should be read, and relegates the values she associates with the Orient to a lowly place in the English scheme of things. She identifies orientalism with anti-didacticism, and this allows her implicitly to stigmatize English oriental tales as inauthentic—neither Western nor authentically and originally Eastern—at the same time as she makes her liberal gesture. The result is that in her account the oriental tale appears at the very margins of English culture, further from the didactic-realistic center than the native varieties of fantasy, which are amenable to allegorization or Addisonian concealment.

This extreme marginality might well explain why the oriental tale flourished during the rise of the novel: its position in the generic system freed it from commitment to a specific set of values and allowed it a variety of uses. It provided hedonistic readers with entertainment; it provoked spokesmen for the dominant ideology to produce moralized and allegorized adaptations; and it afforded satirists an external and critical rhetorical locus from which to survey culturally more central discourses. Those discourses, most clearly represented in literature by novelistic realism, privilege English experience, defining the real in terms of the culturally familiar, producing and reproducing in fictional form England's view of itself. At the same time, these discourses proclaim the uniformity of human life, denying cultural differences in experience.[10]  By constituting itself as a genre through its departure, however superficial, from this anglocentrism, the oriental tale necessarily also makes a gesture of revolt, however perfunctory. The oriental tale may thus be seen as a direct counter-discourse to the novel, asserting some measure of cultural difference and sometimes seriously questioning a realism based only on the familiar. It was supplanted in this function at the end of the century by the Gothic tale, but not until it had created a broadly anti-empirical basis for narrative.

This tendency, inherent in the genre, resulted in a cautious and distrustful treatment of oriental materials by the writers most closely associated with the cultural center and its discursive forms, of which the periodical essay is perhaps the most notable. Indeed, the founders of the periodical essay, Addison and Steele, are drastic assimilators of the oriental tale to Western discourse. One example is Addison's essay on "Our Ideas of Time" (*The Spectator*, No. 94),[11] where two oriental tales illustrate Locke's and Malebranche's accounts of time-consciousness. The first concerns Mohammed's split-second tour of the universe, from which he returns in time to catch a pitcher of water upset at his departure; the second is roughly the middle third of the tale of Chec Cahabeddin, about the sultan who lived for several years, through several reversals of fortune, between sticking his head in a tub of water and pulling it out again. But Addison's introductory description of the latter keeps his use from being entirely innocent: he calls it "a very pretty Story in the *Turkish* Tales which relates to this Passage of that famous Impostor [Mohammed], and bears some Affinity to the Subject we are now upon." The affinity is imposed by Addison himself and extends no further than is allowed by Western ideology. In their original context, these stories exemplify the power of Allah; Addison relocates them and attributes a new meaning to them by giving them a function—to illustrate European philosophy—in a new discourse. They carry a new meaning imposed by their function, but they appear silly in a "realistic" context. He also repeats an ancient slur on Mohammed (that he is a pretender to Christ's role rather than the prophet of a different religion)[12] by which he asserts an occidental view of the Orient as a degenerate and parodic version of itself.

Steele's retelling of "The History of Santon Barsisa" (*The Guardian*, No. 148)[13] shows a comparable hostility. Like Addison, he draws attention to the otherness of the Orient, giving as his epigraph a quotation from Ovid that tells us it is good to learn even from an enemy. Though the tale originates with an enemy, "The Moral to be drawn from it is intirely Christian, and is so very obvious, that I shall leave to every Reader the Pleasure of picking it out for himself." In Steele's version, the Devil tempts a saintly man by appealing first to his fleshly lust, then to his fear of discovery, and finally to his credulous hope. The Santon is self-condemned, and his tale is a kind of oriental rake's progress, an inversion of the temptation of St. Anthony. A number of morals can be seen here, and, because the tempter is not clearly oriental even in trappings, one of them is that a Muslim holy man cannot hold out against the Christian devil. Steele does not trivialize his materials as Addison does, but the effect is very similar, for the underlying assumption is that the true understanding of this oriental tale can only be achieved by a Christian in search of a moral.

Sheldon Sacks's definition of an apologue as "a work organized as a fictional example of the truth of a formulable statement or a series of such statements"[14] helps us see Steele's practice as the imposition of an apological pattern to guide the Western reader, presumably because the original could not be trusted to evoke that kind of reading in itself. This apologizing of the oriental tale is common in the eighteenth century. Eliza Haywood's *Adventures of Eovaai, Princess of Ijaveo* (1736) includes footnotes, one of whose functions is to draw attention to formulable statements dramatized in the narrative. Addison's "The Vision of Mirzah" (*The Spectator*, No. 159), ostensibly set in Persia and translated from an oriental manuscript, is structured as an allegorical dream-vision, a Western didactic genre, and invites a correspondingly moral reading. John Hawkesworth's *Almoran and Hamet, An Oriental Tale* (1761) combines a romantic plot with didactic case-histories like those in William Law's *A Serious Call to a Devout and Holy Life* (1728). Perhaps the most striking example is Johnson's *Rasselas* (1759), which is remarkably bare of exotic local color and rich in observations on general human nature. These and other variations agree in one significant respect: all are dedicated to evoking apological readings.

Appropriately, the position of the oriental tale mirrors the position of William Beckford: English in citizenship but not in spirit. Indeed, André Parreaux has precisely stated the nature of Beckford's radical marginality:

En Angleterre, Beckford ne pouvait être le porte-parole authentique d'aucun groupe social ascendant, parce qu'il représentait une forme de richesse et un style de vie condamnés par l'histoire, tandis que, malgré tous ses liens avec la France, il restait étranger, non à notre esprit ni à notre langue, mais à la réalité sociale dont ces philosophes de chez nous (avec lesquels il avait tant d'affinités intellectuelles) traduisaient les aspirations.[15]

Such a suspension between European cultures is visible in both Beckford's life and the publication history of his book, and both author and tale have been seen as the complex and odd results of several conflicting forces. To summarize Brian Fothergill, *Vathek* is a study of the damnation of an evil man written out of personal experience by a self-indulgent sensualist with a guilty Calvinist conscience.[16] Like the moralized oriental tales of Addison and others, *Vathek* has an overall apological structure, and a conventional code of behavior provides the formulable statements illustrated in that structure. Beckford's personal involvement in the fortunes of his protagonist, however, creates an ironic sympathy for the evil Caliph which often leads to ridicule of the morality uncovered by an apological reading. A further complexity emerges when we consider that the notes to *Vathek* display considerable oriental erudition, reflecting Beckford's great interest in the East. We may take these as satire of the morality and criticism of the erudition of Addison, Steele, Johnson, and the rest, in the sense that, compassed with Beckford's notes, their orientalism and their view of humanity are made to appear superficial.

*Vathek*, as published in 1786, poses a set of interesting problems in orientalism, morality, and characterization. These often appear within the text as disharmonies that create a discontinuous and confusing whole. Beckford's orientalism, even without Henley's help, is much more recondite and comprehensive than that of his predecessors, and historical critics have taken this to denote accuracy. But this view is based on the notes and the local references in the narrative; when we look at other aspects of "accuracy" in the tale, such as its textual representation of human behavior, we must acknowledge strange incongruities. Similarly, it is possible to see the morality of Vathek's damnation as perfectly consistent with eighteenth-century practice, as Conant and others have argued; but style and tone are at odds with the resolution of the plot: Robert Kiely, for one, states that "Vathek is a character without moral dimension," and Alan Liu argues that the moralistic ending is ironic.[17] It is also possible to argue that *Vathek*, far from being Beckford's psychologically troubled attempt to write an accurately oriental apologue, is an attack on the apologue form and on the occidental discourse of orientalism. It is a notably vigorous counterdiscourse to empirical and novelistic realism, privileging entertainment over morality, parodying earlier apologues, and asserting a vision of the oriental Other in a way that questions the conventional certainties of occidental ideology.

*Vathek* deploys a variety of strategies to establish an oriental reality that is distinct from but equal in authority to the occidental, and this happens most obviously in the notes. In them we see the crossing of East and West, for they are drawn from many sources, including some, like Homer and Ovid, of high authority in Western culture, and their purpose seems to be to document factual details of locality and behavior by setting the East and West side by side to exhibit their similarities. They appear, thus, to support the view that human nature is everywhere the same. At the same time, many of these details are strange, and the notes treat them with a bland unconcern that views the strange as familiar. For instance, when the embassy to Mecca returns with the sacred besom which is to be presented to Vathek, the Caliph, who "happened at this instant to be engaged in an apartment by no means adapted to the reception of embassies" (p. 39), commands the besom to be brought to him.[18] The "reverend Moullahs" approach the apartment, which they take to be an oratory, and present the besom, which Vathek promptly uses to brush cobwebs from the ceiling. This is a profanation and the Moullahs are scandalized, but the note of 1786 calmly quotes Harmer's *Observations* to the effect that "The dishonouring such places as had an appearance of being devoted to religious purposes, by converting them to the most abject offices of nature, was an Oriental method of expressing contempt, and hath continued from remote antiquity."[19] Vathek's act is outrageous, and indeed the note hints at how outrageous it is, for Vathek is clearly at his close-stool, but the outrage is passed over, coolly annotated as an ancient practice. A Western source is used to support the reality of Vathek's perverse act and the implication is that such acts are common; what the occidental reader and the oriental Moullah regard as shocking is presented by a Western author as representative of real behavior. In this way, the peculiarities of *Vathek*'s characters come to seem not peculiar but normal.

The ramifications of such characterization will be dealt with in a moment; that the function of the notes is at least partly to disrupt novelistic expectations is, however, clear.

More generally, the notes create a discourse, separate from but intimately linked with the narrative, in which details of the narrative are validated: Vathek, Carathis, Gulchenrouz, and others behave strangely, but they participate in the oriental strangeness of the whole tale, its setting, and its supernatural machinery. They construct a picture of human experience that transcends Western realism—indeed, a picture in which the West is made marginal. They do this by marshalling a great mass of Western scholarship whose ultimate effect is to demonstrate the culture-bound narrowness of the assumptions implicit in the realistic novel, with its emphasis on the normal and the familiar. Human life may be everywhere the same, but that does not mean that it is everywhere such as the novelists make it seem.

The strange behavior of the characters does more than that, for it mocks the conception of character developed by the novelists and thereby creates some of Beckford's best jokes. For example, Carathis is, if anything, yet worse than her son, but she has her own paradoxical morality. She cheerfully sacrifices the loyal subjects who rush to put out the fire in Vathek's tower (pp. 34–5); she looses vipers and scorpions on her guests, and "would have left her friends to die, were it not that, to fill up the time, she now and then amused herself in curing their wounds, ... for this good Princess abhorred being indolent" (pp.

38–9). She thinks nothing of starving the guides who are leading her to Vathek, nor of offering their corpses to be eaten by ghouls, but when her negresses ask to be allowed time for amorous dalliance with those ghouls, " ... Carathis, being chastity in the abstract,and an implacable enemy to love intrigues and sloth, at once rejected their prayer ... " (p. 92). Her prudishness intrudes on her otherwise hearty and good-humored enjoyment of her evil doing, and she even undoes some of it to avoid idleness. This chaste and industrious moral monster is novelistically unintelligible because the chief textual signs of immorality in the bourgeois discourse of the novel are sexual license and sloth. She is not marked with these signs, but she is not good, and the macabre delight she takes in her crimes shows her to be deficient in the essential sentimental-novelistic virtue of sympathy. In the discourse of the novel, lechery and sloth are forgivable because they offer the possibility of repentance, but a lack of sympathy undermines the very concept of morality,[20] and thus the possibility of repentance. Her character is a violation of probability, as constituted by novelistic discourse, that far outruns any merely supernatural apparition.

Vathek himself is comparably unnatural but rather more complex. His early devotion to sensuality, especially gluttony, seems to mark him as doomed in the novelistic discourse of morality, and the first three episodes with the Giaour expose his utter lack of self-control, promising a sticky end. But the protagonist of a moral tale, even one that culminates in his damnation, will be constructed so as to exhibit moral principles clearly, with a minimum of additional attributes. Vathek is not such a character: his immoderate hunger and thirst, his orgies of kicking, his profanation of the sacred besom, his mockery of the holy men, his eating of abominations, and much else establish him as damnable, but the main effect is not that of moral illustration. The sacred besom is ridiculous; the holy men are too stuffy; Vathek himself is a zany whose aberrations exceed purely moral purposes, and the process whereby he earns his punishment contains some wickedly entertaining episodes. Indeed, the Giaour's three appearances at the beginning, from his arrival with the marvellous inscribed sabres to his demand for fifty child sacrifices, repeat a triple pattern characteristic of folktales. This reduplication is also excessive, overdemonstrating the violent incongruity of Vathek's behavior. His nature includes an exoticism that is based not just on differences between the Orient and the Occident but also on a systematic violation of consistency in characterization, a principle important in both apologues and novels. He is consistently self-indulgent, but the active expression of this trait is such as to make surprise and humor operate against the discourse of realism and morality.

*Vathek*'s arrangement of plot elements is also such that apological reading, the mode of reading appropriate to moralized oriental tales, is subverted. Parreaux has noted the close similarity between Addison's original tale of Helim the physician, his daughter Balsora, the tyrant Alnareschin, and prince Abdallah (*The Guardian*, No. 167) and the episode in which Emir Fakreddin fakes the deaths of Nouronihar and Gulchenrouz in order to prevent Vathek's marrying Nouronihar. Parreaux's point, however, is largely based on his claim that Addison's tale "ne comporte aucune morale,"[21] since he argues that even in Addison's hands the oriental tale is exotic and unclassical. This is very dubious, and it obscures an important consideration. Addison gives us a comic romance of wisdom triumphant in which Alnareschin's desire for Balsora is thwarted, freeing her to join with Abdallah in cultivating their private virtue and converting their secluded dwelling into an image of paradise. Using the same plot-motifs, Beckford concocts a perverse tale of wisdom vanquished, in which Vathek's meeting with Nouronihar discloses Fakreddin's ruse, subverts the tendency toward virtue that the loss of Nouronihar has awakened, and leads straightforwardly to the eventual damnation of both. How this happens deserves some attention.

Vathek clearly corresponds to Alnareschin, Fakreddin to Helim, and Balsora to Nouronihar; other clear correspondences include the use of a soporific drug, the seclusion of the lovers, and the eventual disclosure. One of Beckford's disquieting modifications is the correspondence between Gulchenrouz and Abdallah; another is the irony that Shaban and Sutlememe, the servants whom Fakreddin provides, try to persuade their charges that they are genuinely dead and that they are to be chastised for an "indolent and voluptuous life" by being nourished on nothing but sermons and rice (p. 80). Nouronihar comes to regret her lost grandeur and falls out of love with Gulchenrouz, who is happy in morally edifying isolation. Her accidental meeting with Vathek parallels the meeting between Abdallah and his brother, Ibrahim, after Alnareschin's death, but far from being a confirmation of virtue this episode ends with her yielding to his will "with the most bewitching submission" (p. 85). Vathek, unlike Alnareschin, has some psychological interiority: events change him, if only temporarily, and he reacts to the loss of Nouronihar by becoming pious. For a time it appears as if the novelistic discourse of moral characterization will be applicable, but Beckford is only teasing his reader. In Addison's tale, the recovery of the loss, which is the main ingredient of the sentimentally happy ending, is the reunion of Abdallah and Ibrahim, because the lovers have not been parted, and Alnareschin remains the loser. The reunion of Vathek, who has become better as a result of the separation, with Nouronihar, who has become worse, is at best ironically happy, for it leads to their eternal remorse and mutual hatred in the Palace of Subterranean Fire.

The twist that Beckford gave to these correspondences shows that, though he adopted the same plot-motifs as Addison, he redistributed the roles so as to create an incongruity between the sentimental appeal of the outcome and its moral significance. This, in turn, undermines Parreaux's contention that Addison's tale has no moral—it has several that are deeply inscribed in the conventions of sentimental storytelling: good defeats evil and lives happily ever after; good is clever; evil is stupid; good finds contentment far from palaces and places of power; evil is suspicious and discontented. The list of morals can be extended to the limits of the reader's ingenuity. What Beckford has done is to prevent such a reading: the good and, in some respects, wise Fakreddin is exposed as a liar, while Nouronihar is too taken with the carbuncle of Giamschid to benefit from moral lessons, and Gulchenrouz is too taken with the dwarfs who recite the Koran to be of continued narrative interest. Beckford's tale does not indulge the occidental attitudes that clearly structure Addison's, and in his handling of the characters of Vathek and Nouronihar and of the role of chance in shaping events he is repudiating a sentimental, moral heritage. His use of Addisonian motifs allows him to reproduce the outward form of an apologue, even as he frustrates the apological impulse.

The full force of this frustration will appear more strongly if we examine a slightly more remote but still similar episode in Johnson's *Rasselas*. There, in Chapters 33 to 37, Pekuah is abducted by the Arab, and Nekayah, deprived of her favorite, exhibits "the progress of sorrow," which gives Imlac an opportunity for some Johnsonian psychologizing. Just when Nekayah is over her crisis, the Arab offers Pekuah for ransom, and the group is reunited. The initial kidnapping seems to promise exciting adventures after the fashion of entertaining romances, but what Johnson actually gives us is the case history of Nekayah's grief, subverting a convention to serve a didactic purpose. Indeed, Johnson tells the joke a second time, for Pekuah's account of her captivity is a parallel history of boredom. We have here the separation promoting the cultivation of virtue and culminating in a happy reunion which in Addison's version patterned a moral oriental romance and which Beckford revised to eliminate the moral subtext. Johnson revises it in a different direction, for under its oriental dress his tale is a powerful expression of the Western moral order which declares the uniformity of mankind and deals with differences by abolishing them. In a breathtaking act of cultural imperialism, Johnson annexes Cairo to London by asserting that they are the same, and he proves this by analyses such as the one that Imlac gives of the pyramids. They are, he says, products of "that hunger of imagination which preys incessantly upon life."[22] This explanation is drawn from Johnson's moral thought and his cultural tradition, and it is given instead of one based on Egyptian tradition. In a parallel way, Imlac's account of Nekayah's states of mind as she traces the progress of sorrow emphasizes European psychological theory, expelling the exoticism of the oriental mind.

By a series of such manoeuvres, Johnson explains away cultural difference, reducing the oriental to the occidental, even as he frustrates entertainment, reducing the romantic to the apological and the realistic.[23] *Rasselas* is thus the inverse of *Vathek*, for Beckford's subversion is directed at realism and Western ideology, freeing the entertaining romance of its load of didactic morality. These complementary transformations leave *Rasselas* and *Vathek* as radically opposed yet radically similar texts in more than their uncommon exploitation of common generic conventions. The characters have some affinities— Rasselas with Vathek, Nekayah with Nouronihar, and Imlac with Carathis—and they form analogous associations. As Liu has recently argued, this generalized alignment serves to focus the differences. He has shown them to occupy opposing poles within a shared discourse of good and bad taste, but the principle he has pointed out applies with equal force to their relative positions in the discourse of orientalism as well. Johnson adopts Lockean psychological realism; Beckford chooses an incongruous and unpredictable fantastic mode of characterization. Johnson dismisses orientalism; Beckford dismisses occidentalism. *Rasselas* occupies a secure position near the center of the culturally privileged ideology, and this is reflected in its authoritative discourse on human experience; *Vathek* is ironic and macabre because it locates itself at the cultural periphery and it speaks in resistance to authority.

In adopting this stance, Beckford does not manage to escape the occidental discourse, because his orientalism depends on that discourse much as blasphemy depends on belief or crime on the law, but he adds something to it. Jorge Luis Borges remarks, "There is an untranslatable English epithet, the epithet 'uncanny,' to denote supernatural horror; that epithet (*unheimlich* in German) is applicable to certain pages of *Vathek*, but not, as far as I recall, to any other book before it."[24] The uncanny is a category of acute philosophical and psychological unease inspired by the supernatural and the unnatural.[25] In *Vathek*, the rejection of empirical epistemology entails supernatural occurrences, allowing the creatures of Arabic mythology to inhabit the tale without apological/apologetic allegorization, and the offense against novelistic discourse entails unnaturalness, allowing nominally human beings to exist who are nevertheless unreadable in the discourse of realism. The rejection and the offense take place within the structural framework of an apologue, and this is one source of Beckford's uncanny effect. Part of the time, the reader sees the apological framework, with all its conventional alignments to the real and the familiar, and part of the time that framework comes to seem unreal because through it are visible signs of other realities that are normally suppressed in occidental discourse. By thus disclosing something "that needs to remain hidden if the world is to be comfortably 'known'"[26] in his attack on the comfortable discourse of realism, Beckford became one of the inventors of modern fantasy.

Indeed, the thematic structuring of *Vathek* anticipates a pattern that, according to Tobin Siebers, became common in romantic fantasy: Beckford "transforms the social participation of supernaturalism into the aesthetic participation of the fantastic by duplicating the superstitious patterns of persecution and exclusion that influence social life."[27] Beckford's own experience of social persecution and exclusion undoubtedly informs the thematics of his tale. He projects the forces of persecution and exclusion into his tale both as the supernatural Giaour commanded by Mohammed and as the scholarly apparatus of explanatory notes, while the superstitiously excluded and persecuted victim is the main focus of narration. Thus it is that Vathek's psyche is the locus of an anti-novelistic personality, and all around him are the signs of his

crimes—the ironies and jokes that cripple the apological structure—
but we are puzzled how to read him, for the notes imply that the uniformity of human life includes him as well. Vathek is accused, he is
guilty, and he is punished, but this simple sequence encompasses
supernatural and unnatural occurrences, so it does not yield a moral
fable based on a world that is comfortably known. Instead, it involves
the reader in a complex paradox:

A crucial aspect of every fantastic story is the relation between the reader and the
accused. If the reader decides to embrace the accused agent of the fantastic, the
logic of superstition is allowed to endure. Expelling the accused serves to eliminate the supernatural. Yet the formula is not this simple. Whereas embracing the
accused admits the supernatural, expelling him reproduces the essential logic of
superstition.[28]

*Vathek* clings uncannily to the discourse it attacks, disclosing its operations, showing its repressiveness, and entrapping the reader by con-
fronting him, whichever way he turns, with its falsehoods.

   *Vathek* constructs a further uncanny effect on the foundation of this
dilemma. The reader who attempts to reject the tale as oriental and
superstitious, full of Islamic supernatural machinery and non-realism,
is shown by the notes to be rejecting Western thought as well in a gesture that is itself superstitious. One who attempts to embrace the tale
because its notes show how it extends the occidental discourse of universal human nature similarly allows the unreal, the oriental, into that
discourse. The point is not that Beckford's uncanny orientalism is
more authentic than that of his predecessors, though it is more heavily
annotated, but that Beckford has transformed the marginality of the
oriental by establishing in it a tendentiously non-western centre of dis-

cursive authority from which he can attack occidentalism. He may, in fact, be vicariously attacking his tutor, John Lettice, and his guardian, Lord Chatham, two staunch exponents of occidentalism, who forced him in 1773, when he was thirteen, to burn "at the shrine of good taste" the oriental drawings and other treasures he had accumulated.[29] Thirteen years later, in a tale that flouts conventional good taste and that draws constant attention to its own orientalism, he had a telling revenge.

University of Calgary

## REFERENCES

[1]See Martha Pike Conant, *The Oriental Tale in England in the Eighteenth Century* (New York: Columbia Univ. Press, 1908); James K. Folsom, "Beckford's *Vathek* and the Tradition of Oriental Satire," *Criticism*, 6 (1964), 53–69; Robert J. Gemmett, *William Beckford* (Boston: Twayne, 1977); Kenneth W. Graham, "Beckford's Adaptations of the Oriental Tale in *Vathek*," *Enlightenment Essays*, vol. 5, no. 1 (1974), pp. 24–33; Alan Liu, "Towards a Theory of Common Sense: Beckford's *Vathek* and Johnson's *Rasselas*," *Texas Studies in Language and Literature* 26 (1984), 183–217; Fatma Moussa Mahmoud, "Beckford, *Vathek*, and the Oriental Tale," in *William Beckford of Fonthill 1760–1844: Bicentenary Essays*, ed. Fatma Moussa Mahmoud (1960, rpt. Port Washington: Kennikat, 1972), pp. 63–121; Mahmoud Manzalaoui, "Pseudo-Orientalism in Transition: The Age of *Vathek*," in Mahmoud, ed., *William Beckford*, pp. 123–50; Temple Maynard, "The Landscape of Vathek," in *Transactions of the Samuel Johnson Society of the North West*, vol. 7, ed. Alan Fisher (Seattle: SJSNW, 1975), pp. 79–98; André Parreaux, *William Beckford auteur de* Vathek *(1760–1844)* (Paris: Nizet, 1960).

[2]Manzalaoui, p. 124; Gemmett, pp. 19–20, 102, and *passim*.

[3]Edward W. Said, *Orientalism* (New York: Pantheon, 1978), p. 1.

[4]Said, *Orientalism*, p. 71.

[5]Arthur J. Weitzman, "The Oriental Tale in the Eighteenth Century: A Reconsider-

ation," *Studies on Voltaire and the Eighteenth Century*, 58 (1967), 1842–6.

[6]Clara Reeve, *The Progress of Romance and the History of Charoba, Queen of Aegypt* (1785, rpt., 2 vols. in 1, New York: Facsimile Text Society, 1930).

[7]George Granville, Lord Lansdowne, "An Essay Upon Unnatural Flights in Poetry," *Critical Essays of the Seventeenth Century*, ed. J. E. Spingarn, 3 vols. (1909, rpt. Bloomington: Indiana Univ. Press, 1957), III, 295.

[8]*The Spectator*, ed. Donald F. Bond, 5 vols. (Oxford: Clarendon Press, 1965), III, 570–3.

[9]The eighteenth-century distrust of fantasy and medievalism is discussed in Arthur Johnston, *Enchanted Ground* (London: Athlone Press, 1964); Samuel F. Pickering, Jr., *John Locke and Children's Books in Eighteenth-Century England* (Knoxville: Univ. of Tennessee Press, 1981); and Geoffrey Summerfield, *Fantasy and Reason* (London: Methuen, 1984).

[10]This principle is asserted by many authors. David Hume's version shows its importance in both moral philosophy and the theory of the novel:

> It is universally acknowledged that there is a great uniformity among the actions of men, in all nations and ages, and that human nature remains still the same, in its principles and operations. The same motives always produce the same actions: The same events follow from the same causes. Ambition, avarice, self-love, vanity, friendship, generosity, public spirit: these passions, mixed in various degrees, and distributed through society, have been, from the beginning of the world, and still are, the source of all the actions and enterprises, which have ever been observed among mankind.

*Enquiries Concerning Human Understanding and Concerning the Principles of Morals*, ed. L. A. Selby-Bigge, 3rd ed., rev. P. H. Nidditch (Oxford: Clarendon Press, 1975), p. 83.

[11]*The Spectator*, I, 398–402.

[12]See Said, pp. 60, 65–6, 68–9.

[13]*The Guardian*, ed. John Calhoun Stephens (Lexington: Univ. Press of Kentucky, 1982), pp. 483–5.

[14]Sheldon Sacks, *Fiction and the Shape of Belief* (Berkeley: Univ. of California Press, 1967), p. 26.

[15]Parreaux, p. 313.

[16]Brian Fothergill, *Beckford of Fonthill* (London: Faber and Faber, 1979), pp. 129–34. There are a number of studies that adopt this psychological orientation; see James Henry Rieger, *"Au Pied de la Lettre*: Stylistic Uncertainty in 'Vathek,'" *Criticism*, 4 (1962), 302–12; and Robert Kiely, *The Romantic Novel in England* (Cambridge: Harvard Univ. Press, 1972), pp. 43–64.

[17]Kiely, p. 53; Liu, p. 195.

[18]William Beckford, *Vathek*, ed. Roger Lonsdale (London: Oxford Univ. Press, 1970).

[19]I quote from the only recent edition that reprints the notes of 1786: *The Castle of Otranto* by Horace Walpole, *Vathek* by William Beckford, *The Vampyre* by John Polidori, and *A Fragment of a Novel* by Lord Byron: *Three Gothic Novels*, ed. E. F. Bleiler (New York: Dover, 1964), p. 208.

[20]For the importance of sympathy as the basis of morality, see Hume, pp. 218–26.

[21]Parreaux, p. 316.

[22]Samuel Johnson, *The History of Rasselas, Prince of Abissinia*, ed. Geoffrey Tillotson and Brian Jenkins (London: Oxford Univ. Press, 1971), p. 85.

[23]For a discussion of *Rasselas* as a subversive tale, see Earl R. Wasserman, "Johnson's *Rasselas:* Implicit Contexts," *Journal of English and Germanic Philology*, 74 (1975), 1–25.

[24]Jorge Luis Borges, "About William Beckford's *Vathek*," *Other Inquisitions 1937–52*, trans. Ruth L. C. Simms (Austin: Univ. of Texas Press, 1964), p. 140.

[25]For a discussion of the uncanny, see Rosemary Jackson, *Fantasy: The Literature of Subversion* (London: Methuen, 1981), pp. 63–72.

[26]Jackson, p. 65.

[27]Tobin Siebers, *The Romantic Fantastic* (Ithaca: Cornell Univ. Press, 1984), p. 46.

[28]Siebers, p. 56.

[29]Fothergill, p. 41.

# VATHEK—MEGALOMANIAC CALIPH OR PUNDIT OF THE AVANT-GARDE?

## Michel Baridon

A few years before Beckford wrote *Vathek*, a Frenchman of some distinction, M. de Monville, began the construction of a strange tower in the extensive grounds he was improving at Chambourcy, near Paris. This tower was meant to present the appearance of a colossal column in ruins; it was large enough to offer comfortable lodgings to the genius of the place and yet, seen from the garden, it served as a fabric which filled the mind of the astonished visitor with sad musings on the mutability of all things. This strange ruinated structure thus served a double purpose: it enabled M. de Monville to philosophize in the open and to enjoy the sweets of life indoors, and no knowledgeable visitor can see the Désert de Retz, where it still stands,[1] without having a thought for the megalomaniac fantasies of Vathek and of his creator William Beckford.

Whether Beckford knew M. de Monville or whether he had occasion to visit the grounds of the Désert de Retz is not known to modern critics, but the convergence which exists between the Frenchman's gigantic "folly" and the Englishman's dreams of psychic architecture cannot pass unnoticed. Like M. de Monville, Beckford admirably knew how to let his imagination roam about the shape and atmosphere of imaginary dwellings; like him also he succeeded in bringing together the pleasures of refinement and the terrors of nightmares; and like him again he achieved the blending together of the immaterial and of the ponderous by transforming the shape of arches and the weight of stone into the flimsy substance of dreams.

The purpose of the present paper is to explain why this bringing together of extremes was a decisive advance in post-Burkean esthetics. It is also to assess its lasting importance in the romantic age and even later, for Mallarmé would never have resurrected *Vathek* if he had not felt that its avant-garde character did in fact contain revelations and intimations which were to prove essential to the development of aesthetics in the eighty-odd years extending between the rise of the Gothic novel and Cézanne's *Une Moderne Olympia*.

* * *

Before studying Beckford's aesthetics in relation to Romanticism, it is perhaps necessary to explain why it has been defined as "post-Burkean." Burke's *Enquiry* established criteria which have remained famous and which can easily be traced in Beckford's text. Sublimity and Beauty are categories used by Beckford in his delineation of characters: Gulchenrouz and Nouronihar present all the characteristics of "beautiful" human beings because they are lovely, small, sociable, graceful and amiable, whereas Eblis fills the reader with impressions truly "sublime" because he dwells in mystery and solitude behind huge doors of ebony and because he strikes all around him with terror. Setting and character are made to harmonize since Gulchenrouz is always to be found in places of luxury and comfort while Eblis reigns supreme over colossal palaces deep in "the very entrails of the earth, where breathes the sansar or the icy wind of death."[2] The delights enjoyed in palaces where everything seems contrived to refine upon the pleasures of Man are thus contrasted with the horrors of unbounded expanses in which destruction reigns supreme. A single example can serve to illustrate Beckford's use of the fundamental categories of Burkean esthetics; it is taken from the scene in which fifty young children are massacred by the caliph:

They approached the plain full of sportiveness, some coursing butterflies, other culling flowers, or picking up the shiny little pebbles that attracted their notice. At intervals they nimbly started from each other for the sake of being caught again and mutually imparting a thousand caresses.

The dreadful chasm, at whose bottom the portal of ebony was placed, began to appear at a distance. It looked like a black streak that divided the plain. Morakanabad and his companions took it for some work which the caliph had ordered. Unhappy men! Little did they surmise for what it was destined (25).

None of the requisites listed by Burke in his analysis of the "efficient" causes of the Sublime and the Beautiful will be found missing here: horror, verticality, infinity, endless repetition, apprehension, and gloom provide suitable oppositions to smallness, sociability, pleasurable occupations, and smoothness. Neither did Beckford neglect sensations; since they were considered by Burke, in perfect conformity with the teachings of Locke, to be vital to mental activity, Vathek is submitted to an unceasing bombardment of sensory impressions; the poor Caliph falls in fact a victim to experimental aesthetics and all his true friends will forever remember how he is put to the test by the stench of the "venomous oil," the wailings of the dwarfs, and the taste of the medicines concocted by Carathis. None of the five wings of the palace of Alkoremi were meant to be inferior to the others; since they were destined "for the gratification of each of the senses" (1) they must be given equal importance. Beckford was so brilliant a disciple that he improved on his master's ingenuity: *Vathek* teems with olfactory and gustatory sensations in which the *Enquiry* is notoriously defective.

Beckford's insistence on sensations and his illustrations of the sublime and the beautiful seem to point to a definition of *Vathek* as a pure illustration of Burkean aesthetics; yet the book contains so many distortions of the categories defined by the *Enquiry* that the nature and the justification of these distortions must be analyzed if Beckford's modernity is to be understood. The distortions which have just been mentioned can be found in the multiplication of objects supposed to form unending series. Burke did see in "Succession and uniformity" one of the "efficient causes" of the sublime caused by what he called "artificial infinity"[3]; of this "artificial infinity" Beckford made a very extensive use: the fifteen hundred stairs of the tower, the twenty thousand shining lances (4), the endless succession of chambers, halls, and galleries (115) to say nothing of the "forty thousand kicks" bestowed on the guards constitute many instances of multiplied repetitions destined to open the reader's imagination to the wonders of the sublime.

Sublimity as generated by Beckford's artificial infinity was a decisive advance on Burke, however, for the *Enquiry* only took as examples a "rotund" in which, "turn which way you will, the same object still seems to continue and the imagination has no rest," and "the grand appearance of the ancient heathen temples" in which "a range of uniform pillars" stamps "on bounded objects the character of infinity."[4] Islamic sublimity as it was felt in *Vathek* afforded much greater possibilities than Burke's classic or Gothic examples; it derived from Arabic sources a use of great numbers which borders on the fantastic and by means of which echoes of d'Herbelot serve to expand the Burkean categories into which they are infiltered.

Before *Vathek* was written, oriental fiction had already established itself as one of the received genres. When, in the field of aesthetics, reason slowly declined and yielded to the superior powers of sensibility, the sensuousness of the Orient could well appear as a means of using climates of sensibility corresponding to Lockean psychology. Since, according to the *Essay upon Human Understanding*, sensations were the basic fabric of mental life, and since the modes of sensation were pleasure and pain, the literatures of the East could well appear as models. They displayed a wealth of sensations which suited the educated reader's conception of the new "way of ideas." In more ways than one, what Voltaire called "le beau style oriental" was used to supersede the formality of neo-classicism without falling into the barbarity of the Gothic. The orientals appeared as models who had brought sensuousness to perfection. Voltaire himself, while he professed the greatest admiration for the "Siècle de Louis XIV," could thus yield to the charm of a more modern inspiration. And he did so all the more willingly as caliphs and magi enabled him to depict the charms of a world in which there were no monasteries and no Church administration to deny men the joys of the flesh. Montesquieu's *Lettres persanes* were written in the same vein. Gibbon followed in Voltaire's and Montesquieu's steps and he made a lavish use of "the splendours of the East" because they displayed climates of sensibility totally antagonistic to the Christian spirit of self-denial.

Needless to say, there were great differences between the "beau style oriental" as used by Voltaire and the modernized version produced by Gibbon. The *Decline and Fall* is more truly sensuous and more truly expressive of the greatness of Islam than *Zadig*. But the differences are even greater between Gibbon and Beckford. While the former delights in the charming irrationality of magic, the latter exerts the powers of the imagination in such a way as to transport his readers into the regions where the bearings inculcated by "Western" aesthetic criteria are totally lost. Gibbon could still write:

Our education in the Greek and Latin schools may have fixed in our mind a standard of exclusive taste; and I am not forward to condemn the literature and judgement of nations of whose language I am ignorant. Yet, I know that the classics have much to teach and I believe that the Orientals have much to learn ...[5]

With Beckford, things changed completely; whatever sympathy he felt for Gibbon,[6] he considered that the Orientals had much to teach and he conceived his *Vathek* in such a way as to make it the very image of the modern psyche. His hero was to be an experimentalist in a new science, the "physics of the soul," to quote Voltaire's definition of Lockean psychology; he was to haunt the palaces of the senses until he could frame a philosophy best suited to the taste of a rational voluptuary; and it was this philosophy which made him an aesthete. The truths of things were in the sensations they provoked; to refine on sensations was to intensify life, to purify it to an essence which contained its ultimate meaning. The rationality of the classics was too drab, too cold, to favor the quest for beauty; it must be disposed of at all costs, and the magic of oriental or Gothic mythology, either in *Vathek* or at Fonthill, could best serve the purpose of promoting new art forms.

Hence his association with artists like de Loutherbourg, the Cozenses, Romney—the Dr Jekyll and Mr Hyde of fashionable portrait painting—and Wyatt. Not only was Beckford interested in the visual arts as such; what he sought when he associated with architects and painters, was the possibility of supplying his imagination—the "waking thoughts" so vital to his inspiration—with a variety of concrete forms; and the artists who have been named were then actively researching into the creation of new virtualities of expression. Alexander Cozens was experimenting on blots to explore the possibilities offered by associationism; de Loutherbourg was the landscape painter of natural sublimity as well as the mystagogue and enchanter of Fonthill; Wyatt was one of the Gothicists who supplanted palladianism; Romney's secret dreams led him to imagine witches, monsters and strange visionary scenes.[7]

Like all fiction writers, Beckford created an artificial world in order to give life to the innermost movements of his own thoughts. The creations of his artist friends enabled him to confirm the expressive character of his visions; it made them more objective. This led him to positions much more uncompromising than those hitherto adopted in the 18th century. He radically transformed the oriental imagination by pushing it to the limit of its artistic possibilities. He took advantage of its absolutely unbounded freedom—in this respect he displayed all the qualities of his caliph—and he peopled his pages with creatures, objects and episodes as freely disposed as the blots used by Alexander Cozens. Hence the distortions which may well constitute Beckford's most original contribution to late 18th century English literature. Such distortions are to be found in the cripples and the dwarfs who appear here and there in the tale. Their littleness preserves, however, some of the characteristics of beauty as described by Burke: they are not ugly and they can be admired for the symmetry of their bodies. Such is not the case whenever Beckford, instead of miniaturizing things, enlarges them to monstrous proportions. Just before Vathek and Nouronihar fall into "the most abject affliction" at discovering Soliman's heart enveloped in flames, they discover him "on the loftiest elevation and placed immediately under the dome."(112) Similar manifestations of gigantic distortions are to be found in the building of the tower, in the depth of the chasm into which the fifty children are precipitated, in the dilatation of the sun whose "pure gold yielded to a sanguine red"(66), in the planets "which seemed almost to blaze" after Vathek's blasphemous promises to the Giaour, in the prodigious size of the palace of Istakar in front of which "stood forth the colossal forms of four creatures, composed of the leopard and the griffin, and though, but of stone, inspired emotions of terror" (107).

The importance given to the gigantic in *Vathek* points to one conclusion: whenever Beckford meant to strike his reader with "sublime" impressions he resorted to the gigantic; and yet, the gigantic as he used it had little to do with Burke's static "causes of the sublime"; whereas in the *Enquiry*, colonnades, mountains, cascades, domes reach, in Burke's own terms, to a "great extreme of dimension,"[8] they remain static; motion is never suffered to become part of the discussion of architecture as a cause of sublimity. Beckford makes use of architecture in a totally different way; he confers on the shape of buildings a dynamic character which is wholly original and which makes us feel that, with *Vathek*, the sublime as defined in the age of sensibility is undergoing a mutation which leads to the romantic age.

Other examples of similar distortions may be found in descriptive passages. Vathek's tower is a sort of catapult from which he would like to project himself into the sky.

His pride arrived at its height, when having ascended, for the first time the fifteen hundred stairs of his tower, he cast his eyes below and beheld men not larger than pismires; mountains than shells; and cities than beehives. The idea which such an elevation inspired of his own grandeur, completely bewildered him: he was almost ready to adore himself; till, lifting his eyes upwards, he saw the stars above him as they appeared when he stood on the surface of the world. He consoled himself, however, for this intruding and unwelcome perception of his littleness, with the thought of being great in the eyes of others;and flattered himself that the light of his mind would extend beyond the reach of his sight, and extort from the stars the decrees of his destiny (4).

Vathek may well leap into the sky, at least in imagination, for his tower is constantly rising by the operation of magic: "When the work-men had raised their structure a cubit in the daytime, two cubits more were added in the night" (4).

In a similar way the Indian creates a general panic by transforming himself into a ball which draws everybody after it like a magnetic comet; he ends his fantastic course by "glancing from the precipice with the rapidity of lightning" and losing himself "in the gulph below" (20). After the sacrifice of the fifty boys, the chasm "closes" silently (28). Similar effects of dilatation and constriction appear in the description of a meteor which strangely prefigures the modern flying saucer:

In the midst of this festive scene, there appeared a light on the top of the highest mountain, which attracted the notice of every eye; this light was not less bright than the moon and might have been taken for her, had not the moon already risen. The phenomenon occasioned a general surprize and no one could conjecture the cause. It could not be a fire for the light was clear and bluish: nor had meteors ever been seen of that magnitude and splendour. This strange light faded, for a moment; and immediately renewed its brightness. It first appeared motionless at the foot of the rock; whence it darted in an instant, to sparkle in a thicket of palm trees: from thence it glided along the torrent; and at last fixed in a glen that was narrow and dark ... Whilst they were debating what was best to be done, the light shot forth so dazzling a blaze that they all fled away shrieking (68–69).

Aurorae borealis were frequently described in the 18th century; they supplied meterologists with opportunities for reports which look like purple patches in the *Philosophical Transactions*. Meteors had always impressed the learned and the vulgar and Beckford knew that he would strike his readers with dismay by describing the mysterious lights which illuminated the sky as they expanded over the stars.

Similar effects affecting the subterranean world accompany the episodes which bring Vathek's story to an end. The first occurs before he is allowed to enter Eblis's palace:

He scarcely had read these words, before the mountain, against which the terrace was reared, trembled; and the watch-towers were ready to topple headlong upon them. The rock yawned, and disclosed within it a staircase of polished marble, that seemed to approach the abyss (108).

The second is to be found when Carathis interrupts the narrations of the four young men:

... when the third prince had reached the midst of his adventures, a sudden noise interrupted him, which caused the vault to tremble and to open. Immediately a cloud descended, which gradually dissipating, discovered Carathis on the back of an afrit, who grievously complained of his burden (116).

When the Caliph, together with his mother, Nouronihar and the four princes receive their ultimate punishment, they are affected by similar deformations. Carathis "glanced off in a rapid whirl that ren-

dered her invisible, and continued to revolve without intermission."
The others "recoiled, with looks of the most furious distraction"(119),
as if they were sheets of inflammable material thrown into an invisible
fire.

As has already been said, oriental magic was used in European literature before Beckford's time. Voltaire, Montesquieu, Gibbon and
others had read their d'Herbelot and they knew how to make use of the
possibilities offered by the *Bibliothèque orientale* to the literary illu-
sionists; flying carpets, instant metamorphoses, and prodigious flights
through space were inseparable from the "beau style oriental"; but
Beckford was the first to terrorize his readers with what had hitherto
delighted them. He managed to effect this mutation of oriental aesthetics by infusing into it some of the elements actively at work in the
transformation of the creative imagination of the age.

Among these elements, three at least ought to be distinguished
because they generated new images and spread new conceptions of a
world picture which widely differed from that of the early phases of
the Enlightenment. They are all connected with the scientific movement: the first concerns the early experiments on electricity and magnetism; the second, the growing interest in biology following on the
rejection of preformational models of reproduction; and the third, the
concept of perfectibility as it had come to assume a growing importance in the philosophical works of the period.

\* \* \*

It would be preposterous to turn Beckford into an 18th-century
Jules Verne, yet he did read scientific books, as his annotations to

Buffon testify, and he had enough interest in aurora borealis to write: "Shall we with Halley regard it as the effect of magnetism, with Meyer and Rowning kindle an assemblage of exhalations or with Meron call down light from the fixed stars?"[9]

Granted that his curiosities lay with the arts rather than with the sciences, he was an esthete with a remarkable flair for the new, and the new is most of the time discovered by scientific observation. Cocteau may not have been much versed in aerostatics, but there are air-pockets in the typography of his early poems; Picasso did not spend his time reading books of ethnology, but he sensed that great advances were being made in this field and he regenerated the creative imagination of his age by giving a mysterious new life to the arts of civilizations almost lost in the depth of time; other examples could be thought of: Klee with modern psychology; Seurat with Chevreul's theory of light, etc. Suggestions and promptings are essential to the development of an avant-garde, and Beckford, like the artists who have just been named, was a born avant-gardiste. Like them also, and like his Vathek, he was an Icarus whose genius lay in immoderateness.

Immoderateness can be a most precious gift if it urges a creator to devote himself wholly to the exploration of new fields. And since Beckford added to the powers of his imagination the sensibility of a true critic, he was able to become the very impersonation of all the revolutionary trends which composed the Zeitgeist of the later Enlightenment. To follow him in his quest for a new type of beauty is to accompany the intellectual progress of Fuseli, Blake, Flaxman, Romney, the Cozenses, West, and several others. All these artists are distinguished by their attraction to the grotesque, the immoderate, the fantastic, the monstrous and the lurid; they distort forms and they favor light effects which emphasize mysterious or dramatic chiaroscuro contrasts.

Such contrasts were not discoverable only by the observation of the sky. Other mysterious phenomena were intriguing the general public and even if we have no positive proof of Beckford's interest in magnetism and electricity, we may assume that he was not ignorant of the discoveries which greatly impressed his contemporaries. De Loutherbourg would never have been called the mystagogue of Fonthill if his curiosities had not lain that way.

\*   \*   \*

In his *History of Science, Technology and Philosophy in the 18th Century*, A. Wolff writes:

While in the seventeenth century the greatest advances in physics had occurred in the department of mechanics and optics, which were among the oldest branches of natural science, the eighteenth century was remarkable for its developments in the realm of frictional electricity which had been opened up by Gilbert and Von Gericke.[10]

He thus sums up the rise of a new science which raised enough enthusiasm to make Napoleon treat Volta like a prince. Before him, Franklin had gained official recognition as the "vainqueur du Tonnerre" and in the popular imagination he stood as a genius who could who could steal the thunder from the hands of the gods at the same time as he brought liberty to men. The very name *electricity* carried with it an aura of power and mystery which can perhaps compare with the one which surrounds nuclear physics today. Experiments were conducted in scientific societies all over the world. No less important than those experiments were the number of impressive electrical machines which went into operation, some of them, says Wolff, of great dimensions. They required the use of a "glass globe which rotated rapidly"; if the feet of a man "hanging in silk cords" were made to touch the revolving globe, he acted as "a prime conductor from which sparks could be taken."[11] Such machines were in use in England; they were described by Priestley in his *History of Electricity*, in which he mentioned "three or four globes rotating simultaneously." It became possible—and fashionable—to provoke discharges of electricity and cause strong impressions on those who watched in the dark. This might explain Beckford's fascination for the strange flame and crystal effects at the end of *Vathek*. It might also explain the Caliph's fascination for the globe of fire on which Eblis sits, as well as the fact that his face has been "blasted by thunder."

Electricity was then so mysterious a phenomenon that quacks made use of it for purposes which were scientific only in appearance. Wolff may be quoted again in connection with mesmerism:

... the advances made, in the course of the 18th century in the study of electromagnetic phenomena, including galvanism or "animal magnetism" did indeed suggest possibilities of electromagnetic treatment ... [I]n London, James Graham, of Edinburgh, established an "Aesculapian Temple" for electromagnetic treatment. It contained a celestial bed, supported on glass pillars, and decorated with magnets and some electrical hocus pocus. It was reserved for the select who could pay £100 per night, and was looked after by Emma Lyons subsequently famous as Lady Hamilton.[12]

One cannot read about Graham's "Aesculapian temple" without

establishing connections between Beckford's imagination, his private life and the circle of his artist friends. We know that Emma Lyons was painted several times by Romney in 1782, the year when *Vathek* was written and when the very same Romney was commissioned to portray young "Kitty" Courtenay.[13] We also know that Romney was a great admirer of Emma Lyons whose beauty he associated with languid attitudes suggesting illness and melancholy, a state of health of which Beckford had personal experience.

The magic of electricity, together with the despair of being ever cured, the strange effect produced by glass and fire, the association of the mysteries of science with black magic and with the beauty of Emma, all suggest that Beckford's imagination was haunted by images popularized by scientific research. Romney himself painted an impressive portrait of Newton holding a prism which discomposes light into its seven components;[14] the great scientist is painted against a pitch black background and he is presented as a magician whose powers conjure up the mysteries of the unseen. In *Vathek*, magnetism and electricity are not only described by the luminous or physical effects they provoke; they are also present by their capacity to attract and to distort. They are invisible agents acting at a distance. Carathis flies in the air and seems to be aspirated into the abysmal sky; her forehead is "corrugated" as if she was struck by fire without even seeing flames. And the reader is all the more impressed by the description of her ultimate dissolution as she seems to have been struck by lightning.

Electricity was considered very dangerous in the days of Beckford. The Dutch scientist Muschenbroek, when he related one of his experiments to Réaumur—himself a friend of Bonnet whom Beckford had met—said that he had been in great danger of being killed by the commotion he had felt.[15] His description of the electrical machine he used brings into play "rods"—Eblis, it will be remembered, "swayed an iron sceptre" in his hand "which thunder had blasted"—as well as silk cords and spheres of crystal used as Leyden jars. No less interesting are the illustrations to some of the experiments conducted on static electricity, for they show that swords were used to produce sparks, which must have made them look like the "fulminating sabres" displayed by the Giaour before he transforms himself into a magnetic ball.[16]

All this proves that Beckford was aware of his contemporaries' interest in the mysteries of electricity and magnetism; his artist friends shared this interest which was often enhanced by political implications as Robert Darnton has proved;[17] nor were these implications, indifferent to somebody whose politics assumed a radical cast.

No less important, though perhaps not so impressive, was the impact of biology on the collective imagination. New images of the world of plants and animals percolated into the general public consciousness. Erasmus Darwin's *Loves of the Plants* was given an enthusiastic reception; it was illustrated by Blake, for whom Beckford had a lasting admiration, and Blake, it will be remembered, often embosomed his figures in foliage. This mysterious union of Man with nature implied that all beings assumed a plastic quality common to both the vegetable and the animal worlds.

In the second half of the 18th century it looks as if the scientific community tended to question the supremacy of geometry in order to establish that of biology. This entailed a change in epistemological conceptions and although it is no easy thing to prove the existence of correspondences between the research of scientists and the creative activity of artists, one cannot deny that in the second half of the 18th century a decline of geometrical systems took place in the arts. Whether we look at the gardens at Versailles or at the "système" in conformity with which the French tragedies were written (the three unities, the congruence of human motivations with a repertory of passions reputed to be eternal) we shall find that the great creations of Neoclassicism depended on very strict rules established by human reason and reputed to provide infallible guidelines for the artist. This triumph of rational formality was also the triumph of the *"méthode des géomètres"* so much praised by Descartes because the *"méthode des géomètres"* suited the mechanistic conceptions underlying the world picture of the neoclassicists. It assumed that human nature was the same in all ages and that the true manner of painting it was by the help of rules; it also assumed that since rules were founded on human reason they were as eternal as human nature itself. Hence the impression we derive from the contemplation of the great creations of classicism: they seem impervious to time as if they had triumphed over its relentless action. They are the *"rêve de pierre"* of which Baudelaire spoke; geometry establishes fixed relations between their different parts and between the parts and the whole. Their harmony results from logical articulations which proclaim the indestructible character of geometrical relations.

When Diderot laughed at a picture because its left half was exactly symmetrical with the right one, when Pope and the English gardenists decided against regularity and formality, it became evident that important changes were occurring. Geometry was losing ground, and it may be interesting to note that it suffered its first obvious defeat in the gardens: many an English landlord stuck to palladianism as a style fit for a house; but he did not object to having a Gothic ruin on his grounds.

The development of biology in the second half of the 18th century accelerated the movement away from the geometric. Whether all members of the ever-growing public who discussed Lamarck, Erasmus Darwin, or Bonnet were conversant with the theoretical views they had expressed is no easy thing to ascertain, but Beckford had seen Bonnet when he was in Switzerland and he certainly knew more about his works than many.[18] It is no exaggeration to consider that he knew why a new conception of organic development was slowly imposing itself. The preformational view, according to which reproduction was achieved by the growth of a germ strictly similar to its genitor, was gradually being abandoned. The prevailing view became quite opposite: the growth of a germ was unpredictable; nature fashioned it as it passed through successive stages and it grew into shape by a process in which an inner energy confronted environmental pressure. Life had to be conceived as a shaping force. Biology introduced so much change in the world picture of the time that it fascinated minds of the very first calibre. Diderot considered himself a biologist; Goethe devoted much of his time to the study of a science which shed light on his artistic conceptions. According to M.H. Abrams:

Goethe is distinctive among aesthetic organologists in that he was himself a research biologist as well as a theorist of art. He deliberately pursued these as mutually illuminating kinds of activity, each new hypothesis or discovery he made in biology duly reappearing in the form of new organizing principles or insights in the field of his criticism.[19]

Other poets and artists might also be mentioned in connection with the percolation of biology into the creative imagination. Blake had illustrated Erasmus Darwin, and his refutation of the use of "central forms" by Reynolds—a true defender of neoclassicism if ever there was one—makes great use of the theory of vegetable genius. One has only to look at the way he elongates the human figure to make it part of the universal life of plants to understand that vital impulses were more important to him than mathematical relations.

But there was no stopping vital impulses. They could not be contained by abstractions. The very mind of Man developed like a plant by a never-ending process of confrontation with the living world. So great were his capacities to develop its knowledge that a new term— *perfectibilité*—had to be coined to express this capital discovery. It appeared in the early works of Turgot and soon became a philosophical watch word among the *encyclopédistes* of the second generation. Rousseau—himself an enthusiastic botanist—used it in his *Discours sur l'Origine de l'Inégalité* and then it passed on to Condorcet, Godwin, Kant, and later Hegel. Perfectibility implied that the truth of things was only found in "a longing for the beyond," since life was a process in which things to come were struggling for existence in the inner core of things present. But the present itself appeared as the ultimate stage of the past, a sort of ever-moving point where history and futurity met; hence the intellectual temptation to become a Janus projecting visions into the future and images into the past. Hence also the double-faced problematic so often encountered in the Romantic age, with its empyrean utopias confronted or contrasted with a hankering after the mystery of origins. The *Urmensch* on one side, ideal cities on the other. To take but a few examples which were known to Beckford, Turner painted *The Opening of the Walhalla* ("the morning ray/Beams on the Wallhalla [*sic*], reared to science and the arts," to quote his own description of the picture) but he also made a picture of *The Decline of the Carthagian empire*. Similarly Blake reconstituted a primitive Nebuchadnezzar half man, half animal, and he also conceived paradisaical visions of floating angels. The visionary architects of the late 18th century designed grottoes and the huts of primitive men but this did not prevent them from dreaming of huge palaces of the mind, dedicated to the sciences and the arts—see Ledoux's *Mausolée de Newton* for example.

*Vathek* offers similar contrasts between primitivism and utopia. Beckford introduces his reader into the chamber where the pre-Adamite kings lie, and he leads him deep down into the entrails of the earth where the sound of a primeval cataract is heard; but he also dreams endlessly of colossal buildings whose perfect cosmic forms answer Ledoux's definition of beauty, for they are *"pure[s] comme celle que décrit le soleil dans sa course."* His cosmic obsession corresponds to a quest for the faultless beauty of utopia where the nature of man is in harmony with its environment and where the pleasures of the intellect prolong and crown those of the senses. But Vathek remains torn between the two worlds; he hankers after the brave new world of utopia; he wishes "to know everything; even sciences that did not exist"(3); he is "almost ready to adore himself"(4), and after he has failed in the conquest of space he wildly throws himself into the chasms from which he hopes to wrench the mystery of his origins and the meaning of his existence; the "endless parchment"(35) held by Carathis stands for this mystery, a mystery which is symbolically hidden from him by his mother. He meets her in the abysmal depths into which he descends with Nouronihar. But the stairs which lead them there are very typical of the endless perspectives opened by the prospects of perfectibility:

The only circumstance that perplexed them, was their not arriving at the bottom of
the stairs. On hastening their descent, with an ardent impetuosity, they felt their
steps accelerated to such a degree, that they seemed not walking but falling from a
precipice (108).

The dreams of utopia have transformed themselves into their very
reverse, an unending nightmare, and Vathek's quest for his origins
ends in disaster just like his quest for universal knowledge. Primitivism and perfectibility thus provide the basic themes on which Beckford's imagination builds the phantasmagoric variations which have
turned Vathek into a mythical figure embodying the hopes and the
nightmares of avant-garde thought.

\* \* \*

As such, he is immortal, like all great myths. But the lasting quality
of a creation, whether artistic or literary, does not depend on the universality of its subject. It depends on the way the subject is treated. By
exploring all the creative virtualities opened by the age of perfectibility, Beckford managed to explore the mazes of thought in which his
contemporaries were trying to form a new world picture. He opened
literature to the mysterious world of magnetism and electricity. He
allowed fiction to be permeated by organicist thought. He transformed
the Burkean sublime into an aesthetic perception of the plastic imagination so dear to Coleridge, thus making *Vathek* a sort of slender
bridge which soars with superb audacity over the age of Johnson and
lands the reader in the Romantic age.

Like M. de Monville's tower, *Vathek* stands as an image of the avant garde measuring the empyrean height of its dreams and the depth of the chasms over which it hovers. The greatness of this little book lies, as I hope to have shown, in its unique capacity to express this predicament by revealing what was essential to the modernity of its age. It also lies, but this is a point I did not mean to discuss, in its secret enjoyment of this predicament. As well as acute perceiving of what was modern in his age, Vathek, the satanic yet kindly caliph, also found the idea deeply funny that he must rule over men and yet be an iconoclast. It was this side of his personality which charmed Mallarmé, and more recently Peter Greenaway. Such indeed is the magic of his history, that it has captured the mental energy which went into the discoveries of its age and turned it into a myth which will forever haunt the imaginations of men. Long may it assert the rights of the avant garde, for it has few equals to disturb the wise and to dismay the dumb!

Université de Dijon

## REFERENCES

[1]*Jardins 1760–1820, Pays d'Illusion, Terre d'Expérience* (Paris, Caisse Nationale des Monuments historiques et des Sites: 1977), pp. 89–97.

[2]William Beckford, *Vathek*, ed. Roger Lonsdale (London: Oxford University Press, 1970) p. 118. Subsequent references will be given in parentheses after the quotation.

[3]Edmund Burke, *A Philosophical Enquiry into the Origin of Our Ideas of the Sublime and the Beautiful*, ed. J.T. Boulton (London: Routledge & Kegan Paul, 1958) p. 75.

[4]*Ibid.*, p. 74.

[5]Edward Gibbon, *The History of the Decline and Fall of the Roman Empire*, ed. J.B. Bury, VI (London: Methuen & Co., 1898) p. 33.

[6]Boyd Alexander, *England's Wealthiest Son: A Study of William Beckford* (London: Centaur Press Ltd., 1962), p. 121.

[7]See *Drawings by G. Romney*, Exhibition selected and catalogued by P. Jaffé, The Fitzwilliam Museum, Cambridge, 1977.

[8]Burke, *Sublime and Beautiful*, p. 72.

[9]Marcel May, *La Jeunesse de William Beckford et la Genèse de son Vathek* (Paris: Les Presses Universitaires de France, 1928) p. 69.

[10]Abraham Wolf, *A History of Science, Technology and Philosophy in the Eighteenth Century* (London: G. Allen & Unwin Ltd., 1938) p. 213.

[11]*Ibid.*, p. 219.

[12]*Ibid.*, p. 494.

[13]André Parreaux, *William Beckford, auteur de Vathek* (Paris: A.G. Nizet, 1960), p. 59.

[14]Romney's portrait of Newton is exhibited at the Iveagh bequest, Kenwood, London.

[15]Wolf, *History*, p. 223.

[16]*Ibid.*, illustration 103: Gralath's experiment.

[17]R. Darnton, *Mesmerism and the End of the Enlightenment in France* (Cambridge, Mass.: Harvard University Press, 1968), chapter 4.

[18]May, *La Jeunesse de William Beckford*, pp. 67–70.

[19]M.H. Abrams, *The Mirror and the Lamp* (New York: W.W. Norton & Company Inc., 1953), p. 206.

# BECKFORD TREASURES REDISCOVERED: MYSTIC GLOW OF PERSIAN SUFISM IN *VATHEK*

Devendra P. Varma

Alike for those who for TO-DAY prepare,
And those that after some TO-MORROW stare,
A Muezzin from the Tower of Darkness cries,
"Fools! your Reward is neither Here nor There."

*Rubáiyát of Omar Khayyám*

## I

On 6 July 1977, the literary manuscripts and letters of William Beckford, reputedly England's wealthiest son, were sold for £120,000 at Sotheby's—an English auction record for a collection of 24 boxes of manuscripts, "personal, detailed and sad," the "literary remains of the late William Beckford."[1] This important archive of entombed papers, a treasure which had passed on Beckford's death to his daughter, the Duchess of Hamilton, and had long remained sealed in family vaults, was sold by order of the Duke of Hamilton and Brandon, and bought by the Oxford dealer Blackwell.

This collection contains the only surviving fragments of the original manuscript of *Vathek*, Beckford's most celebrated work, the story of a Caliph who quested for the powers of evil; autographed manuscripts of later works, drafts of poems, a collection of unpublished verses, some 28 musical scores including an opera, architectural sketches, drawings and other intimate trivia revealing glimpses of his private life. There are boxes full of some 1,500 letters written by Beckford, and 1,000 letters from his correspondents; the drafts and original diary of *Dreams, Waking Thoughts and Incidents*; the manuscript of *Italy with Sketches of Spain and Portugal*; as well as various interesting unpublished works. There is also the original unexpurgated manuscript of *Memoirs of William Beckford* by Cyrus Redding, editor of the weekly *Bath Guardian* (1834) and Beckford's first biographer. Redding's manuscript had found its way into the Beckford papers at Hamilton Palace, and "It would be a splendid contribution to Beckford studies if the Manuscript were now published."[2]

Beckford studies are by no means complete. As far back as 1961 the *Times Literary Supplement*, reviewing Andre Parreaux's sustained labors, had called Beckford "a major English eccentric" and noted that "no remotely comparable study of Beckford's imagination and literary achievement exists."[3] But the life and works of William Beckford are sufficiently documented by Boyd Alexander and Brian Fothergill. H. A. N. Brockman, who wrote "Fonthill Abbey" for the *Architectural Review* for June 1944, produced *The Caliph of Fonthill* (1956). Guy Chapman had earlier written his *Beckford* in 1937. The scholarly publications by Fatma Moussa Mahmoud[4] and Kenneth W. Graham[5] have given an added dimension to Beckford research. And James Lees-Milne, the living doyen of Beckford studies, published a precise account of his life and works,[6] and proved that an eccentric's worth can only be assessed on the strength or charm of his foibles. Beckford was a great connoisseur with lashings of gold, crimson, and purple about him.

However, the Beckford Commemorative Exhibition in Bath, which lasted from 14th June to 3rd July 1966, at least proved that all his stories and jottings are highly autobiographical. Even as a youth he uncannily prophesied his boredom and isolation in his future Abbey, and what he imagined to be his emotional and spiritual doom in a present and future Hell. Lonely and bitter, he turned into a semi-introvert and romantic, in upon himself, in the green unvisited depths of his Fonthill Abbey, which was to be the fulfillment of Vathek-fantasies, a stucco-gothic miracle. "Beckford's Fonthill estate fed Coleridge's dream of Kubla Khan's Xanadu."[7]

Reputed to have received music lessons from Mozart, Beckford performed on the piano and harpsichord with brilliance, polish, yet idiosyncrasy. Sir W. Chambers had instructed him in architecture; he learnt drawing and painting from Alexander Cozens, from whom he acquired a taste for the oriental and fantastic. He had mastered Greek, Latin, French, Italian, Spanish, Portuguese, and Arabic. And his writings in French were admirable in style and idiom.

Naturally, Fonthill excelled in paintings by Raphael, Rembrandt, Tintoretto, Holbein, and Turner. The range of Beckford's collection seems limitless: besides furniture, books, and objects of art, there were missals, psalters, miniatures, bronzes, jades, Venetian glasses, ebony cabinets and procelain. But his love of flowers and perfume came from the Persians.

The events in the Old Egyptian Hall at Fonthill House at Christmas, 1781, take us to the origins of *Vathek*. "It was, in short, the realization of romance in its most extravagant intensity. No wonder such scenery inspired the description of the Halls of Eblis."[8] The strange necromantic lights, the glowing haze, the mystic look, the intricacy of this vaulted labyrinth caused the dream of a "Demon Temple deep beneath the earth set apart for tremendous mysteries."[9] Beckford's note dated 9 December 1838 describes the splendor of gilded roofs "obscured by the vapour of wood ascending in wreaths from cassolettes placed low on the silken carpets in porcelain salvers of the richest Japan."

Roger Lonsdale has cleverly summed up the story of its origins and publication as "a bizarre episode as strange as the tale itself," and has explained "the difficulty of attaching any clear meaning or satiric purpose to *Vathek*."[10] But a forewarning of *Vathek* is also to be found in one of the dreams reported in Beckford's *Dreams, Waking Thoughts and Incidents*:

I hurried to bed, and was soon lulled asleep by the storm. A dream bore me off to Persepolis; and led me, thro' vast subterraneous treasures, to a hall, where Solomon, methought, was holding forth upon their vanity.[11]

Equally, the domain of Vathek came to be represented in Fonthill, and, just as Walpole's *Castle of Otranto* is the embodiment of a building, *Vathek* is a man, a building, and a mode of thought all remarkably hypostatized as a novel.[12] Critics have often suggested that Carathis is modelled after his imperious mother; Nouronihar's real-life name was Louisa, the wife of Beckford's cousin; Vathek is William himself, and Louisa in her letters addresses him as her "infernal beloved," compares him to a "new Lucifer," and remains always willing for any criminal undertaking he may suggest.

Among the Romantics, Byron was the most enthusiastic admirer of Beckford, and made warm references to *Vathek* in his final note to the *Giaour* (1813). Other admirers include Poe, Mallarmé, and Swinburne.

Roger Lonsdale has admirably summarized the contemporary reviews of *Vathek* in his introductory piece.[13] *The European Magazine* in August 1786 (X.102–4) praised the portrayal of the manners and customs of the East and the ending as "picturesque description, which more than borders on the sublime." It commented upon the punishment of unrestrained longings and aspirations, and the fate of those who pursue unlawful and immoral pleasures.The reviewer compared the quality of description to "the sombrous grotesque of Dante; and the terrific greatness of Milton."[14]

Mario Praz has drawn attention to the fact that the vast ruins and royal sepulchres in *Vathek* were inspired by Piranesi's *Carceri*.[15] The moment that Vathek and Nouronihar descend by torchlight the marble steps into the palace of subterranean fire, and the Giaour opens the ebony gate to usher them in the presense of Eblis, "the pen one had thought Voltairian is dipped into blacker and blacker ink: it is the pen of Edgar Poe, of Baudelaire, of Lautréamont."[16] But Vathek's evil eye, his pact with the Devil, the intervention of good angels (episode of the shepherd with his magic flute), the torments of the damned (the burning heart seen through the crystal transparency of the breast), the blend of the marvellous and the grotesque—all come from the Persians.

*Vathek* has been pronounced "a vehicle for the imaginative projection of private fantasy and emotional turmoil."[17] Vathek's unrestrained indulgence of senses and appetites; his restless, impatient, insatiable curiosity and pursuit of forbidden knowledge; his crimes against the pious and sacred; and the final vision of the lonely damned, despite their sombre and tragic power, are reminiscent of Sufi poets and their philosophical concepts.

Beckford's own occult speculations and fastidious orientalism, were imbued with the lonely grandeur of Eastern Kings. Often alone he mounted the gloomy tower and became wrapped in his own meditations, perhaps with thoughts like those that haunted the minds of creatures with which he peopled the Hall of Eblis, gazing upon the pre-Adamite Sultans and the accumulated treasures of a lost world.

From the mists of time Beckford emerges as a fascinating figure. He excelled in many roles: as writer, collector, traveller, gardener, architect, and eccentric. He used to say that "Pleasure is in the pursuit not in the attainment of an object." His own maxim rings as true today: "There is no obtaining anything worth obtaining without taking the most perseverent pains."

Even his funeral was the most splendid that Bath had ever seen. Twenty thousand people lined the route to the Abbey to watch the cortege. The funeral cavalcade was reminiscent of the burial of an ancient Pharaoh. Amidst breathless silence the sarcophagus was laid to rest on a circular plot of ground in "a landscape so picturesque" and "overlooking a vale of Italian-like beauty, varied with richly tinted foliage, streams of water, and hanging woods."[18] In the cemetery below Lansdown Tower, his mausoleum is constructed of solid Aberdeen granite, in "a mode of sepulcher" that "was general amongst the Assyrians, Egyptians, and many of the eastern nations, and was the ancient usage in this country."[19] The Saxon Kings, from whom Beckford claimed descent, were buried in tombs of this description: the solidity presented to the eye is so entire that the whole appears to have been hewn out of one primitive rock.

On one side of his tomb is the following quotation adapted from *Vathek*: "Enjoying humbly the most precious gift of Heaven to man—hope." On the other side is a touching "prayer" drawn from verses written years before his death:

> Eternal Power!
> Grant me through obvious clouds one transient gleam
> Of thy bright essence in my dying hour!

# II

While the Hellenic spirit left its impact upon Western art and litera-ture, the subtle spirit of Persia exerted its quiet influence through a litera-ture of human aspiration. Persian literature tries, by intertwining fact with fiction, to lift the veil which hides from mortal sight the mystery of exis-tence, building its mansions on earth, and its castles in the air. In Beck-ford one listens to distinct echoes from Firdáusi, Sa'di, Omar Khayyám, and Háfiz, the stars of Persian poetic genius. His romantic interest looked to Persia for inspiration; we smell in *Vathek* the fragrance of the rose-gardens of Tus and of Shiraz.

Omar Khayyám, the twelfth century mystic-astronomer-poet of Persia, whose *rubáiyát* has titillated the Western senses, was after all a sufi phi-losopher. Within all his exuberant fancy and delight for carousing, the intoxication of wine, love, and bright eyes of lovely maidens, there flows an undercurrent of deep, settled melancholy, misanthropy, and a realisa-tion of the utter worthlessness of the Ego. Traces of mysticism emphasize his profound longing for some knowledge of the invisible; and even as a great astronomer he succumbs to sceptical despondency. He points to man's inevitable Doom. And there was Sa'di (born 1184), known as the Singer of Shiraz, who with great depth and spiritual insight wrote the *Gulistan,* or "Rose-Garden," which gives an account of the lives of Kings who have passed away into oblivion.

The *Divan* by Háfiz (14th century) has been even more popular than

Omar's quatrains. A thorough Sufi, his extravagant imagery and use of veiled language made everyday objects appear as symbols of highest transcendentalism. "God guard thee from Kamal's malefix eye!" writes Háfiz in the *Divan* (Kamal was an Arab whose glance inflicted death). Dante places Epicurus in the furnace-tombs of his Inferno. But Háfiz says of himself:

"Open my grave when I am dead, and thou shalt see a cloud of smoke rising from it; then shalt thou know that the fire still burns in my dead heart—yea, it has set my very winding-sheet alight."

Firdáusi (born 933 A.D.) in his *Sháh Námah* presents a fantastic crowd of demons, *peris,* and necromancers. King *Zohak* mounts on the ladder of *Zerdusht* from earth to heaven:

> surprised he saw
> Something in aspect terrible—its eyes
> Fountains of blood; ...
> Fixing its gaze upon that hideous form ...

He relates of *Jemshid*, distinguished for learning and wisdom, who commanded his demons to construct a splendid palace:

> He taught the unholy Demon-train to mingle
> Water and clay, with which, formed into bricks,
> The walls were built, and then high turrets, towers,
> And balconies ...

When *Jemshid* was dispossessed of his empire, and turned into an unfortunate wanderer, he took refuge in Zábulistan:

> Flying from place to place, through wilderness,
> Wide plain, and mountain, veiled from human eye,
> Hungry and worn out with fatigue and sorrow,
> He came to Zabul.

Gureng, the King of Zábulistan, had a daughter of extreme beauty and charm:

> With dignity and elegance she passed—
> As moves the mountain partridge through the meads;
> Her tresses richly falling to her feet,
> And filling with perfume the softened breeze.

In *Sháh Námah* there is reference to *Kai-Kobád*, the first King of Persia, a benevolent monarch, who had established a throne at *Istakhar*, also called *Persepolis* and *Chehel-Minar*, or the *Forty Pillars*. This city was said to have been laid in ruins by Alexander after the conquest of Darius. Kai-Kaus who succeeded Kai-Kobad (about 600 B.C.):

> ... feasted and drank wine continually ... in the midst of his luxurious enjoyments he looked upon himself as superior to every being upon the face of the earth, and thus astonished the people, high and low, by his extravagance and pride ...
> One day a Demon, disguised as a musician, waited upon the monarch ...

According to Firdáusi he was a foolish, tyrannical prince. Yet he applied himself much to the study of astronomy, and founded two great observatories, the one at Babel, the other on the Tigris.

Beckford displays a fine sensitivity to Persian art and miniature painting. In the undisturbed tranquillity of Gulchenrouz there is hint of "the pure happiness of childhood"; his sweet accents, dancing steps and languishing looks suggest that "one has to become a child to enter the Kingdom of Heaven." Nouronihar, the daughter of Emir Fakreddin, is like a *peri* come down from the heavens: she is slender in form, sprightly, nimble-footed and full of wanton gaiety, attended by a troop of gracious damsels on tip-toe, her golden tresses floating in the breeze at twilight hour. We see her radiant eyes, listen to the sweet tinkle of her voice from honeyed lips, and glance at the faces by the light of perfumed lamps. It is all Persian.

The bevy of beauties and the interior of the harem, the Persian blinds through which Vathek "perceived large soft eyes, dark and blue, that came and went like lightning"; the troops of *Houris*, fragrant flowers, exquisite perfumes, aromatic lamps and cisterns of gold, and essence of roses distilled on faces in accompaniment of music and *sherbet* and wines of Shiraz and grapes from the banks of the Tigris—are Persian to the core.

The Caliph arrayed in robes in his capacious litter upon cushions of silk; the tinkling bells of a Cafila, the richly-laden kneeling camels with sumptuous burthens; the dreams of the diadem of Gian Ben Gian, the talismans of Soliman and the treasures of the pre-Adamite Sultans— these Persian pictures are exquisitely painted. And finally Vathek makes the resolution: "I ... am resolved to go and drink of the stream of Rocnabad."

The panoramic vista near Samarah is "swarded with wild thyme and basil" and "thickets of eglantine and other fragrant shrubs"; there are roses, jessamine and honey-suckle; clumps of orange trees, cedar, and citron; waving palm trees, pomegranate, and the vine to regale the eye and taste. The ground is strewn with violets, hare-bells, and pansies, with tufts of jonquils, hyacinths, and carnations. The serene evenings and clear skies transport us to perfumed Persia.

The Oriental tale, often written as a vehicle for criticism, moral sentiment, or allegory, came to be used as a frame for most fantastic fancies. Beckford's contribution lies in the imagination, and in his evocation of the sense of wonder that permeated Islamic stories. "His was a recreation of the Gothicism of Islam, a cultural milieu as medieval as the European Gothicism of Walpole," notes E. F. Bleiler. "Beckford created afresh the Magic culture in its most delightful and its most horrific form."[20] He adds that "The story is original with Beckford, for no Islamic sources have ever been found, although there does seem to have been a Caliph Watik."[21]

But Beckford's inspiration is not solely Oriental. When Vathek "wildly gazed at the stars" and "lo! on a sudden, the clear blue sky appeared streaked over with streams of blood", the passage recalls Marlowe's: "See, see, where Christ's blood streams in the firmament!" And like Faustus, the Caliph "muffled up his face in the folds of his robe." Then "one night, however, while he was walking as usual on the plain, the moon and the stars were eclipsed at once, and a total darkness ensued." This cataclysmic disorder reminds us of Shakespeare:

> "It should be now a huge eclipse
> Of sun and moon, and that the affrighted globe
> Should yawn at alteration" (*Othello*, V.ii)

To chart in stars the decrees of destiny, to solve the mysteries of astrology, to penetrate the secrets of Heaven, are Vathek's methods for resolving the theology in Islam. There had been obelisks of Pharaohs, tapering columns at Luxor and Qutb-Minar in Delhi, for towers have functioned as links between earth and heaven since the days of Babylonian sanctuaries. They are symbolic of an ecstatic journey; the pilgrim experiences a breakthrough from plane to plane; he enters a "pure region" transcending the profane world. It is a class of fancy, according to Poe's *Marginalia*, applicable to the shadow of shadows, psychical rather than intellectual. Towers arise in the soul only at points in time where the confines of wakefulness blend with those of dreams in an ecstasy far beyond the pleasurable. The Heaven in theology lies beyond its Hell. This ecstasy is a glimpse of the outer world, an experience of the mystical, and the remote vacancy "sets vibrating chords of the numinous along with the note of the sublime."[22] A tower raises the soul to the level of its journey into the sacred.

According to the Muslims, a thick mist envelopes a narrow and tottering bridge, the only pathway between Time and Eternity. This symbolism of a perilous passage in funerary rituals and mythologies takes us into the bottomless pit where "the yell that went up to the Heavens from out of that mist, I dare not attempt to describe."

The tombs of Istakar, the stately black-marble terraces and vast staircase, the ruins of the royal mausoleum embossed with grotesque figures, and the shades of lofty columns in moonlight ring true of "an architecture unknown in the records of the earth." But there *is* a Persepolis, there *was* a Soliman the Wise; there were Pharaohs, and there still are mummies. Beckford's imagination was not altogether *fantastic*.

We enter the infernal empire of Eblis, the "doleful mansion," "the abode of vengeance and despair" in camphorated vapors ascending like a cloud. The darkness, silence, and sublimity of those ruins, lit by an occasional flare, suggest by analogy the realm of existence that lies hidden behind the world of material reality. The mystic visions have come true; the quest of Vathek for the sabre and the talismans and treasures of pre-Adamite sultans is nearing its end. Before the rites of fire, as he walks hand in hand with lovely Nouronihar over the pavements strewn with gold and saffron, the aroma wafting from the tables loaded with viands, wines, and vases of crystal, recalls the banquet scene of Corinth in Keats's *Lamia*. It is different from the horrific rituals of Carathis in the tower which engulfed the setting in thick dun vapor and stench of infernal powers as the venomous oil leapt into blue flames dissolving the mummies and catacombs of the ancient Pharaohs.

Vathek gazes at the fleshless forms of the pre-Adamite kings. "At their feet were inscribed the events of their several reigns, their power, their pride, and their crimes." In their dejected look one may read Shelley's *Ozymandias*. It proves an ancient Persian proverb that "Behind every resplendent glory lies the shadow of Doom."

*Vathek* is a mystic vision of Truth, and Realization that unbounded thirst for Knowledge takes one to the Well of Disaster; that our sins and foul deeds point to Istakar and Eblis; that Towers of Ambition collapse, and even Grand Mausoleums are fragments of skeletons. But even in this sad predicament of man's fate there are always flashes of light, moments of joy, and dream visions of romantic loveliness under the arch of stars, in this wonderful architecture of the universe. There is Love, Hope, and may be even Perdition.

Dalhousie University

## REFERENCES

[1]Boyd Alexander, "The Sale of Beckford Papers", *Times Literary Supplement*, 8 July 1977, p. 833.

[2]Jon Millington, "Beckford Tower Trust: *Newsletter*," Spring 1984. p. 8. An illuminating critical essay.

[3]"The Mask of Beckford," review of Andre Parreaux's work. *Times Literary Supplement*, 10 February 1961. pp. 82–83.

[4]Fatima Moussa Mahmoud, *Bicentenary Essays*, (Port Washington: Kennikat Press, 1972).

[5]Kenneth W. Graham, "Beckford's Adaptation of the Oriental Tale in *Vathek*", *Enlightenment Essays* V (1974); "*Vathek* in English and French," *Studies in English Bibliography* XVIII (1975); "Beckford's Design for the Episodes," *Papers of the Bibliographical Society of America*, LXXI (1977).

[6]James Lees-Milne, *William Beckford*, (Tisbury: Compton Russell, 1976).

[7]Beckford's Estate, *The Observer Review*, 2 May 1976.

[8]J. W. Oliver, *The Life of William Beckford*, (London: Oxford University Press, 1932) pp. 89–91.

[9]J. W. Oliver, *The Life of William Beckford*, pp. 89–91.

[10]William Beckford, *Vathek*, ed. Roger Lonsdale. (Oxford: Oxford University Press, 1983), pp. vii–viii.

[11]William Beckford, *Memoir of William Beckford Dreams, Waking Thoughts and Incidents*, vol. I of *The Travel-Diaries of William Beckford of Fonthill*, ed. Guy Chapman (Cambridge: Constable and Company Limited & Houghton Mifflin Company, 1928), p. 30.

[12]William Beckford, *Vathek*, ed. E. F. Bleiler. (New York: Dover Press, 1966), p. xxx.

[13]Lonsdale, ed., *Vathek*, pp. xix–xxi.

[14]Rev. of *Vathek*, *The European Magazine*, 10 August 1786, p. 102–104.

[15]Mario Praz, ed. *Three Gothic Novels* (London: Penguin, 1968) p. 21.

[16]Praz, *Three Gothic Novels*, p. 21.

[17]Lonsdale, ed., *Vathek*, p. xxviii.

[18]Rev. of Beckford's Funeral, *Bath and Cheltenham Gazette*, 22 May 1844.

[19]Funeral, *Bath and Cheltenham Gazette*, 22 May 1844.

[20]Bleiler ed., *Vathek*, p. xxix.

[21]Bleiler ed., *Vathek*, p. xxix.

[22]Rudolf Otto (1860–1937), *Idea of the Holy,* (Oxford University Press, 1958). Otto was Professor of Theology at Marburg University.

# *VATHEK:*
# THE INVERSION OF ROMANCE*

Randall Craig

# I

Those who approach *Vathek* expecting a feast of the Orient receive instead a bitter pill of reality—with Milton's Adam and Eve and Beckford's Vathek and Nouronihar, "they greedily reaching to take of the Fruit, chew dust and bitter ashes."[1] Readers are, in fact, feted with the "exquisite dainties" that the eighteenth century had come to expect as the oriental tale's standard bill of fare; however, Beckford's menu includes not only "delicate cakes ... baked in silver ovens ... rich manchets; amber comfits; flaggons of Schiraz wine; porcelain vases of snow; and grapes from the banks of the Tigris," but also "roasted wolf; vultures à la daube; aromatic herbs of the most acrid poignancy; rotten truffles; boiled thistles; and such other wild plants, as must ulcerate the throat and parch up the tongue."[2] The two banquets—the one bountiful, the other baneful—dramatize the central tension in the novel between indulgent sensuality and excessive orientalism, on the one hand, and austere moralism and restrictive protestantism, on the other.

Eighteenth-century readers seemed untroubled by this contradiction between escapism and didacticism, accepting the tale's moral conclusion as justification for its sensual excess and grotesque humor.[3] But subsequent critics rejected the "didacticism, inevitably of a ... simpleminded character [that] had been an especial feature of English 'orien-

tal' tales," and some classified *Vathek* as a straightforward but excessive "oriental Tale of Terror," one of a "gang of wild and *fauve*
romances" for which polite scholarship must make "Zeitgeist
excuses."[4] But this reading, focusing on the novel's escapism, ignores
the irony of Vathek's Faustian quest and of Beckford's use of the
oriental tale, an irony symbolized by the drastically different repasts
offered to the Caliph.[5] While both bills of fare exemplify the highly
imaginative, often purely entertaining elements of oriental romance, as
well as the comic exaggeration that typifies Beckford's use of them,
the tension between the appetizing and the nauseating frustrates the
reader's taste for a steady diet of fantasy. The humorous serves a serious end as Beckford invokes but inverts the conventional structure of
the romance. This inversion not only unifies aesthetics and ethics,
orientalism and didacticism, but also complicates the moral vision of
romance by presenting a dark view of the human condition.

Beckford's familiarity with the lore of the East and his own exotic
sensibility have long been accepted as informing the novel, which both
adopts themes common to tales such as the *Arabian Nights Entertainments* and includes extensive explanatory notes drawn from
d'Herbelot's *Bibliotheque Orientale* and other works on Eastern religion, culture, and manners.[6] H. P. Lovecraft's comment typifies the recognition accorded Beckford for capturing "the atmosphere with
unusual receptivity and ... reflect[ing] very potently the haughty
luxury, sly disillusion, bland cruelty, urbane treachery and shadowy
spectral horror of the Saracen spirit."[7] Less obvious, however, is Beckford's adaptation of the structure of romance, a mode that to the eighteenth century was directly associated with orientalism.[8] While it has
been pointed out that the demonic quest and Faust are the archetypal

form and figure of much Gothic fiction, yet to be recognized and explained is the extent to which *Vathek* conforms to these patterns.[9] The rigid structure of the novel contains and controls the comic tension, producing a vision of humankind's limited place in the world from which the exoticism of the fiction seems to be far removed.

The structure of romance is tripartite and marks the progress of the hero from the *agon*, or conflict, to the *pathos*, or death-struggle, to the *anagnorisis*, or discovery. These terms come from Northrop Frye, although Joseph Campbell's monomythic categories—separation, initiation, and return—are equally appropriate.[10] In either case, Vathek's quest is an inversion of the traditional hero's; Beckford's adaptation of the third category is ironic, abrogating the cyclic structure and establishing a linear descent: aesthetically, from the fifteen-hundred-step tower on the Hill of Pied Horses down the "staircase of polished marble" to the Hall of Eblis (108); psychologically, from wish-fulfillment and hope to frustration and despair; and metaphysically, from a vision of humanity as unlimited potentiality to humanity as finite actuality in an alien world. The action begins with the promise of pre-Adamite kingdoms, moves to the enjoyment of an edenic interlude, and concludes with the attainment of postlapsarian punishment.

This novel, which appears to be so random, is in fact architectonically constructed on a principle of triads. Each of the three sections— conflict, struggle, and discovery—itself contains three segments. Even seemingly minor details reinforce this controlling principle; for example: Vathek's genealogy is traced through three generations—he is the "son of Motassem, ... the grandson of Haroun al Raschid" (1)—and three women urge him on his quest, ultimately joining him in hell: his mother, Carathis, a favorite sultana, Dilara, and his betrothed, Nouronihar. The ubiquity of this triadic motif reinforces Beckford's themes, first, that underlying the apparent randomness of existence (and of this episodic novel) is a rigid and remorseless structure, and, second, that the pleasures of the world (and of fiction) are not unlimited and self-justifying ends. For Vathek to ignore the structure of reality (or for readers to indulge in the sensuality of the text, oblivious to its structure) is to embark on an ironic rather than a heroic journey. The magic sabres, which foretell "of a place where all is wonderful," also warn: "Woe to the rash mortal who seeks to know that of which he should remain ignorant; and to undertake that which surpasseth his power" (11). Vathek's path from wonder to woe is traced out in the three stages of his inverted romantic quest.

## II

The "conflict" that prompts the quest is not, as is conventionally the case, with an enemy that threatens the hero's people but with the limitations of human existence itself. Vathek pursues uncircumscribed knowledge and power, unsurpassed wealth and pleasure. The *agon* begins with his Faustian pact with the Giaour—abjuration of Mahomet in exchange for "the treasures of the pre-Adamite sultans" (36). It should be noted that the Giaour assumes three shapes—that of a merchant, of a long-bearded old man, and of an Indian—before disappearing into a chasm and tricking Vathek for a third time: the first occasion was his escape from jail, the second his transformation into a rubber ball, and the last his accepting the sacrifice of fifty boys without granting Vathek's wish. Frustrated by the Giaour, Vathek nevertheless resolves to obtain the pre-Adamite treasures. The unfortunate result of this quest is foreshadowed by three scenes atop the tower, which he has built "from the insolent curiosity of penetrating the secrets of heaven" (4). On the first occasion, he

cast his eyes below, and beheld men not larger than pismires; mountains, than shells; and cities, than bee-hives. The idea, which such an elevation inspired of his own grandeur, completely bewildered him: he was almost ready to adore himself; till, lifting his eyes upward, he saw the stars as high above him as they appeared when he stood on the surface of the earth. (4)

Whatever his position with regard to other people, Vathek cannot overcome the division between the terrestrial and the celestial. The hiatus is, in fact, widened by his inordinate pursuit of the divine. Thus, the Caliph is often subject to fits of dehumanizing madness, and his thirst for spiritual truth, for example, leaves him so desiccated that "he would prostrate himself upon the ground to lap the water, of which he could never have enough" (14). Instead of approaching God, he "assimilate[s] [him]self to a dog" (14)—the orthographical and substantive inversion of his goal of deification.

Throughout this and other scenes, a direct ratio exists between spiritual and physical hunger. The very attempt to rise above human nature provokes physical responses that frustrate the effort. Thus, on his second ascent of the tower, "the Caliph, ... instead of the visions he expected, had acquired in these unsubstantial regions a voracious appetite" (31). Once again the pursuit of the ethereal produces only the grotesquely corporeal, and Vathek is "abandoned ... to grief and to the wind that ravaged his entrails" (32).

The final ascent of the tower occurs on the night before his departure for Istakar. As he did upon first climbing the tower, Vathek presupposes the success of his endeavor, already "imagin[ing] himself going in triumph to sit upon the throne of Soliman" (41). The progress of Vathek's vision, directed upward to the stars in the first scene but toward the recesses of the earth and the Palace of Subterranean Fire in this one, foreshadows the fate of his journey.

That journey (which functions as *pathos*) is from Samarah, Vathek's capital, to Istakar, the entrance to the Hall of Eblis. Corresponding to the three tower scenes are the three segments of the journey: from the tower to the "happy valley of Fakreddin" (52), from there to the curtained valley, where he shares a nuptial interlude with Nouronihar, and from there across "the spacious valley of Rocnabad" (100) to Istakar. In the traditional romance quest, the temptation to abandon the journey must be overcome if the quest is to be successful. Although such is the case in *Vathek*, the temptation is ironic because to succumb would be to accept Mahomet, thereby to avoid damnation. Vathek is so tempted three times: when terrified by the cosmic storm, he curses the Giaour "and bestowed upon Mahomet some soothing expressions" (50); when he believes that Nouronihar has been killed, "he thundered out: 'Perfidious Giaour! I renounce thee for ever ... and I supplicate the pardon of Mahomet'" (81); and finally when a good genius in the form of a shepherd pipes a holy siren's song to dissuade the errant Ulysses from his demonic journey, he, "depressed with fear, was on the point of prostrating himself at the feet of the shepherd ... but, his pride prevailing, he audaciously lifted his head" (105). In each case, then, the Caliph overcomes fear and resumes the search for illicit knowledge.

Although unfaithful to Mahomet, he is also incapable of keeping the agreement made with the Giaour. The parchment that has replaced the sabres as the medium of demonic communication promises Vathek "all kinds of delight" (30), but it also prohibits entering any dwelling on the journey to Eblis. Although he consults the magical tablets three separate times (44, 50, 52), Vathek ignores the injunction. Immediate gratification of his appetites invariably distracts him from the promised rewards of the pre-adamite sultans. Describing himself as "not over-fond of resisting temptation" (102), he manages, nevertheless, to arrive at Istakar, having earned a place in the Palace of Subterranean Fire. Paradoxically, by not fulfilling the terms of the agreement, Vathek proves himself worthy of it.

The first leg of the journey to Istakar is ended by a cosmic storm after three days of travel. Vathek's response to the cataclysm is typical of his reliance upon physical or mechanical means to solve spiritual or intellectual difficulties. In building the tower, for instance, he confuses vision and insight: "he flattered himself that the light of his mind would extend beyond the reach of his sight" (4). Likewise, when the Giaour disappears in the chasm, he "ordered a thousand flambeaux to be lighted ... and attempted by the help of this artificial splendour, to look through that gloom, which all the fires of the empyrean had been insufficient to pervade" (21). At the outbreak of the storm, the "ten thousand torches" (56) that are lighted cause a fire that forces Vathek "to touch, with his sacred feet, the naked earth" (47). The Caliph thus reaches middle ground in his descent to hell. He is "bespattered, like an ordinary mortal" (48). Mortified, he retreats, in violation of the agreement with the Giaour, to the palace of Emir Fakreddin. He does not, however, remain long with the pious Emir and his holy dwarfs because, although he "found the waters refreshing, ... the prayers [were] abominably irksome" (60).

Against Fakreddin's wishes and in violation of "the rights of hospitality" (74), he elopes with Nouronihar, who initially poses the most serious threat to successful attainment of Eblis's subterranean kingdom. Vathek says to her,

Your lovely little person, in my estimation, is far more precious than all the treasures of the pre-adamite sultans; and I wish to possess it at pleasure, and, in open day, for many a moon, before I go to burrow underground, like a mole. (84)

Although the reference to Vathek's "inflamed bosom" (64) suggests that he will finally achieve his destination, the journey to the curtained valley, where the lovers pass their days enjoying one another's charms, is a diversion from the true course. Only Dilara's jealousy and greed, Nouronihar's growing impatience for the wealth awaiting them, and Carathis's harangues provoke the resumption of the quest.

On the final leg of the journey, Vathek attempts to compensate for violating the Giaour's interdict by insulting the santons and holy men of Schiraz (102)—as he had previously treated his own and Fakreddin's holy men—and by razing the valley of Rocnabad. The lovers, "fired with the ambition of prescribing laws to the powers of darkness" (106), overcome all obstacles, including one another.

The *pathos* is easily the longest section of the novel, and it contains three intervening episodes. In the first incident, Nouronihar is introduced and established as Vathek's double. Her mischievous indulgence in whim at her father's court is a feminine and adolescent echo of the Caliph's gargantuan appetites. She shares his vanity (66), his fatal curiosity (69), and ultimately his greed (106). In a vision, which anticipates the landscape of Eblis, she is promised, as Vathek had been, the possessions "'which belong, not only to the sovereigns of the

earth, but even to the talismanick powers!'" (71). In the second episode, Fakreddin fakes the deaths of his daughter and nephew in order
to deceive Vathek. The cousins' state of death-in-life portends the life-
in-death that awaits the worshippers of Eblis. The relation between the
two scenes is emphasized by Beckford's descriptions of them. Gulchenrouz and Nouronihar are convinced "that the angel of death had
opened the portal of some other world" (79) and believe they are being
punished for their "indolent and voluptuous life" (80). Vathek and
Nouronihar are later admitted through "the portal of ebony" (108) by
an angel of death, the Giaour, "to wander in an eternity of unabating
anguish" (108)—also because of the voluptuousness of their lives. In
the third incident, Carathis, motivated by a lust for power and in a fury
of ironic maternal concern, sets out to correct Vathek's inclination for
immediate gratification. Her comic troop, with its "particular predilection for a pestilence" (90) and "tender connexions with the gouls" (92),
to say nothing of her own wish for "intercourse with the infernal
powers" (31), provides an ironic comment on Vathek's entourage. The
comedy of the Caliph's bargaining with the Giaour, for example, is
exaggerated when compared to his mother's bartering with the grave-
yard ghouls and exchanging the "fresh corpses" (92) of her guides for
information. Her grotesque and unsuccessful pursuit of Gulchenrouz,
who is safely ensconced in a nest above the clouds, also anticipates her
similar assault upon the throne of the pre-Adamite sultans in hell,
where she arrives in a descending cloud (116).

Gulchenrouz himself plays a part in each episode. In the first two,
he is established as Vathek's rival in love. Although alike in their relation to Nouronihar, they are opposite in character. Gulchenrouz is
decidedly unheroic, having been "brought up too much on milk and

sugar" (85). He is effeminate, timid, cloyingly sentimental, and mor-
bidly sensitive—petted by men, women, children, and heavenly spirits
alike. His role of negative analogue to Vathek is reaffirmed in the third
episode, in which Carathis sets out to save her son and to kill Gulchenrouz. Each attempt achieves its opposite: Vathek is damned and Gulchenrouz is apotheosized, along with the fifty boys whom Vathek had
sacrificed. All are saved by "a good old genius" and taken to a heaven
"remote from the inquietudes of the world; the impertinence of
harems, the brutality of eunuchs, and the inconstancy of women" (97).
The chiastic paths of the rivals are completed by the third stage of
romance, Vathek's ironic *anagnorisis*.

In this section, Vathek reaches his destination, and many commentators, including Jorge Luis Borges, base the novel's merit on Beckford's descriptions of the Palace of Subterranean Fire.[11] The structure
of the final stage of romance recapitulates that of the novel as a whole:
the judgments of Eblis and Soliman are followed by a brief reprieve
and ultimately by their enactment. The lovers enter the palace by
descending a staircase, as Vathek had done earlier. Although "they
already esteemed themselves spiritual intelligences" (108), they soon
learn that they are mere "'Creatures of clay'" (111). They are unable to
detect the irony of Eblis's message until Soliman tells his story (112-
13), which parallels Vathek's desertion of his people because of lust
and "a curiosity that could not be restrained by sublunary things"
(113). When the Giaour announces their doom—"Know, miserable
prince! thou art now in the abode of vengeance and despair. Thy heart,
also, will be kindled like those of the other votaries of Eblis" (114)—
they realize that the knowledge of the pre-Adamite sultans is that of a
post-edenic fate. Given a few days to enjoy the pleasures of the under-

world before their punishment is enacted, Vathek and Nouronihar iron-ically have lost their appetites: "Every reservoir of riches was dis-closed to their view: but they no longer felt the incentives of curiosity, of pride, or avarice" (114–15). The Caliph, a true denizen of the under-world, is capable only of vengeance and summons his mother, who, in turn, announces the imminent arrival of Dilara. The party is complete; only Carathis's comic assault on the secrets of Eblis intervenes before the ironic fulfillment of the quest takes place, at which point: "Their hearts immediately took fire, and they, at once, lost the most precious gift of heaven:—HOPE" (119).

## III

Beckford's use of the romance form, that is, his retaining its struc-ture but inverting its action, results in a modification of the vision of romance. He, of course, depends upon the symbolic relationship between romance and reality. The fantastic setting and improbable plot of the oriental tale, like the symbolic landscape and action of myth and fairy tale, are rooted in a fundamental expression of personal and social experience. G. S. Kirk, for example, explains that myths

can possess... significance through their structure, which may unconsciously rep-resent structural elements in the society from which they originate ... They may also reflect specific human preoccupations, including those caused by contradic-tions between instincts, wishes and the intransigent realities of nature and society.[12]

The structure of *Vathek* expresses just such a contradiction between human aspiration and limitation. The clearest formulation of the analo-gous relationship of romance to reality is found in Joseph Campbell's

*The Hero with a Thousand Faces*:

Through the wonder tales—which pretend to describe the lives of legendary heroes, the power of the divinities of nature, the spirits of the dead, and the totem ancestors of the group—symbolic expression is given to unconscious desires, fears, and tensions that underlie the conscious patterns of human behavior ... Exhibited here as in a fluoroscope, stand revealed the hidden processes of the enigma *Homo Sapiens*—Occidental and Oriental, primitive and civilized, contemporary and archaic.[13]

*Vathek* has been criticized, however, because its vision is too personal, its dreamlike expression of wish-fulfillment insufficiently displaced to avoid "repulsive mockery and sensuality."[14] According to one critic, in reading this oriental fantasy,

one enters upon a realm of hallucination and daydream as surely as Coleridge claimed to have done with opium. In such a world ... the only limits to action, experience, and passion are those of one's own personality. If the personality in question is warped and tormented as Beckford's was, the djinns and demons summoned from the depths will be those of neurotic nightmare.[15]

But the very form of the novel shows that Beckford achieves something more than the creation of a "totally subjective world, indeed, almost a private mythology."[16] The vision is neither neurotic nor private; it is, as Otto Rank suggests of myth, "a dream of the masses of the people."[17]

That dream expresses not merely the pleasures but also the fears of indulgence; ultimately, it is a dream not of wish-fulfillment but of frustration. Beckford relies on romance only to deny its vision of the fundamental and radical polarity of good and evil. According to Frye:

Romance avoids the ambiguities of ordinary life, where everything is a mixture of good and bad, and where it is difficult to take sides or believe that people are consistent patterns of virtue or vice. The popularity of romance, it is obvious, has much to do with its simplifying of moral facts.[18]

This dichotomy and simplification break down in *Vathek*, which presents a world of mixed good and evil, from Mahomet to the general populace. Mahomet, the force of good opposing Eblis, is not a uniformly benevolent divinity. He can be as vindictive as the evil gods and says of Vathek: "Let us leave him to himself ... let us see to what lengths his folly and impiety will carry him: if he run into excess, we shall know how to chastise him. Assist him, therefore, to complete the tower ... he will not divine the fate that awaits him" (4). And, as we have seen, Vathek does follow a more or less direct path to a demonic underworld. The epicene Gulchenrouz, however, is whisked away to a heaven of "perpetual childhood" (98), seemingly for no other reason than that he is the object, first, of Carathis's search for a propitiatory sacrifice to the Giaour—to whom there is "nothing so delicious ... as the heart of a delicate boy palpitating with the first tumults of love" (95)—and, second, of the attentions of an old genius with an inordinate "fondness for the company of children" (97). Both hero and heaven seem pale in comparison to the demonic grandeur of Vathek and Eblis. While both heaven and hell seem to be characterized by appetiteveness—at least concerning young boys—the middle world of human existence is no less concupiscent. Even the Caliph's subjects, while occasionally motivated by altruistic loyalty to their sovereign, share his epicurean tastes. Being great admirers of women and apricots from Kirmith (10), ...they are easily bribed. For example, although incensed by the loss of the children who have been sacrificed to placate the Giaour, they are soon mollified by the money thrown to them by Bababalouk (30). Their loyalty extends no further than to the satisfaction of physical desire. Thus, nothing in the fictional world is without limitation: gods, heroes, and humankind are flawed.

Keeping in mind "the close relationship maintained in the Orient [and the oriental romance] between myth, psychology and metaphysics," readers encounter a dark picture of human status in a limited world.[19] The irony of the tale does not serve, as Edmund Wilson suggests, merely "to satisfy a perverse impulse," but rather to comment on the nature of reality.[20] The vision of existence presented in *Vathek* negates that of romance; there are no reductionist illusions of a clearly defined world of good and evil or of human freedom. Supernatural powers interfere at will, manipulating, enticing, and victimizing. The narrator of the tale does not share the delusion of the Persians, who, after chasing and kicking the Giaour, fail to suspect

that they had been impelled by an invisible power into the extravagance, for which they reproached themselves: for it is but just that men, who so often arrogate to their own merit the good of which they are but instruments, should also attribute to themselves absurdities which they could not prevent. (20)

The fantastic and improbable, the meaningless and unmotivated, the fated damnation and gratuitous salvation all express the human position in an irrationally deterministic world. The Giaour ironically comments at the entrance to hell, "you will soon be acquainted with all" (110), and for readers this knowledge is that there is little or nothing that humanity can know. The "moral" of the tale is not ethical, but metaphysical, not prescriptive but descriptive—"the condition of man upon earth is to be—humble and ignorant" (120).

The meaning of romance, that there is "the release potential within us all, and which anyone can attain—through herohood,"[21] is denied by Beckford. With the installation of Vathek, Nouronihar, and Carathis in a world of suffering, isolated in the midst of the "accursed multitude" (120), the picture of the human condition is complete. The dish served up by Beckford is finally such that readers lose the appetite which has been whetted by promises of "the most exquisite dainties ... the most delicious wines and the choicest cordials" (2). Presented with the truth of their state, readers, like Vathek, respond to the prospect of another meal by saying, "there is no time left to think of such trifles" (107). Doubtless, Beckford savored the pun on the Caliph's just desserts.

SUNY Albany

## REFERENCES

* This essay was originally published in *Orbis Litterarum* 39 (1984), pp. 95–106.

[1]John Milton, "Argument, Book X," *Paradise Lost*, in *Complete Poems and Prose*, ed. Merritt Y. Hughes (New York: Odyssey Press, 1957), p. 406.

[2]William Beckford, *Vathek*, ed. Roger Lonsdale (London: Oxford Univ. Press, 1970), p. 49. All subsequent references to the text will be from this edition and are cited in the paper.

[3]For a summary of contemporary reviews, see Lonsdale's "Introduction" (vii–xxxv) to *Vathek*.

[4]See Lonsdale, p. xxiv; Edith Birkhead, *The Tale of Terror* (New York: Russell and Russell, 1963), p. 94; Sacheverell Sitwell, *Beckford and Beckfordism* (London: Cambridge Univ. Press, 1930), p. 34; and Rayner Heppenstall, *The*

*Fourfold Tradition* (London: Barrie and Rockliff, 1961), p. 80.

[5]Kenneth Graham's, "Beckford's 'Vathek': A Study in Ironic Dissonance," *Criticism*, 14 (1972), 243–52, insightfully analyzes the novel's ironic elements, and my own reading is indebted to him. Stylistic dissonances are the subject of several essays: James Henry Rieger, "Au Pied de la Lettre: Stylistic Uncertainty in 'Vathek,'" *Criticism*, 4 (1962), 302–12; and Stanley J. Solomon, "Subverting Propriety as a Pattern of Irony in Three Eighteenth-Century Novels: 'The Castle of Otranto,' 'Vathek,' and 'Fanny Hill,'" *Erasmus Review*, 1 (1971), 107–16.

[6]See Martha Pike Conant, *The Oriental Tale in England in the Eighteenth Century* (New York: Octagon Books, 1966); Fatma Moussa Mahmoud, "Beckford, *Vathek* and the Oriental Tale," in *William Beckford of Fonthill: Bicentenary Essays*, ed. F. M. Mahmoud (Cairo: Costa Tsoumas and Co., 1960), 63–111; and Robert J. Gemmett, *William Beckford* (Boston: Twayne, 1977).

[7]Howard Phillips Lovecraft, *Supernatural Horror in Literature* (New York: Dover Publications, 1973), p. 73.

[8]See Arthur Johnston, *Enchanted Ground: The Study of Medieval Romance in the Eighteenth Century* (London: The Athlone Press, 1964). As Johnston points out, the origin of fiction itself was attributed "to the Egyptians, Arabs, Persians, and Syrians with their fondness for allegory, fable, and metaphor" (16). More generally, he argues that "romance was synonymous with magic, with the incredible and the impossible, with the abandoning of accounts of plain matter of fact, in actions and characters" (9).

[9]See G. R. Thompson, "Introduction: Romanticism and the Gothic Tradition," and Robert D. Hume, "Exuberant Gloom, Existential Agony, and Heroic Despair: Three Varieties of Negative Romanticism," in *The Gothic Imagination: Essays in Dark Romanticism*, ed. G. R. Thompson (Pullman: Washington State Univ. Press, 1974), pp. 1–10 and 109–27.

[10]Northrop Frye, *Anatomy of Criticism* (Princeton: Princeton Univ. Press, 1957), p. 187; and Joseph Campbell, *The Hero With A Thousand Faces* (Princeton: Princeton Univ. Press, 1968), p. 30.

[11]Jorge Luis Borges, *Other Inquisitions* (New York: Simon and Schuster, 1964), p. 138. See, too, J. W. Oliver, *The Life of William Beckford* (London: Oxford Univ. Press, 1937), p. 102.

[12]G. S. Kirk, *Myth: Its Meaning and Functions in Ancient and Other Cultures* (Cambridge: Cambridge Univ. Press, 1971), p. 252.

[13]Campbell, pp. 255–56.

[14]Conant, p. 69.

[15]Rieger, p. 309.

[16]Mahmoud Manzalaoui, "Pseudo-Orientalism in Transition: The Age of *Vathek*," in Mahmoud, p. 148.

[17]Otto Rank, *The Myth of the Birth of the Hero* (New York: Random House, 1959), p. 8.

[18]Northrop Frye, *The Secular Scripture: A Study of the Structure of Romance* (Cambridge: Cambridge Univ. Press, 1976), p. 50.

[19]Campbell, p. 164. Relevant here is Frederick Garber's argument about the significance of Orientalism: "The Oriental is the Other .... The Oriental is a version of that which stands over against us and, by virtue of its unlikeness, helps us to understand what we are in ourselves." See "Beckford, Delacroix and Byronic Orientalism," *Comparative Literature Studies*, 18 (1981), 321–32.

[20]Edmund Wilson, *The Shores of Light* (New York: Farrar, Straus, and Giroux, 1952), p. 266.

[21]Campbell, p. 151.

# THE ENLIGHTENED OCCULTIST: BECK-FORD'S PRESENCE IN *VATHEK*

## R. B. Gill

*athek* repays frequent reading with an increased sense of its complexity and tight structure. Throughout the novel Beckford has carefully prepared for many aspects of his striking conclusion: the curiosity theme, for example, the loss of hope, even little details like the whirling of Carathis. And that worrisome moral at the end, "that the condition of man upon earth is to be—humble and ignorant," is foreshadowed in a multitude of ways. This moral, which we might call the public voice of *Vathek* and Beckford, is the key to continuing interest in the novel, for many readers sense that it does not coincide with Beckford's emotional concerns, however much its surface details may have been foreshadowed. The result is a tension that leaves the end somewhat unfocused. As Roger Lonsdale notes, "the official moral framework is in practice constantly subverted by the conduct of the tale."[1] We suspect Beckford of hidden motives and begin looking for psychological explanations, for a private Beckford lurking beneath the public persona.

But the biographical Beckford is not hidden within *Vathek*. Rather, Beckford has included himself as a public and prominent part of the novel. Robert Kiely writes that Beckford "created an image of himself which became almost inseparable from his literary achievement."[2] I would drop the word "almost" from Kiely's statement and claim that this image is an integral and indispensable part of Beckford's literary achievement, for it is a created, public image that appears in the novel. Our modern impulse to psychoanalyze causes us to look for an inner man, but the eighteenth-century Beckford was entirely ready to accept his created, public image as his real self.

An important consideration as we look for Beckford in his novel is the fact that the fundamental style or approach of *Vathek* is an exterior one. It is a public work whose surface meanings are the intended meanings. In some respects *Vathek* is a philosophical tale like *Candide* and *Rasselas*, but it rejects their moderate and personal conclusions; Beckford has used the external forms of Enlightenment moderation without belief in their internal justification. Although each of these works is a series of variations on the vanity of human wishes, a consideration of the self being accommodated to its world, Beckford relies on the literal meaning of his story, avoiding its potential as an exploration of inner psychology or a statement of universal significance, in spite of its closing moral.

Similarly, *Vathek* includes satire on extreme beliefs and actions as the philosophical tales do, although it fails to develop an inner philosophy that can sanction the satire. From the beginning the novel rejects religious asceticism just as it condemns pride and sensuality. Mahomet gives Vathek another chance to moderate his irreligious excesses (103), yet some of the best moments of the novel ridicule religion—the pious graybeards, for instance, and their colorless lives. On at least three occasions the Caliph is brought to the brink of thoughtful examination of his conditions (50, 81, 104). Although Carathis remains insatiable in Eblis, Vathek himself assumes a new, thoughtful demeanor as he comes to realize the vanity of his search for the extremes of pleasure (117).

There are other satirical aspects of the novel that seem to be shaping it into a parable of philosophical moderation like *Candide* and *Rasselas*. Beckford exposes a Vathek who has not learned the line of demarcation between himself and the public world. His mode is indulgence, an engulfing the outside world into himself as if he were an infant who had not yet learned to distinguish between the self and the other. He exists in an unweaned state encouraged by his approving mother. The evil Giaour reinforces this disinclination to distinguish between private desires and public world by promising even more indulgence. It is appropriate, then, that the punishment in Eblis of this failure to limit the aggrandizing self is a condemnation to the private self, an eternity of inner pain. Vathek orders Carathis removed from his presence and sinks into apathy, aversion, and despair. Heaven's most precious gift, "hope," the possibility of rescue from the self, is lost (119).

These are the components of a philosophical dialogue between the self and its world, an accommodation between the desires of the self and the restrictions demanded by the world. But these external forms of Enlightenment moderation lack an inner justification. For example, *Vathek* differs from *Candide* and *Rasselas* in its lack of cosmic somberness. While its call for humility and ignorance is related to cultivating one's garden or resolving to return home to Abissinia, it is conceivable that a person could prosper in the world of *Vathek* in a way not possible in *Candide* or *Rasselas*. It is the hunger of the senses rather than the hunger of imagination that Caliph Vathek seeks. His is a less metaphysical hunger, one not made impossible by the inherent nature of things. His story, then, has the potential of achieving a moderate and enlightened fulfillment. But Beckford has no interest in

Enlightenment moderation. There is, in fact, no reason in *Vathek* for moderation other than the perfunctory pronouncements of Mahomet and an occasional unconvincing genius. Although the pose of satire is present, critics have repeatedly noted that the satiric spirit is absent. There is no substratum of values in the novel to substantiate and justify satire of immoderate actions.

Furthermore, Beckford shows no interest in the general implications of his narrative, nor does his moral attempt Voltaire's and Johnson's philosophic universality. The Orientalism is so pervasive that it resists generalizing and the Caliph's actions so hyperbolic and evil that they deny him the status of an everyman figure. *Candide* and *Rasselas* are wisdom literature: the vicissitudes of life impart experiential truth and assent to their pensive messages. But *Vathek* does not respond to the inwardness of mature reflection. It is a young man's book and reaches no reconciliation with things. For *Rasselas* and *Candide* the solution was an inner one, a retreat into self-sufficiency, a victory over the "hunger of imagination" by an enlightened life. Significantly, however, Beckford's public sensibility reverses this solution. No moderate and internal conclusion is possible in *Vathek*, for Beckford's solution—obedience to an imposed law of humility and ignorance—is externally given rather than internally realized during the progress of the story. Loss of the public self that once fed the hunger of Vathek's imagination is punishment; in Eblis the Caliph must live with the inner pain of a burning heart.

Many critics have sought to explain this disparity between the forms and the spirit of *Vathek*, between the moral and emotional interests, by appeal to Beckford's biography. Lonsdale speaks for these readers when he writes that "the difficulty of attaching any clear meaning or satiric purpose to *Vathek* has also tended to force its readers back on the author himself for enlightenment."[3]  The result is frequently a portrait of a young, unconventional Beckford at odds with the mores of bourgeois English society. The young rebel makes the novel's perverse materials its emotional center; yet a very eighteenth-century public Bedford attempts to put a conventional veneer on it all. It is as if Beckford's ego were not able to reconcile the conflicting claims of his id and superego. In such a view, Beckford petulantly concludes with humility and ignorance rather than submit to the dull moderation of a return to one's garden or Abissinia. It is the most immoderate little hothouse character, Gulchenrouz, whom Beckford places in the last paragraph as chief example of rewarded humility. Despised by the Caliph, perhaps but not by Beckford (for the novel never makes him a contemptible person, however lowly), Gulchenrouz's pretty effeminacy, his ambivalent sexuality, his pampered indulgence of the senses, and the "many little freedoms" he has taken with his cousin Nouronihar are indeed beyond the pale of bourgeois morality. Nevertheless, Gulchenrouz is the only positive model in the novel. In fact, Beckford rejected Henley's suggestion that the final reward of Gulchenrouz be omitted, insisting that "the contrast between the boisterous Caliph & the peacable innocent Gul [is] not ill imagined."[4]

But this inner, unconventional Beckford is not the self that the novel puts on public view. Its exterior focus gives us, instead, an ingenious but highly decorous and sophisticated eighteenth-century gentleman. A Romantic author like Baudelaire or Poe achieves a memorable portrayal of irrational material by either subordinating himself to his subject or making himself part of it. The effect in either case is to lessen the aesthetic or psychic distance between the reader and the occult subject matter. But exactly the opposite happens in the exterior style of Beckford, where a rational and public sensibility purposely distances itself and the reader from the irrational material. Beckford does not turn *Vathek* into an allegory of the unfamiliar, unexplored depths within us. Rather, he takes care to avoid such implications in his material, preferring that we journey through the occult without dwelling there. Much as Beckford traveled to Portugal or observed voyagers from the East in Venice, we satisfy our normal and justifiable curiosity in *Vathek* with Beckford as our entirely knowledgeable guide. The novel carefully creates a sense that Beckford is in control of its irrational subject matter.

Even when the occult is imaginatively gripping, his rational style holds back, distancing the enlightened author and reader from its excesses. In descriptions of the awful gloom of Eblis there is an architectural precision, and the pained hearts of the doomed are described from the outside. When Carathis first entered this infernal empire, she perceived "in all the inmates who bore their hands on their heart, a little singularity, not much to her taste" (118). Here the understatement and incongruity of "a little singularity" and the use of the fine word "taste" in such dire circumstances intellectualize and diminish the felt horror of its truth, another example of Beckford's irony removing us from the character, causing us to think rather than to feel. Edgar Allan Poe's irony draws readers into the turmoil of an inner psyche, while Beckford watches coolly from the outside, keeping readers and his public self quite apart from his fable. T. S. Eliot notes that Baudelaire elevated his imagery "to the *first intensity*—presenting it as it is, and yet making it represent something much more than itself..."[5] Beckford, in contrast, regards the *outré* more as ornament than as symbol of inner experience. His strange subject matter is what it is rather than "something much more than itself."

Emphasis on Orientalism as an end in itself, on "correctness of costume" as Byron put it, removes Beckford from the strangeness of his material by implying that he presents to us not so much his own imaginative being as his knowledge of the East. The multitude of names and allusions in *Vathek*, the careful use of Oriental settings, and the evocation of an exotic Arabian tone are carried beyond the mild references in *Rasselas*, the *Lettres persanes* of Montesquieu, and the Eastern tales of Goldsmith. Beckford and Henley need not have added their notes in order to draw attention to the correctness of their setting; that they did append those elaborate glosses leaves no doubt about the self-referential nature of their work. It is to himself as knowledgeable author that Beckford draws attention.

Further, the novel abounds in what psychologist Paul McGhee has called "fantasy cues," which affect a reader's orientation to the work.[6] What we would regard with horror in life or serious fiction we view with amusement in works that cue us to expect comedy or fantasy. Henry Fielding's comic cues in *Tom Jones* elicit a different reaction to sexual imprudence than does his sterner demeanor in *Amelia*. In *Vathek,* fantasy cues frequently cause depraved and occult material to be regarded lightheartedly, thus freeing Beckford from suspicion of having intended it seriously. He uses these self-conscious references to the fantasy as he used the Orientalism: both call attention to himself as ingenious author and enlightened eighteenth-century gentleman. Among the fantasy cues we find incongruous linkings or zeugma — "the caliph ... abandoned himself to grief and the wind that ravaged his entrails" (32); extravagant, exaggerated situations—it is not just some cripples but "a superb corps of cripples" (61); humorous understatements and frequent use of litotes—"Carathis, whose antipathy to wine was by no means insuperable" (36); rhetorical parallelism—"he ... beheld men not larger than pismires; mountains, than shells; and cities, than bee-hives" (4); use of numbers with irrelevant connotations—"seven empalements of iron bars," "forty thousand kicks" (7,8); dry jokes; half-concealed incongruities; and so on, with a multitude of literary devices that act as fantasy cues.

The dry jokes and humorous incongruities are also means of calling attention to the skills of Beckford the author. Of three hundred dishes offered to Vathek at a meal, "he could taste of no more than thirty-two" (7). Here we might concede that the fastidious connotations of "taste" ironically applied to the extravagant size of even thirty-two dishes characterize the sensuous excesses of the Caliph. But the figure thirty-two, the number of our permanent teeth, calls attention to its own humorous incongruity and to Beckford's wit rather than to the message, and thus it is typical of the many such instances where Beckford halts our attention at the exterior style. (This sort of simple and delightful incongruity, enjoyed for purposes other than its message, is characteristic of children's literature as well as an important contributor to the fable-like tone of *Vathek*. In children's literature, though, these incongruities are reader- rather than style- and author-oriented, their purpose being not to call attention to themselves but to lead the child to the pleasures of his or her own logical discoveries.)

There are other types of fantasy cues that remove Beckford from suspicion of taking his occult subject matter with undue seriousness. The opening paragraph of the novel, with its succession of exotic names, its quick summation (reminiscent of fables), the exaggerated powers given to Vathek, and its concluding ironic joke, sets the detached tone of the novel. That last joke concerns Vathek's ability to destroy people with the gaze of his terrible eye. The paragraph concludes, "For fear, however, of depopulating his dominions and making his palace desolate, he but rarely gave way to his anger." This dry, rational humor requires us to consider the gulf between Vathek's reason for not killing people and what a more appropriate reason would be. It smiles knowingly at the understated implications of Vathek's rarely giving way to his anger. It pulls from us wry condescension rather than empathy. Throughout the novel the third-person, omniscient point of view and the external description of characters preserve a distance between the author and his material. For instance, Vathek's murder of the fifty amiable and innocent children is an intellectually repulsive but emotionally neutral act, our feelings having been distracted by the brittle irony of Beckford's style, the disconcerting implications of Vathek's stripping both his victims and himself, and the grotesque farce of the Giaour's mutterings for "more! more!" (27). This self-conscious passage admits a few perfunctory adjectives like "dreadful," but, in fact, its removed, third-person viewpoint never contemplates an empathic identification with the boys, who become only factors in a distant, fabular narrative.

Yet, like a fable, Beckford's quick narrative and third-person, omniscient point of view do not require more than external description. When Vathek rejects the beneficent genius's last offer of redemption, a complex interaction of fear and greed within the Caliph can be summed up in the phrase, "his pride prevailing ... " (105), an assertion that is external and unreflective but adequate for Beckford's purposes.

The fantasy cues allow us to accept assertions without demanding greater depth of characterization and motivation. They allow us to view repugnant crimes as comic, and they impose a tone of detachment even on acceptable moral judgements such as Mahomet's early condemnation of Vathek's insolent curiosity. The result of such detachment is that the moral lessons of the novel arise more from Beckford's own assertions than from the inherent meaning of the narrative. Having been led by the fantasy cues to separate our feelings from the horror of its subject matter and to regard Beckford as a stylist, an Orientalist, a detached observer himself, we cannot easily return to a felt commitment to his conclusion. The assertion that man's condition is to be humble and ignorant is just that—an assertion rather than a realization of value judgements inherent in the work. The fable-like narrative does not require it to be otherwise.

We find, then, that Beckford chose material with potential for the most morally engaged and personally intense treatment. It was, however, his gift to turn this pervervid material into a work whose exterior calls attention to its own skill and wit. It is not so much a world as a style that Beckford has created. His particular genius was not as an explorer of inner character and morals but as a transformer of exotic material into an exterior style, making the occult accessible as ornament, as one might use arabesques and Oriental designs in fine china, rugs, and handsome eighteenth-century wallpaper. Beckford's desire for an acceptable public demeanor withdraws from involvement, focusing instead on the wit and skill of the aloof author. It is, then, Beckford's public self that becomes a functional part of what I am calling the "exterior" style of *Vathek*. He constantly withdraws from those private interests that a reader senses beneath the elegant surface.

An early paragraph describing Vathek's "reasonable" persecution of zealots illustrates this complex process and foreshadows the energetic but somewhat unfocused tone that is perhaps the chief source of readers' interest in the novel:

Vathek discovered also a predilection for theological controversy; but it was not with the orthodox that he usually held. By this means he induced the zealots to oppose him, and then persecuted them in return; for he resolved, at any rate, to have reason on his side. (3)

On one level the passage characterizes the Caliph by stating that he regards persecution of zealots as reasonable. The obvious reading of this statement is as simple irony, a way of condemning Vathek's willful and cruel excesses. Here is the public voice of Beckford.

But on a second level the passage speaks in a less obvious and orthodox manner. The connotations of excess in the term "zealots," the concession of problems contained in the aside "at any rate," and the humorous ironic understatement in "predilection" encourage the reader to suspend seriousness and, rather, to entertain a sophisticated amusement at the "reasonableness" of rending an apt justice to these fanatics. This is an example of "double irony," the judgement turning on itself, that William Empson thought characteristic of *Tom Jones*.[7] Double irony is a trait of an intellectualized and self-conscious style that sees both sides of an issue and leans towards the less orthodox but more human one. Its equivocations are inner musings rather than public certainties.

But Beckford never trusts this private voice. As readers we please ourselves with finding implications of anti-social, dream-centered, childish, and sensual ideas. Yet Beckford withdraws from all such implications, as if he heard over and again the voice of Lady Hamilton cautioning him to consider his honor and reputation. He may have complained about family pressures to conform, but he also complied with them. Thus, on a third level, the paragraph goes off idiosyncratically at right angles to the unorthodox implications of its double irony. Fielding's double irony stems from a humane and serious moral sensibility, but, as we have seen, Beckford's removed, exotic material does not lead to reflections of this type.

To speak truly, he really has little to say one way or the other about persecution; the point of the paragraph is its highly self-conscious and sophisticated wit. This third turning in a willful direction of its own is similar to the style of Laurence Sterne: both authors approach their material in an external, self-conscious, and intellectualized manner. Both tell us that the fiction itself must share attention with the writer and the act of writing. It is not to the occult as metaphor for the antisocial but to his own skill in handling it that Beckford calls attention. His public abilities rather than his private fantasies are the subject of *Vathek*.

As the levels of irony and the twistings of interpretation in this paragraph show, there wavers throughout *Vathek* an interference pattern of unfocused impulses, cancelling and augmenting each other in their various combinations. The novel's energetic but socially questionable subject matter conflicts with its attempt to present a socially acceptable public image. This conflict prevents the clearly focused philosophical message that we find in *Rasselas* and *Candide* but nevertheless creates the unreconciled tension that continues to make *Vathek* one of the most energetic and fascinating examples of eighteenth-century literature. Although speculation about the inner author is irresistible in such a work, it is the voice of a rational wit, an enlightened gentleman of taste and sensibility, an orthodox if not convincing moralist, who speaks from the surface of *Vathek*, most concerned to appear detached from his occult subject. It is possible that Beckford never resolved the dissonances of his own life, that he never came to peace with the reality of his several selves. But it is clear that his public self is the subject of the only intensely felt fiction that he ever wrote.

Elon College

## REFERENCES

[1]William Beckford, *Vathek*, ed. Roger Lonsdale (London: Oxford Univ. Press, 1970), p. xxviii. All further references to this work appear in the text.

[2]Robert Kiely, *The Romantic Novel in England* (Cambridge, Mass.: Harvard Univ. Press, 1972), p. 45.

[3]*Vathek*, p. viii.

[4]*Vathek*, p. 160.

[5]T. S. Eliot, "Baudelaire," in *Selected Essays* (New York: Harcourt, 1960), p. 377.

[6]Paul E. McGhee, "On the Cognitive Origins of Incongruity Humor: Fantasy Assimilation Versus Reality Assimilation," in *The Psychology of Humor*, ed. Jeffrey H. Goldstein and Paul E. McGhee (New York: Academic Press, 1972), pp. 61–80.

[7]William Empson, "Tom Jones," *The Kenyon Review*, 20 (1958), 217–49.

# VATHEK, HEAVEN AND HELL*

### Peter Hyland

William Beckford's *Vathek* appears to have presented great difficulties for critics and scholars. Those who have examined the tradition of the Gothic romance, while usually accepting *Vathek* as part of that tradition, have hardly known how to treat it. Others have been more interested in Beckford's eccentric life than in his novel. Some of the most valuable work has been done in France, notably by André Parreaux, but even his monumental book on *Vathek* is concerned with textual problems and with placing the novel within the traditions of the Gothic and Oriental tales, rather than with analyzing it as a literary work. One editor of *Vathek* sees it mainly as a projection of its author's private fantasy and emotional turmoil, a supposition which suggests that its true interest is for psychiatrists. Another critic calls the book simply a romantic novel, and, while rightly pointing out its eclecticism, again stresses that the book is about Beckford himself.[1]

Much of this work is not especially helpful, but one possible method of coming to an understanding of *Vathek* might be to examine it in the light of Leslie Fiedler's identification of the major symbols of Gothic fiction.[2] Fiedler's list, of sinister protagonist, persecuted maiden, haunted castle and ruined landscape, reflecting a world of infantile fears and dreams, covers most of the stock paraphernalia of the Gothic novel; and although it will become apparent, I think, that *Vathek* fails to exhibit all, or even most, of these symbols; nevertheless a recognition of the way in which its symbols differ from those of Fiedler's catalogue will prove instructive.

In one sense, Vathek is a conventional figure within the Gothic tradition, a hero-villain who makes a pact with the devil; what is of special interest in this novel, however, is not so much the hero himself, as his relationship with the landscape of the book, and a clearer understanding of his function can be gained by turning attention from Vathek to the landscape through which he moves. At the outset of the story he is associated with, and defined by, his palace, a building dedicated to the pursuit of pleasure in the satisfaction of the five senses, and surmounted by a high tower. According to Eino Railo, the theme of *Vathek* is "uncontrollable surrender to the lust for pleasure, which proves insatiable and demands ever new food,"[3] but this interpretation appears to be insufficient, since it fails to acknowledge that the tower is as important a symbol as the palace of the senses. The tower, whose purpose is to penetrate the secrets of the heavens, is related to the idea of the search for ever more knowledge, represented by Vathek's insatiable curiosity: "He had studied so much for his amusement in the lifetime of his father, as to acquire a great deal of knowledge, though not a sufficiency to satisfy himself; for he wished to know every thing; even sciences that did not exist" (3). It is, of course, for his curiosity and ambition, rather than his libertinism, that Vathek is finally punished, and so it must be of importance that, when his curiosity is most aroused, he closes the palace of the five senses and retires to his tower.

Vathek's curiosity leads him to damnation through a series of places which are types of paradise, each of which he abandons or destroys. Ironically, it is paradise that he is seeking: "he did not think ... that it was necessary to make a hell of this world to enjoy paradise in the next" (1). But in his moral confusion he fails to recognize paradise when he sees it, and he fails to discern that a man can create his own hell, but must find heaven. He starts from a place which Beckford specifically relates to "the Paradise destined for the faithful," a mountain with four fountains which resembles "the garden of Eden watered by four sacred rivers" (13). But Vathek's thirst for new knowledge drives him out of this first paradise, and eventually to the valley of the Emir Fakreddin. This valley is another figure of paradise, "the asylum of pilgrims, the refuge of travellers" (54), and is, further, essentially the place of the family, with the happy relationship between Nouronihar and her father, and her cousin Gulchenrouz, to whom she is betrothed. The family, whole but vulnerable, is itself a basic type of paradise, and Vathek destroys this one by breaking its harmony. It is also significant here that the last time Nouronihar feels any remorse it is for causing "the desolation of her family" (104). The final paradise Vathek encounters is Rocnabad, a valley watered by a stream, inhabited by "pious persons" who cultivate "little gardens." Vathek reacts to this Eden by treading underfoot the gardens and oratories. The destruction of paradise is the destruction of rest and peace, and ironically the only place where Vathek's curiosity can come to rest is in hell; the Lucifer-figure Eblis tells him: "There, insatiable as your curiosity may be, shall you find sufficient objects to gratify it" (111).

Paradise has its standard landscape of pleasant gardens, airy, flower-clothed mountains, and especially streams and fountains: there is always water there to quench the thirst. The landscape of hell consists of crags, caverns, and abysses, and the somber ruins of Istakhar. The imagery of hell is often associated with figures who are heading for damnation: to Vathek's mother Carathis, "there is nothing so pleasing as retiring to caverns" (42); when Vathek first sees Nouronihar, she is "running on the brink of the precipice" (63), and the light she follows in her vision leads her to a cavern. And, of course, it is the subterranean palace that is always Vathek's objective. So his progress through the novel is a steady descent from the mountain and the tower of intellectual curiosity into the abyss of the unconscious.

Vathek himself is a somewhat ambivalent figure. The strange power of his eye, frequently described, makes him superhuman if not supernatural. As Caliph, he has supreme power in the world; his appetites are all projected on a monstrous scale, and he is free to do whatever he will. His first step toward damnation comes on his symbolic destruction of innocence when he willfully, if remorsefully, throws the fifty "lovely innocents" into the Giaour's chasm. This question of the functioning of Vathek's will is a central one. Throughout the novel he chooses evil, and it is made to appear that his choice is a free one; his final choice at Istakar, where the good genius offers him a last chance for mercy, is certainly an act of will:

Whoever thou art, withhold thy useless admonitions: thou wouldst either delude me, or art thyself deceived. If what I have done be so criminal, as thou pretendest, there remains not for me a moment of grace. I have traversed a sea of blood, to acquire a power, which will make thy equals tremble: deem not that I shall retire, when in view of the port; or, that I will relinquish her, who is dearer to me than either my life, or thy mercy. Let the sun appear! let him illumine my career! it matters not where it may end. (105)

This is an important passage, recalling the offer made by the Old Man to Marlowe's Faustus, and in it Vathek performs irrevocably the action which makes him a Faust-figure. To use Fiedler's term, he chooses to

be damned, "whatever damnation is. Not to fall into error out of a passionate loss of self-control, not even to choose to sin at a risk of damnation; but to commit oneself to it with absolute certainty for 'as long as
forever is.'"[4]

But running counter to this theme is a suggestion that Vathek's
progress to damnation is not, in fact, subject to his own control. The
whole series of events which leads him to damnation is really an elaborate trick set up by the Giaour — presumably acting on behalf of
Mahomet, who is angered by Vathek's desire for knowledge.
Mahomet's hostility is defined at the outset: "Assist him ... to complete
the tower, which, in imitation of Nimrod, he hath begun; not, like the
great warrior, to escape from being drowned, but from the insolent curiosity of penetrating the secrets of heaven:— he will not divine the fate
that awaits him" (4). This suggestion that Vathek's will is not actually
free is underlined by a series of images related to thirst. Vathek's curiosity is often described as a thirst, and this metaphor is made actual in
the novel when his curiosity is first aroused by the Giaour, and is represented by the uncontrollable thirst which overtakes him: "So insatiable
was the thirst which tormented him, that his mouth, like a funnel, was
always open to the various liquors that might be poured into it, and
especially cold water, which calmed him more than any other" (12).
Thus there is the paradoxical suggestion that choice is subject to free
will, and at the same time that the curiosity which dictates the choice
allows no freedom.

It is this contradictory suggestion about the question of will which
causes a corresponding complication in the question of good and evil—
a complication which, when clarified, suggests that distinctions
between good and evil are irrelevant. At this point, a closer examina-

tion of the Gothic symbols defined by Fiedler, and of the way in which they are modified in *Vathek*, may prove helpful. The Gothic novel generally sets up the hero-villain who has chosen evil against the forces of good, usually figures of traditional, established virtue or authority. This circumstance produces what Fiedler calls the chief of the Gothic symbols, the maiden in flight.[5] But this figure, so common in the Gothic tradition, is lacking in *Vathek*. Nouronihar, the "maiden" here, does not fly; on the contrary, she is only too willing to join Vathek and, in the end, to share his damnation. In fact, the figures which represent "good" in *Vathek* are all minor, and, far from having their virtue rewarded, are ridiculed or destroyed. The one apparent exception is Gulchenrouz but, as Parreaux has pointed out, a closer examination shows him to be a somewhat ambivalent figure; the best that can be said for him is that he is innocent rather than good.[6] What Parreaux does not add, but something that seems equally true, is that the traits embodied by Gulchenrouz are, in the terms of this novel, essentially negative. Vathek is too ironically treated to be considered admirable even by his creator, but there is virtue in the energy he shows in his unending search, and courage in his final choice of evil and damnation. He, Nouronihar, and Carathis, essentially different aspects of the same idea, embody energy, vitality. On the other hand, innocent, humble Gulchenrouz has neither energy nor courage, and no curiosity: his heart always trembles "at anything sudden or rare" (69). It is this attitude which makes him pathetic; and the very things, lacking in Gulchenrouz, that bring about the damnation of Vathek are things which make it possible, if only in part, to admire him. Vathek is not damned for the evil he does, but for the energy, curiosity, and ambition which drive him to choose evil.

The fact that good is located in minor characters is important in another way, since the good people are all pious representatives of Mahomet. Another common Gothic symbol listed by Fiedler is the symbol of authority in decay—the ruined abbey or castle. By extension, the father-figure in these novels is also someone who must be destroyed because he, like the abbey and the castle, is a symbol of repressive authority.[7] In *Vathek*, the question of repressive authority is treated in a different way. As Vathek is supreme ruler of the world, the only possible father-or authority-figure for him is Mahomet himself, who withdraws from the scene at the beginning of the book. The Giaour, it is true, can eat more and drink more than Vathek, and Vathek fears his sexual powers; but the Giaour appears to be an extension of Mahomet's anger (the Giaour is, of course, diabolic, but as God is essentially a father-punishment figure in works of this sort, He tends to become identical with the devil). But Mahomet's representatives appear throughout the book and are all treated in the same way. The ruins of abbeys and castles are here replaced by the ruins of men—old men and dwarfs. All are easily destroyed. Early in the novel, the venerable man who brings the sacred besom from Mecca "expires on the spot" when Vathek uses the besom to sweep away cobwebs from his "oratory." The devout Fakreddin apparently also expires after Vathek has abused his hospitality and taken away his daughter. The good dwarfs are murdered, and the old men who meet Vathek before Istakar are trampled underfoot. Thus the old and devout, and the repressive authority of the past and of religion which they represent, are rejected and destroyed.

The religion that gave the law and defined the "good" is frequently seen as repressive in novels of the Gothic tradition, because the "good" is so generally hostile to energy. A crucial point in M. G. Lewis's *The*

*Monk* comes with the burning of the convent, an attack upon traditional authority similar to Vathek's own. To a hero like Vathek, God appears at best like Blake's Urizen, and the enclosing circle of His law must be broken. However, another of the ways in which the lawgiver is attacked in the Gothic tradition is omitted in *Vathek*. In Fiedler's catalogue there is, related to this destroyed, paternalist past, a figure representative of the mother with whom the hero-villain commits incest, the primal "offense against the father."[8] The central relationship in *Vathek* is between the Caliph and his mother Carathis. There is no incest here, Carathis being "chastity in the abstract." Essentially Carathis, Nouronihar, and Vathek are aspects of the same thing: mother, maiden, and hero-villain follow the same course. The women, far from embodying any sentimental virtue, outdo even Vathek in curiosity, prodding him on when he is slowed by sensual pleasure, and walking as willingly into hell. Figures which have quite separate functions in the Gothic tradition here follow a common route to a common damnation. So of all the Gothic symbols in Fiedler's catalogue, the only ones much in evidence in *Vathek* are those related to anti-religious and anti-authoritarian themes. The women of the Gothic tradition—the Clarissa-inspired maiden in flight, and the wronged mother—are here transformed into extensions of the ambitious, energetic hero-villain. The essential concern of the novel is Vathek's attempt to free himself of all restraining forces, and the consequent descent into hell.

It remains to ask: What exactly is the hell of *Vathek?* Much of the movement of the novel is suggested in conflicts between the four elements, hell being defined especially by fire and earth, heaven by air and water. Air suggests paradise, the place high above the clouds to which Gulchenrouz is taken; but air is vulnerable to the foul vapors which

Carathis conjures up, and a move from clear to poisoned air marks the descent of Nouronihar into hell: "she abandoned, without hesitation, the pure atmosphere, to plunge into these infernal exhalations" (108). Earth is related to hell; the journey to hell is to take "the way to the mineral kingdoms and the centre of the earth itself" (42). As Carathis says of the Giaour, "the terrestrial powers are always terrible" (29). But the most significant opposition is between fire and water. Hell is, in fact, the kingdom of subterranean fire. The bitter irony of the book is that the eternal fire is not the fire of creation, but the fire of guilt, of iso- lated self-consciousness, which burns in the human heart. Water, on the other hand, is generally associated with heaven. It is a feature of all the symbolic paradises of the novel, while hell can only offer an imitation: "the terrace... was flagged with squares of marble, and resembled a smooth expanse of water, upon whose surface not a blade of grass ever dared to vegetate" (107). As soon as Vathek and Nouronihar discover the reality of their damnation, they find "their tears ... unable to flow" (114). The only man in hell who is allowed hope is Soliman Ben Daoud, whose hope is signified by a cataract of water. So the theme of thirst, the journey inspired by curiosity, comes to an end in this sterile place. Here thirst can be quenched, but the sinners have no more thirst: "Every reservoir of riches was disclosed to their view: but they no longer felt the incentives of curiosity, or pride, or avarice" (114–115). Curiosity and energy end in apathy, and even Carathis forgets "her thirst for that knowledge which should ever be hidden from mortals" (119).

It is highly significant that this hell does not come after death, for the central characters do not die. Gulchenrouz's life is extended into eternal childhood; in the same way, Carathis, Nouronihar, and Vathek are damned to the suffering of eternal guilt and isolation, "as if alone on a desert where no foot had trodden" (110), again without death. This is why the final image of the book is so disturbing; for the most part the cool irony of the treatment allows us to take nothing seriously, and this necessity gives greater power to the final suggestion that in life the individual is isolated within the crowd, deprived of contact with others by his absorption with the pain in his own heart. This conclusion makes more poignant the contradiction whereby the negative, passive Gulchenrouz is allowed salvation, while Vathek, active and energetic, is damned.

We seem to be left with a choice between Vathek and Gulchenrouz, the choice, perhaps, between acting out a myth of rebellion or acting out a myth of regression. As the last words of the novel describe the final state of Gulchenrouz (indeed, the last word is "childhood"), regression seems to be suggested as the more viable possibility. Gulchenrouz is saved by his effeminacy. Vathek is presented as strongly heterosexual, and it is the women, in effect, who destroy him. And Soliman Ben Daoud says of himself, "I basely suffered myself to be seduced by the love of women" (113).

The ironies and contradictions in *Vathek* make it impossible to suggest any clear-cut moral meaning. The novel projects a world of great moral confusion, where the authority of the past is ignored or destroyed; where categories of "good," "innocence," and "virtue" are dubious indeed; where the greatest duty is to oneself, to satisfy whatever appetite is most immediate; and where action taken in a hostile universe leads inevitably to damnation.

Huron College

# REFERENCES

\* A version of this article was originally published by the Washington State University Press in *Research Studies* 50/2 (1982).

[1] Eino Railo, in *The Haunted Castle* (New York, 1964), while dedicating much space to Walpole and Lewis, mentions *Vathek* only in passing. Montague Summers, in *The Gothic Quest* (New York, 1938), fails to treat *Vathek* at all. Edith Birkhead, *The Tale of Terror: A Study of the Gothic Romance* (New York, 1921), and Devendra P. Varma, *The Gothic Flame* (London, 1957), give the book only cursory treatment. Elizabeth MacAndrew, *The Gothic Tradition in Fiction* (New York, 1979), has some illuminating comments, but, again, treats *Vathek* only in passing. Sacheverell Sitwell, in *Beckford and Beckfordism* (London, 1930), and Guy Chapman, in *Beckford* (London, 1952), are mainly concerned with the author's life. The best starting point to read about Beckford is Andre Parreaux, *William Beckford, Auteur de "Vathek" (1760-1844)* (Paris, 1960). See also Robert Kiely, *The Romantic Novel in England* (Cambridge, Massachusetts, 1972), 43–64. All quotations from *Vathek* in the present paper are from the edition by Roger Lonsdale (London, 1970) and are cited in the text.

[2] Leslie A. Fiedler, *Love and Death in the American Novel* (1960; rpt. New York, 1966), pp. 126–141.

[3] Railo, p. 322.

[4] Fiedler, p. 133.

[5] *Ibid.*, p. 131.

[6] Parreaux, pp. 349ff., shows that Beckford undermines any possibility of our considering Gulchenrouz to be the embodiment of good in the novel by stressing his effeminacy, the nature of his intimacy with Nouronihar, and the occasional guilt he feels for this attachment.

[7] Fiedler, pp. 129, 131.

[8] *Ibid.*, p. 129.

# THE GOTHIC *VATHEK* : THE PROBLEM OF GENRE RESOLVED

Frederick S. Frank

This short essay investigates the problem of genre or genres in Beckford's *Vathek*.[1] The paper develops an argument for a Gothic *Vathek*, a work that is structurally, thematically, and symbolically in harmony with the central motifs of an emergent Gothic tradition. The critical argument is built upon four propositions about the generic characteristics of Beckford's orientalized Gothic novel, those features of form and theme which *Vathek* shares in common with other Gothic examples taken from the period. The four Gothic aspects that I want to examine are: first, the pattern of the demonic quest or perverse pilgrimage, a Gothic version of the long and dark voyage of the hero; second, the physical and psychological nature of the protagonist, since I want to argue that Vathek himself is an early manifestation of the heroic villainy so characteristic of the Gothic novel's tormented tormentor, those towering and terrifying beings who have risked all for evil or those "grand, ungodly, godlike"[2] men who can slay with the eye or paralyze with the voice or immobilize their victims in other unusual ways; third, the preference of the characters for diminishing enclosures and similar forms of architectural sequestration as denoted by such Gothic locales as towers, grottos, caverns, contracting corridors, and subterranean theatres of hellish anguish; and finally, the evocation of a hypothetically malignant cosmos, an ontologically unreliable and ambiguously deceiving Gothic universe in which all moral norms are inverted or twisted, where disorder is far more likely than order, and where universal darkness can bury all without warning and at any moment.

If we take the metaphoric aspects of *Vathek* seriously, the novel makes its statement about God, the self, and the world in a speculative manner similar to other models of high Gothic fiction. Like other Gothic writers active at the end of the eighteenth century, Beckford uses his own Gothic novel to confront the moral ambiguities of an inexplicable universe; nor can we overlook the fact that Beckford ends *Vathek* with an austere moral concerning nothing less than "the condition of man upon earth."[3] *Vathek*'s Gothic, like other varieties of Gothic within the genre, certainly does amuse and entertain us, and no one would want to overlook the role of the ludicrous in Beckford's Gothic text. But the risible diversion of the reader is not always its sole aim or end. Gothics such as *Vathek* are also concerned with matters of first and final causation as well as fundamental issues of existence. Furthermore, Gothics such as *Vathek* project a disquieting *Weltanschauung* and by so doing, they engage us in final questions by displaying for the reader a world in which evil is stronger than good, instability more probable than stability, and unnatural passions closer to the true core of human behavior than the calm control of the intellect. Inquisitive characters in Gothic fiction (the inordinately curious caliph Vathek is a prime example) are forced to ask their questions and seek their answers in a sort of intellectual vacuum without the support of stable value systems to affirm any answers their quest might lead them to. Symbolically speaking, they must move through a landscape of collapsed ego-ideals wherein the older symbols of authority, secular and divine, lie everywhere in ruin. Beckford's characters, like the entrapped casts of other Gothic novels, are never free, although they may delude themselves with the dream of freedom by their sensual and sadistic conduct. At issue throughout *Vathek*, as one pro-Gothic reader of the novel has stated it, is the "contradiction between the illusion of man's freedom and the reality of his imprisonment in a necessitarian universe."[4]

From the advantageous retrospective of literary history, *Vathek* can be studied as a prototype of the subjective and subversive Gothic tendencies in the late eighteenth century which were beginning to challenge and displace an exhausted classicism and a moribund rationalism in the arts. The Gothic novel attained its astounding pre-eminence (in the form of literally thousands of horrid titles) in the late 1790s in the maiden-centered romances of Mrs. Radcliffe and the outrageous supernaturalism of Lewis's *The Monk*. Nearly four decades separate *Vathek* from the masterworks of Gothicism, Mary Shelley's *Frankenstein* (1818), Maturin's *Melmoth the Wanderer* (1820), and James Hogg's *Confessions of a Justified Sinner* (1824). But at the beginnings of the Gothic movement, Beckford's *Vathek* enjoyed the unique status of being a model for the emergent energies of the Gothic. Yet, the *Vathek* of 1786 has no close literary equivalent, unless the irrational itself be denominated a genre. Preceding *Vathek* were several narrative experiments important to recognize in summarizing the rise of the Gothic genre: Thomas Leland's *Longsword, Earl of Salisbury* (1762); Horace Walpole's *Castle of Otranto* (1764); Clara Reeve's *Old English Baron* (1777). Leland's *Longsword*, an elaborately plotted romance of chivalry set in an imaginary Middle Ages, contained both the quest and a panorama of grandly gloomy architectural settings. Walpole's *Otranto* supernaturalized the sinister properties of Gothic architecture and added the pursuing hero-villain and the fleeing maiden as they performed their violent minuet in "the long labyrinth of darkness,"[5] the basement of the haunted castle. Clara Reeve relaxed and normalized the irrational atmosphere already associated with the new genre, but she also cleverly installed a forbidden chamber within the castle, thus donating a mandatory fixture to the Gothic interior. At the climax of *Vathek*, we have an enlarged version of Clara Reeve's chamber of horrors. These romances were the only available Gothic models when Beckford sat down to compose his *Vathek*. Beckford was very much aware of these Gothic contemporaries and conscious too of the rational malaise that had generated their Gothic endeavors. The Gothics of Leland, Walpole, and Reeve had challenged the efficacy of rationalism both as an outlook and a response to existence. In its abhorrence of limits and its repudiation of a meaningful universe, the Gothic *Vathek* of Beckford is an extension of the darkening vision of these first Gothics.

The first reviewers of *Vathek* found no difficulty in assigning Gothic traits to the work. *The English Review* for 1786, to choose just one instance, discussed *Vathek* in terms of vigorous extremes and grotesque energy. "The characters," noted the reviewer, "are strongly marked though carried beyond nature; the incidents are sufficiently wild and improbable; the magic is solemn and awful, though sometimes horrid; anachronisms and inconsistencies frequently appear; and the catastrophe is bold and shocking."[6] The sadistic absurdities and diabolical climax aroused the moral fury of the reviewer of the 1834 edition. Writing in *The Southern Literary Messenger*, the reviewer denounced the novel's Gothic qualities as "obscene and blasphemous in the highest degree. ... We should pronounce it, without knowing anything of Mr. Beckford's character, to be the production of a sensualist and an infidel—one who could riot in the most abhorred and depraved conceptions—and whose prolific fancy preferred as its repast all that was diabolical and monstrous, rather than what was beautiful and good."[7]

Modern criticism of *Vathek*, however, has tended to dismiss or ignore the novel's affinities with "the monstrous and diabolical" currents of Gothicism in order to stress Beckford's predisposition to irony and his cynical undercutting of *Vathek*'s carefully built moods of terror. With the exception of the conclusion of the quest far down within the fiery Hall of Eblis, *Vathek*, is viewed as a work which shows so much vacillation between hilarity and horror that to call it Gothic in any sense is to misrepresent its literary essence and its generic category. The anti-Gothic view is expressed by one of the best twentieth-century editors of *Vathek*, who believes that any concession to Gothic responses would deny Beckford's comic purposes. "There was nothing in *Vathek*," Roger Lonsdale assures us, "which obliged reviewers to connect it with contemporary 'Gothic' tendencies in the novel. It is not easy to see that *Vathek* sets out to exploit the imaginative terror, the suspense of psychological shock tactics which were entering the English novel about this time."[8] The case against a Gothic *Vathek* gathers additional impetus from the opinions of R. D. Hume and Frederick Garber, two sympathetic and perceptive interpreters of Gothic fiction. Garber, who has edited Mrs. Radcliffe's *The Italian* (1797) and written many incisive commentaries on the place of the Gothic in literary history, nevertheless can find no place for *Vathek* in the annals of Gothicism. Writes Garber: "*Vathek* has been called a counterpart of the Gothic but it shows none of that calculated fuzziness through which the Gothic exposed the uncertainty of our daily perceptions of experience."[9] And R. D. Hume, whose 1969 *PMLA* essay, "Gothic Versus Romantic: A Revaluation of the Gothic Novel," is something of a landmark in the debate over the Gothic genre's crucial importance and its growing scholarly respectability, finds *Vathek* to be too flippant, ironic, and burlesque in tone to merit a Gothic classification. Writes Hume: "*Vathek* is often treated as a Gothic novel on the grounds that it exploits horror and magic scenery in *Schauer-Romantik* fashion. Yet I must agree with the work's recent editor that *Vathek* is not centrally of the Gothic type. Its horrors reach the point of burlesque, and its continual return to a detached and even comic tone set it apart."[10] For Hume, and his position may be regarded as the orthodox position on *Vathek*'s Gothicism, the work is best comprehended within the subgenres of comedy such as farce, burlesque, and harlequinade, "a dark-tinged but high spirited comedy" and "an existential crisis defused by comic exaggeration."[11]

Beckford shares with other early Gothic writers a paradoxical sense of the chaotic whereby images of former order are demonically reversed. Thus, it is Satan (or Eblis, as the archfiend is called in the Muhammadan tradition) who is the prime mover and highest authority in *Vathek*'s anarchic and nihilistic universe; the unspeakably repulsive becomes the attractive or the hilarious blurs into the hideous; the infernal replaces the celestial as the objective of the quester's journey; and the desire for damnation supplants salvation as the pilgrim soul's sharpest desire. These bizarre inversions directly connect *Vathek* with some major Gothic themes found in other specimens of Gothicism from Walpole's *Otranto* to Maturin's *Melmoth*. After consciously choosing evil, Beckford's Satanic hero makes a first voyage of no return in his profane quest for an infernal Xanadu. In the dark voyage of the hero may be seen a composite of Gothic motifs: a displacement of soul and loss of self which the hero attempts to counter by a descent to the lower depths; the hero's mounting awareness of the futility of spiritual values and the pointlessness of human wisdom and intelligence; realization of a universe controlled by a fiendish deity devoted to man's confusion and despair; the Faustian problem of the overreacher's limitless desire in a limited cosmos; and the ridiculousness of suffering as symbolized by the proximity of pleasure and pain in many of Vathek's adventures en route to hell.

The mythic and philosophic elements of the Gothic outlook first converge in the physical and psychological aspects of Vathek himself, a model Gothic protagonist. Whether he be a debauched monk, rapist nobleman, cruel count, ferocious brigand, or malicious caliph, the Gothic villain is a two-sided personality, a figure of great power and latent virtue whose chosen career of evil is the result of a clash between his passionate nature and the unnatural restraints of conventions, orthodoxy, and tradition. Moreover, Vathek is the first Gothic villain whose moral and physical features are given in detail. Vathek's predecessor, Manfred, in *The Castle of Otranto*, is barely described at all and one looks in vain for any lavish description of the hideous Gothic face and frame, always a landmark passage in later varieties of the Gothic. But in the makeup of Beckford's caliph, we find the progenitor of almost every single later Gothic villain, for Vathek's Satanic personality is inscribed in his face and single overwhelming eye. The lethal optic, like Vathek's private tower, is an image of absolute and pernicious power. It connotes his contempt for rational and mortal limits and functions as it will in later Gothic figures as a weapon of visionary penetration. Vathek is first introduced to the reader by way of the awesome eye: "His figure was pleasing and majestic; but when he was angry, one of his eyes became so terrible, that no person could bear to behold it; and the wretch upon whom it was fixed, instantly fell backward, and sometimes expired."[12] Vathek's deadly glance, the single eye that can maim or slay, is almost immediately transplanted to the Gothic features of Mrs. Radcliffe's Montoni and Schedoni, Lewis's Ambrosio, and attains its demonic zenith first in the blazing eyes of Melmoth the Wanderer and eventually in the ocular stimulus to madness in the "vulture eye" of the prostrate old man in Poe's "The Tell-Tale Heart." The Gothic eye which is frequently used to immobilize a reluctant maiden or to paralyze a rival heir to the castle originates with Beckford's caliph.

Complementing the ferocious and supernatural eye in the personage of Vathek is the character's passionate commitment to evil, the final stage of Faustian curiosity and ungratified sensuality. Vathek's passion for the supreme climb culminated by a haughty seclusion within a tower, or its reverse, the ultimate descent to the Palace of Subterranean Fire, are two images of perverted aspiration which give *Vathek* its model Gothic structure. Vathek's toweromania, or compulsion to elevate and isolate himself in contemptuous pride at some supreme pinnacle is counterpointed throughout the narrative by his excessive grottophilia, the impulse to descend to an ultimate darkness there to dwell eternally within a fiery abyss presided over by demons. Inspired by "an insolent curiosity of penetrating the secrets of heaven,"[13] Vathek transmits to the Gothic villains who come after him in the genre a powerful longing for absolutes in a universe devoid of such finalities. Atop one of his flaming towers, Vathek amuses himself with the mass strangulation of his subjects. In the depths of the earth at the opposite end of the novel's axis of Gothic action he joins the vast congregation of the damned upon seeing his breast become "transparent as crystal, his heart enveloped in flames."[14] The Gothic *Vathek* is the genre's first full-length portrait of a tormented tormentor, a metaphysical isolate and a monomaniac who thirsts to realize himself in evil.

Various examples of the Vathekian traits of future Gothic villains might be cited to demonstrate Beckford's major contribution to the making of the Gothic hero. Here, for example, is Count Rudiger of Frankheim, the hero of Monk Lewis's little known Gothic novella, *Mistrust: or, Blanche and Osbright*. When we first see this titanic villain, he is standing in an open grave glaring defiantly upward in a posture of mortal defiance. Note that Count Rudiger derives both the death-dealing eye and the fatal passion from *Vathek*. Those powerful emotions which would certainly prove fatal to any ordinary human being become a source of malignant strength for the Vathekian character who denounces life even as he seeks to triumph over it:

His heart was the seat of agony; a thousand scorpions seemed every moment to pierce it with their poisonous stings; but not one tear forced itself into his blood-shot eyeballs; not the slightest convulsion of his gigantic limbs betrayed the silent tortures of his bosom. A gloom settled and profound reigned upon his dark and high-arched eyebrows. Count Rudiger's stature was colossal; the grave in which he stood, scarcely rose above his knees. His eyes blazed; his mouth foamed; his coal-black hair stood erect, in which he twisted his hands, and tearing out whole handsful by the roots, he strewed them on the coffin, which stood beside his feet.[15]

If the character of the protagonist helps to identify the genre of *Vathek*, the hero's destination and his progressively frustrated experiences as he approaches his journey's end further define just how deeply Gothic the work is. Vathek's Gothic grail is nothing less than damnation for himself and those who accompany him in the voyage downward and inward to hell. The quest is demonic because it begins in torment, proceeds through heightened degrees of self-destruction, and climaxes in the hopeless horror of body and of soul for the disappointed quester. Unlike a traditional epic hero whose descent into the underworld takes him to his heroic limits and yields him a transcendent or victorious release from the darkness of self-doubt, Vathek's descending voyage ends in perplexity, guilt, and despair. Gifted with the power of perpendicular imagination, a necessary angle of vision for realizing the upper and lower limits of Gothic fantasy, Beckford conveys his hero along a vertical axis of exotic anguish and blue fire effects. Enroute to hell, Vathek and Nouronihar traverse an insular landscape rich in diabolical spectacle. Indeed, it is almost as if we were hearing descriptions of Dante's inferno as Laurence Sterne might have written them. The algolagnic terrain offers stairways spiraling downward to black depths of no return, Gothic pits containing chuckling ghouls who must be fed on live children, a pyramid of skulls nearly as high as the Gizeh monument, reptiles with human faces, toxic delicacies and idolatrous banquets consisting of "roasted wolf" vultures à la daube . . . rotten truffles; boiled thistles: and such other wild plants, as must ulcerate the throat and parch up the tongue,"[16] odd lights and bizarre beasts including an omnipresent squadron of vultures, flaming towers, and a kaleidoscopic subterranean amphitheatre in which Vathek's sorceress mother, Carathis, performs obscene

rites amidst an ornate charnel decor to the accompaniment of a shrieking chorus of one-eyed negresses and burning mummies. Across quiv-
ering plains of black sand, through swarms of curious insects, past
batallions of howling cripples and cubit-high dwarfs, into blizzards of
burning snowflakes Vathek makes the Gothic's downward voyage of
no return.

Vathek's precursor, the European Faust had sold his soul out of a
desire for power and pleasure, but Beckford's Islamic Faust already
possesses these and willingly renounces them to seek pain and damnation. One of the deepest and most enduring patterns of the Gothic
quest which brings the ambitious character to the horror of horrors in
an underground of no return is to be observed in Vathek's perverse pilgrimage. The Gothic hero's abhorrence for limits stimulates his
Satanic vanity; his vanity expresses itself in a destructive pursuit of an
ideal of horrid beauty typically depicted elsewhere throughout Gothic
fiction by the maiden and villain performing their deadly duet of flight
and pursuit through the subterranean passageways of a haunted building. The destructive pursuit of beauty culminates in spiritual and metaphysical frustration for Vathek thus implying an irrationally
determined universe in which man is fixed as an eternal victim condemned to occupy forever some chamber of horrors. In Vathek's case,
the destination is an "immense hall ... where a vast multitude is incessantly passing"[17] in a never-ending parade of anguish.

The transcendental or epic hero often climaxes his quest by arriving at some vision of totality, but when Gothic heroes venture into the
heart of darkness their experiences at the dead center often invert the
conventional romance's pattern of achievement and self-fulfillment.
From Beckford's Vathek to Melville's Captain Ahab, the Gothic hero

is a frustrated quester whose pursuit of the absolute ends by condemning him to endless circuits "'round perdition's flame.'"[18] Gothic novels
after *Vathek* adhere to the pattern of the ironic quest, a destructive version of the hero's long journey to a dark place which the Gothic hero
makes not in order to rescue the maiden but to rape her.

The pro-Gothic reading of Beckford's strange novel enables us to
recognize the motif of the dark, inward voyage as a characteristic of
the genre at large. Gothic romances like *Vathek* mock the very form
they feed on for they "retain the structure of romance, but invert the
hero's progress. The result is a linear descent: aesthetically, from the
Hill of the Pied Horses to the Hall of Eblis; psychologically, from
wishfulfillment to frustration; and metaphysically, from a vision of
humanity as unlimited potentiality to humanity as finite actuality in an
alien world."[19] Other characters throughout the Gothic genre who
decide to risk all for evil suffer the fate of Vathek in similar gruesome
confinements of body and soul. In Gothic terms, the Eblis episode
means a permanent condition of disunity between the self and nature,
the self and society, and the self and God. At the end of the novel, we
have entered the zone of ultimate cosmic discord intensified by the
dreadful apprehension that the world is under the control of a demon
and that there is "no exit." The imagery of death-in-life or life-in-death
which typifies the high Gothic through such situations as premature
burial, cadaverous enclosure, and lingering impalement attains its first
full development in the descriptions of Vathek and company in the
Hall of Eblis.

The final point to be made for a Gothic *Vathek* involves the way in
which the work's atmosphere goes beyond comedy, irony, and wild
disorder to evoke the theme of a malignant universe in which the

imagination, always striving to be free of rational bounds, is repeatedly denied its goals. Freedom of mind is perpetually at issue throughout Gothic fiction, the physical flight and pursuit through avenues of
darkness and the other forms of dreadful entrapment all indicating
symbolically the imagination's containment by finite ideas and restrictive ideological structure. Beyond the buffoonery of *Vathek*, the theme
of freedom is powerfully stated through Vathek's continuous contact
with a world that continuously disappoints his suprarational desire to
liberate himself from all mortal restraints. Each of his Gothic ordeals
is a perverse universe's reminder to him of an invincible and limited
reality impeding every effort of the imagination to break through
rational defenses. This menace of limits which a malignant cosmos
fixes upon its creatures of aspiring imagination is at the very core of
*Vathek*'s Gothicism as well as a trait of the Gothic tradition at large,
where characters constantly strive to be free but exist in bondage to
some grotesque enclosure, be it a haunted castle or an arabesque
Hades thronged with the damned in flaming heart postures. In her
important treatise, "On the Pleasure Derived from Objects of Terror,"
(1792) Beckford's contemporary, the Gothic theorist Ann Letitia
Aikin Barbauld, describes the degree of terror experienced when a
character is confronted and overwhelmed by an unholy or perverse
"otherness," as Vathek is each time he attempts to overreach the limits
of self. Higher Gothic horror of the sort we encounter in the climactic
scenes in the Hall of Eblis places *Vathek* in the highest category of the
Gothic genre, the region of total ontological distress, where the
mythology of the imaginative self as an agent of control gives way to
the nightmare of a supreme and malignant "otherness" which cannot
be escaped or transcended. The conditions of such an otherness are

expressed by Mrs. Barbauld as "Solitude, darkness, low-whispered sounds, obscure glimpses of objects, flitting forms [which] tend to raise in the mind that thrilling, mysterious terror which has for its object the 'powers unseen and mightier than we,'"[20] precisely the conditions which prevail at the frustrated terminus of Vathek's imaginative quest.

G. R. Thompson has written that "the Gothic romance is a genre that in its historical development, as well as in individual texts, moves from a stable modality of clearly defined conventions and forms toward an unstable and deliberately indeterminate modality. Frequently, the Gothic veers toward the grotesque, a mode of inherent instability that plays on the dissolution of norms—ontological, epistemological and aesthetic."[21] The Gothic *Vathek* is just such an apocalyptic narrative where the problem of genre can only be resolved by viewing the work as part of the energetic revolt against reason spearheaded by the dominance of the tale of terror during the closing decades of the eighteenth century. In the chaotic landscape of the Gothic tradition it stands like one of Beckford's infernal towers deep within the zone of ultimate Gothic fantasy where we find not just a destabilization of the norms cited by Thompson, but the dark universe's mockery of all human striving.

Allegheny College

## REFERENCES

[1]William Beckford, *Vathek*, ed. Roger Lonsdale (London: Oxford Univ. Press, 1970).

[2]Herman Melville, *Moby Dick*, chapter 16 ("The Ship").

[3]Beckford,*Vathek*, p. 120.

[4]Kenneth W. Graham, "Beckford's 'Vathek': A Study in Ironic Dissonance," *Criticism*, 14 (1972), 252.

[5]Horace Walpole, *The Castle of Otranto: A Gothic Story*, in *Three Gothic Novels*, ed. E. F. Bleiler, p. 36.

[6]*English Review*, 8 (1786), 180–184.

[7]*Southern Literary Messenger*, 1 (1834), 188–189.

[8]Roger Lonsdale, Introduction to *Vathek* by William Beckford, pp. vii–xxxi.

[9]Frederick Garber, "Beckford, Delacroix, and Byronic Orientalism," *Comparative Literature Studies*, 18 (1981), 321–332.

[10]R. D. Hume, "Exuberant Gloom, Existential Agony, and Heroic Despair: Three Varieties of Negative Romanticism," in *The Gothic Imagination: Essays in Dark Romanticism*, ed. G. R. Thompson, pp. 109–117.

[11]R. D. Hume, "Exuberant Gloom," p. 117.

[12]Beckford, *Vathek*, p. 1.

[13]Beckford, *Vathek*, p. 4.

[14]Beckford, *Vathek*, p. 114.

[15]Matthew G. Lewis, *Mistrust: or, Blanche and Osbright*, in *Seven Masterpieces of Gothic Horror*, ed. R. D. Spector, pp. 237–330.

[16]Beckford, *Vathek*, p. 49.

[17]Beckford, *Vathek*, p. 109.

[18]Melville, *Moby Dick*, Chapter 36 ("The Quarter–Deck").

[19]Randall Craig, "Beckford's Inversion of Romance in *Vathek*," *Orbis Litterarum*, 39 (1984), 95–106.

[20]Ann Letitia Aiken Barbauld, "On the Pleasure Derived from Objects of Terror," in *The Evil Image*, eds. Patricia L. Skarda and Nora Crow Jaffe, pp. 10–13.

[21]G. R. Thompson, "The Form of Gothic Romance," a paper delivered at the Modern Language Association Meeting, Washington, DC, December 1984, pp. 1–26.

# VATHEK AND DECADENCE*

Jürgen Klein

for Devendra P. Varma

William Beckford's *Vathek* has been classified as a Gothic novel and as an Oriental tale. It is also an example of decadent literature and it is as such that the other two classifications may be reconciled.

There can be no doubt that eighteenth-century Western authors and intellectuals have been fascinated by the decadence and the intoxicating perfumes of the Orient. Asia always has provided a power of attraction for Europeans, since the quantity and quality of information on this far off region had been scarce for centuries. Eighteenth-century Europe intensified its curiosity concerning the Eastern world. Dr. Johnson chose the setting of Asia Minor for his tale *Rasselas*. Oriental studies became prominent in England as well as in Germany, if one refers to scholars like Robert Lowth and J.D. Michaelis. As Devendra P. Varma has rightly emphasized, Beckford "was deeply saturated in the history and romance of the East, a fact well corroborated by the scholarly and voluminous annotations of his editor Henley."[1]

If we look at *Vathek* as a work of decadent literature, then the Oriental setting acquires a special relevance. Diderot reminds us in his Encyclopedia article "Luxury"[2] that Asian refinement corrupts the virtues and renders its adepts effeminate. What is significant in *Vathek* is not the costume, the gay colors of the Orient with its camels, bazaars, muezzins, and mosques, but something quite different: firstly the spirit of the wondrous and fabulous in its echoes of the *Arabian Nights*, and secondly the "aesthetics of evil," found in an ecstatic sensuality based on unsurmountable excess and over-refinement. Its mode is both decadent and delicate. It stimulates all the senses with the Burkean extremes of the beautiful and the sublime. Evil acquires different shapes as it combines on the one hand with the sensual and earthly to produce the horrible, the cruel, the cannibalistic, and the ugly; and on the other shines forth in an ideal incorporation in the figure of Eblis— a representation of the pure nothing, the hyper-aesthetic glorification of negativity.

As is conventional for the Gothic novel, Vathek begins with a description of the protagonist and his lineage. Caliph Vathek's descent[3] is almost fabulous,—since his grandfather was the legendary Haroun al Raschid. His faculties are superhuman—he can kill people by his basilisk gaze. His stature is beautiful and sublime at the same time, "pleasing and majestic." The Caliph shows himself lavish within his greatness. His life streams like a continuous ecstasy of sensual pleasure. His palaces are devoted to the heightening and intensification of the human senses: the first palace is consecrated to the consumption of dishes and beverages (The Eternal or Unsatiating Banquet), the second to musical entertainment (The Temple of Melody or the Nectar of the Soul); the third contains the rarest treasures and valuables (The Delight of the Eyes or the Support of Memory); the fourth offers all the scents of the orient (The Palace of Perfumes of The Incentive of Pleasure), the last one is consecrated to love itself (The Retreat of Mirth, or the Dangerous).

All these palaces are glittering in their unsurmountable opulence, great splendor and magnificence. Vathek's desire for beauty knows no limits: the most fragrant, the finest, most flowery, the most variegated scents surround him, the most select wines effervesce from golden bowls, the sounds of the musical instruments flatter the ears, and the most beautiful and tempting women respond to the wishes of their sovereign. But all this luxury and pleasure cannot drive away Vathek's melancholia. Vathek longs to escape from tediousness: "What one does not know, exactly that one needs/ And what one knows, one cannot use" (Goethe, *Faust* I, Vor dem Tor). With all his pleasures, Vathek is not content because they have by now lost their quality of particularity. Like Faust, Vathek "wants to know everything." He is going to solve the mystery of the heavens. Similar to Goethe's *Faust*, where God gives Mephistopheles the chance to achieve power over Faust, Mahomet, who watches Vathek's activities, leaves him alone.

Vathek seeks to deify himself. He commands an enormous tower to be built—a counterpart to the tower of Babel—to contemplate with complacency from its airy height the power of his own sovereignty.[4] He wants to look down on his subjects, to see them as swarming ants. The most important use for Vathek's tower is related to astronomy and astrology. By star-gazing, Vathek hopes to find out the mysteries of the heavens. His curiosity is so unbounded that every stranger who passes his capital, Samarah, is forced to present himself to the Caliph.

A stranger appears,[5] a ghastly being to look at, presumably an Indian. This stranger provides Vathek with things unheard of and never seen before, which strike the Caliph with awe and joy at the same time:

There were slippers which, by spontaneous springs, enabled the feet to walk;

knives that cut without motion of the hand; sabres, that dealt the blow at the person they were wished to strike; and the whole enriched with gems that were hitherto unknown.

The sabres especially, the blades of which, emitted a dazzling radiance, fixed, more than all the rest, the Caliph's attention; who promised himself to decipher, at his leisure the uncouth characters engraven on their sides. (5–6)

The stranger on his part does not even try to explain these mysteries: he maintains his silence. Questions concerning the Indian's origin or the source of those miraculous objects are unanswered. Only a shrill laughter does the stranger accord to Vathek's curiosity. Contrary to all the world, which trembles in the face of Vathek, the stranger is indifferent to Vathek's wishes. It becomes obvious that this stranger derives his authority from something which transcends the Caliph's power. Even Vathek's deadly gaze, fatal for human beings, cannot affect the stranger. Typical to the genre, the novel begins with a question mark. At the beginning something happens which cannot be explained: a miracle and a superhuman event.

What follows demonstrates that the stranger possesses a supernatural mode of existence: his actions eclipse the human. Cast into prison, the insubordinate stranger breaks out, "the grates burst asunder, and his guards lying lifeless around him." (7). In a fit of "madness" Vathek beats his servants, who let the Indian escape.

Returning to his senses, Vathek remembers that the planets had announced this weird visitor. To get to know more about this stranger, his mother, Carathis, suggests that the mysterious inscriptions on the sabres should be deciphered.[6] Scholars gather, but traditional learning offers no insights to the meaning of the sabres. Finally, a venerable sage offers this translation:

"We were made where everything is well made: we are the least of the wonders of a place where all is wonderful, and deserving the sight of the first potentate on earth." (11)

The characters hold out the promise of the miraculous. The inscription, though explained, remains an enigma. The miraculous inscription becomes uncanny when it changes without any visible influence. The sage earns Vathek's displeasure with a second translation: "Woe to the rash mortal who seeks to know that of which he should remain ignorant; and to undertake that which surpasses his power." The changing inscriptions are truly *uncanny* or *unheimlich*: "the name for everything that should have remained ... hidden and secret and has become visible." Beckford belongs to those authors, who "...intensify and multiply the uncanny far above the degree possible for experience by letting such events occur, which in reality never or very rarely would have come to pass."[7]

Having driven away the successful scholar, Vathek remains ignorant of the meaning of the changing messages on the sabres. His curiosity leads him nearly into madness. Fever and anxiety cause a collapse. An unquenchable physical thirst seizes him—a copy of his psychic "thirst" to be initiated into the great secret. The dissonance between existence and the shapings of the eternal construe Vathek's problem. At the same time this dissonance constitutes the tension within the novel itself: "the refusal of the immanence of being to enter into empirical life..."[8]

This dissonnance has seized Vathek already as its victim; he has experienced the uncomfortable relativity of his position, far above his subjects but far below the eternal stars. Vathek himself is not important. What matters is his Faustian ambition, his longing for what the stars represent, the idea which keeps aloof over him. Vathek represents curiosity, desire, the response to boredom in the eternal *nevertheless*.[9] Not interested in innocent pleasures, Vathek faces his failure and retires from the world.[10] Powerlessness leads him to lose his capacity to act and he seeks to escape.

Meanwhile, Vathek's mother Carathis tries by magic to exert power over the Indian, now called the Giaour. Vathek, still sick and remaining in retirement, is brought to a nearby mountain garden, about which we read, "... it might have been taken for the Paradise ..." (13). Beckford describes this garden, a synaesthetic as well as orgiastic scene, with an intensity rarely to be found in literature. This unspeakably beautiful landscape, with its interplay of heavy scents and many colors, an ideal region for nineteenth-century authors of the decadence movement. There, however, Vathek's thirst remains unquenched.

At last the stranger returns and frees Vathek from his torments with the help of a magic potion. In his delight Vathek even kisses the nauseating Indian (15) and orders a banquet to be held to honor him. When the stranger is asked to explain the ingredients of the potion he again answers with a yelling laughter. Vathek kicks the Giaour for his impertinence, and he—the terror and fascination of the citizens—coils up to a ball, and disappears into a deep cleft in the "mountain of the four fountains."[11] The metamorphosis of the Giaour into a ball, which is followed after by the excited, ecstatic crowd, shows how an extreme action turns towards the supernatural.

Vathek orders tents to be pitched up in the garden, so that he can keep an eye on the abyss. But the voices which he seems to hear from the depth, are products of his own imagination. Vathek curses the stars—but suddenly blood-red stripes discolor the clear blue sky. The Caliph's inclination to the marvellous keeps him for a long time in this place, until some time later he perceives the stranger's voice again. The Giaour is the true protagonist: he is responsible for the progress of action within the novel.

"Wouldest thou devote thyself to me? adore the terrestrial influences, and abjure Mahomet? On these conditions I will bring thee to the Palace of Subterranean Fire. There shalt thou behold, in immense depositories, the treasures which the stars have promised thee; and which will be conferred by those intelligences, whom thou shalt thus render propitious. It was from thence I brought my sabres, and it is there that Soliman Ben Daoud reposes, surrounded by the talismans that control the world." (22)

The promises offered by the master of the subterranean fire cannot be assessed in a first reading of the novel. During the second reading it is, however, easy to see that the Caliph receives an offer which really cannot free him from his ennui or cure him of his melancholia and frustrated desires. All Vathek can expect is merely a multiplication of what he already possesses and what he does not esteem. Any "surplus" does not help Vathek.

The invitation to make an agreement with the "terrestrial influences" has been voiced. This agreement entails the condition that Vathek abjure his belief. This contract recalls Goethe's *Faust*, though the presuppositions are not identical.[12] The Arabian "Satan" is no fallen angel—*ab initio*—but a *jinn* (spirit), who "was received by the angels into heaven in order to get a better education, but he turned out badly."[13]

Vathek, incited by insatiable curiosity, abjures Mahomet. At once the sky becomes clear and within the abyss a "portal of ebony" becomes visible, "before which stood the Indian, holding in his hand a golden key, which he sounded against the lock." (23) Seemingly at the goal of his wishes, the Caliph demands to be let in, but the Giaour stipulates another, terrible, condition:

"Know that I am parched with thirst, and cannot open this door, till my thirst be thoroughly appeased; I require the blood of fifty children. Take them from among the most beautiful sons of thy viziers and great men; or, neither can my thirst nor thy curiosity be satisfied. Return to Samarah; procure for me this necessary libation; come back hither; throw it thyself into the chasm, and thou shalt see!" (23)

Within this demand the aesthetics of evil come into the open. The negativity of murder is set in fascinating combination with the positives of youth and beauty. This doctrine of negativity defines the novel's subject. The blood sacrifice requires beautiful and noble children. The human detestation of murder is balanced against and outweighed by the exceptional shapeliness and nobility of the victims as well as by the thrill of trespassing ethical laws.[14] Decadence as "Satan's metamorphosis" (Mario Praz) is signalled in this context.

If we compare the murders commited in accordance with the idea of evil in Marquis de Sade's *The 120 Days of Sodom* (1785) with those deeply corrupted scenes in *Vathek*, Beckford's refined, though evil taste, his malicious delicacy and intoxicated beauty, triumphs over Sade, though in *Vathek* the aesthetics of the ugly is partially considered too. The reader of *Vathek* is confronted with a specific exoticism, "which feeds upon a particular cultural atmosphere ... which flourished in the Romantic period." Praz calls it a "sort of ecstasy" and he links it with mysticism.[15]

Corruption and crimes in *Vathek* are cultural actions, and sacrifices are transformed into an aesthetic entity by atmospheric arabesques. On the "mountain with the four fountains" Vathek executes the sacrifice, but the ebony gate, which should have led him into the mystery, remains shut. Disappointed expectation leads the Caliph into a frenzy. With difficulty Carathis manages to soothe the people of Samarah, in uproar over the murders. She retires with her melancholy son into the tower in order to take counsel on the situation. Carathis proves to be more strenuous and more unremitting than Vathek when it comes to reaching her goals. She is willing to take everything upon herself to confront evil itself. The description of the fire, which Carathis uses for sacrifice and conjuration so that she might be able to satisfy the spirit of evil with a devilish stench, represents one of the most remarkable and gruesome scenes within the novel. The smell of the burnt substances contrasts exactly with the perfumes and the rich scents of Vathek's garden.

Vathek finds frustration insupportable. He responds with sadistic eruptions to all the negations he encounters. When Carathis's mute female negro slaves do not serve dishes to appease his hunger, "he began to cuff, pinch, and bite them, till Carathis arrived to terminate a scene so indecent..." (31) The terrible drama, however, takes its course. Black magic with all its psychical power[16] has its effects through the incantation. In devilish excitement and great haste Carathis executes the necessary rites. Abstinence from food[17] is a necessary condition for the success of this magic endeavor, so that Carathis commands Vathek to act accordingly. "At length darkness approached, and Carathis, having stripped herself to her inmost garment, clapped her hands in an impulse of ecstasy ..." (32)[18]

Darkness stimulates the magic scene and Carathis's ecstasy increases. Her abstinence relates not only to food but also to sex. The exhibitionism is nothing more than lust.[19] Exorcisms generally are based on magically exploited sexual abstinence. Influenced by the stench, the negresses are drawn into their mistress's rapture, so that all together they utter hysterical yells. The flames of the poisonous fire mount,[20] so that the scene is tinged in the magical colors black and red. But the dark festivity to honor the "terrestrial influences" has not yet achieved its peak. When the inhabitants of Samarah carry water to the place of the ceremony in order to save their beloved ruler whom they fear to be consumed by the flames, the personified evil in the shape of Carathis sees them as suitable candidates for a human sacrifice.[21] Vathek's subjects, nearly suffocated by the vapors, are strangled by the negresses and, with Vathek's consent, thrown on the pyre.

Carathis, whose presence of mind never forsook her, perceiving that she had carcasses sufficient to complete her oblation, commanded the chains to be stretched across the staircase, and the iron doors barricadoed, that no more might come up.

No sooner were these orders obeyed, than the tower shook; the dead bodies vanished in the flames; which, at once, changed from a swarthy crimson, to a bright rose colour: an ambient vapour emitted the most exquisite fragrance ... and the liquefied horns diffused a delicious perfume. (35)

Here black romanticism is triumphant. Beckford displays an undoubted masterliness in his creation of an atmosphere characterized by transitions from the dark and gruesome scene of the sacrifice to the ethereal and intoxicating beauty in the scene that follows.

With the shaking of the tower, the supernatural force placated by the sacrifices and incantations announces its approval. The scents as well as the sky, lightly tinged in red, demonstrate the contentedness of this being. By marvellous and unexpected operations Vathek sees that the pyre is replaced by a most luxurious dinner-table. His highest principles, lust and pleasure—including the lust for evil—draw him to dinner, during which Carathis discovers a parchment from the devil, a written expression of thanks for the sacrifice. Vathek is invited to travel to Istakar, where he will have the chance to look at the treasures, heaped up by the pre-Adamite sultans.

The devil himself intends to welcome Vathek in the "region of wonders," but he forbids Vathek on penalty of his anger not to enter any dwelling on the way to Istakar. The preparations for Vathek's journey are made. Carathis is commissioned to rule over Samarah during Vathek's absence. The court, including an impressive number of ladies from the seraglio, is equipped for the journey. The stars favour this intention, but Carathis does not neglect to remind Vathek to act according to the devil's condition: "Forget me not then, but the moment thou art in possession of the talismans which are to open the way to the mineral kingdoms and the centre of the earth itself, fail not to dispatch some trusty genius to take me and my cabinet..."(49)

Beckford's novel *Vathek* indulges in ritual performances and aesthetic procedures. Thus it is no wonder that Vathek's leave-taking is acted out in a grand ceremony. The people of Samarah are on their knees before the ruler. Under a flourish of trumpets Vathek climbs into his sedan so that the procession can move forward. The crossing of the mountains is described by Beckford in a way which makes obvious his artistic power to create an atmosphere either of the sublime or of the intoxicatingly beautiful. All the terrors of nature which Burke had listed in his description of the sublime fall upon the procession. The categories of "power", "obscurity," and especially "terror" are put into practice in this description. Storms howl and squalls beat the travellers' faces. Dark clouds announce "horrors of this disastrous night" (45). The ladies of the seraglio tremble in the biting cold. Tigers or devils stare with glowing eyes in the darkness: beasts of prey attack Vathek's caravan. The caravan is so long that the news that the vanguard has been eaten by beasts of prey is slow to reach the main body. "The confusion that prevailed was extreme. Wolves, tigers, and other carnivorous animals, invited by the howling of their companions, flocked together from every quarter. The crashing of bones was heard on all sides, and a fearful rush of wings over head; for now vultures also began to be of the party" (45–6).

Here the natural sublime intensifies into the measureless terrible. It is not the infinity of the sea which gives to human beings the idea of the sublime, but nature in its unconscious and greedy ferocity, in its uncontrolled lust to murder and devour, which fills human spectators with horror. Only when Vathek hears his women scream does he know what horrible events have taken place. Torches are lighted and the caravan stops on Vathek's order at the place of horror where the beasts of prey "[had] made ... a most luxurious supper." Some of them, surfeited and incapable of flight are themselves prepared as a meal (48). Here the *dégoutant*, the ugly, and the terrible are a subject for artistic creation: the indirect cannibalism is in the final analysis transformed into oral profligacy or into ventral perversion.

A glowing heat on the next day calls forth the resentment of Vathek's thirsty followers. Suddenly two dwarfs appear carrying baskets full of the most refreshing fruits, "melons, oranges and pomegranates" (51). Through a *deus ex machina* an aesthetic catharsis changes everything.

By order of Emir Fakreddin the grotesque figures invite the "vice-*gerent* of Mahomet" to visit the "Happy Valley," after they have explained to Vathek that the evil spirit, Deggial,[22] has been responsible for the disaster. Supernatural phenomena occur again and again, as the Caliph receives a message in Carathis's hand warning him not to visit a lodging if he wishes to see the subterranean palace. But Vathek breaks the Giaour's condition and accepts the invitation. Fakreddin's Happy Valley surpasses Vathek's garden, and Samuel Johnson's "Happy Valley" in *Rasselas* appears to be a poor landscape in comparison. Beckford succeeds in describing an enchanting landscape full of luxurious life in Fakreddin's palaces. The opulence and pleasures there fascinate and delight the Caliph:

Vathek found himself beneath a vast dome, illuminated by a thousand lamps of rock crystal: as many vases of the same material, filled with excellent sherbet, sparkled on a large table, where a profusion of viands were spread. Amongst others, were rice boiled in milk of almonds, saffron soups, and a lamb à la crème, of all which the Caliph was amazingly fond. (55)

Vathek's eunuch, Bababalouk, enters the seraglio to discover Nouroni-har, Fakreddin's daughter, in a bath made from black porphyry:

... groups of young slaves were visible; amongst whom, Bababalouk perceived his pupils, indulgingly expanding their arms, as if to embrace the perfumed water, and refresh themselves ... The looks of tender languor; their confidential whispers; and the enchanting smiles with which they were imparted; the exquisite fragrance of the roses: all combined to inspire a voluptuousness, which even Bababalouk himself was scarce able to withstand. (57)

The atmosphere evoked is decadent: a mixture of exoticism and eroticism—"looks of tender languor", a scene producing "voluptuousness," games of the female slaves, characterized by seductive levity within rooms of extreme luxury.

In his religious fanaticism Fakreddin organizes a festivity for cripples and zealots. Sadistic and masochistic performances by fakirs and dervishes offer a truly grotesque pageant.

Wherever the Caliph directed his course, objects of pity were sure to swarm round him; the blind, the purblind, smarts without noses, damsels without ears, each to extol the munificence of Fakreddin, who, as well as his attendant grey-beards, dealt about, gratis, plasters and cataplasms to all that applied. At noon, a superb corps of cripples made its appearance... (61)

As in Marquis de Sade's literary texts, the ill, the ugly, and the disgusting figures are presented in Beckford's *Vathek*. Karl Rosenkranz in his *Ästhetic des Hässlichen* (1853) already remarked, "that from now on the dark sides of beauty's bright figure will be an element of aesthetic science as well, like illness in pathology or evil in ethics ..."[23] Hell is not only a religious and an ethical entity, "it is also an aesthetic phenomenon."[24] As, especially for the novel, the tension between ethics and aesthetics is a constituent, so the ugly must be the counterpart to evil, because aesthetics and ethics in the novel are interrelated in such a way, that they refer to the process of literary creation on one side and to the teleology of actions on the other side. "In the novel ... ethic—the ethical intention—is visible in the creation of every detail and hence is, in its most concrete content, an effective structural element of the work itself."[25]

Vathek's ethical disposition towards evil is based on an extreme as well as totalitarian hedonism, whereas Carathis represents the power of negativity. Driven by hedonism, Vathek sets out on his journey: with pleasure as his only goal, Vathek's quest is subject to interruption.

Among the "elegant forms of several young females, skipping and bounding like roes" (62), the Caliph catches sight of Nouronihar, who bewitches his soul. Her playmate is Gulchenrouz, a youth, "(who) seemed to be more feminine than even herself" (66). The youth figures as a sentimental character, shedding tears of emotion when playing the lute. In his "unresisting languour" and grace Gulchenrouz is so to speak the ideal homosexual. Nouronihar, however, is drawn under Vathek's spell.

A mysterious blinding light appears at the top of a mountain. Nouronihar's playmates flee, but she herself, though terrified, investigates "[u]rged on by an irresistible impulse ..." (69) She continues her way to a cave and hears voices which prophesy her marriage with Vathek and their joint admission to the palace of subterranean fire.

Vathek, unable to resist Nouronihar's beauty, violates the law of hospitality and declares Nouronihar peremptorily to be his wife. The emir deceives the Caliph by drugging his daughter and Gulchenrouz so that he can take them into faraway mountains, to preserve them from Vathek's desires. He reports Nouronihar dead and Vathek falls into a debilitated mourning. He curses the Giaour and charges him with having procured Nouronihar's loss. Vathek renounces him by begging Mahomet's pardon (81). Here the novel arrives at a critical point: the possibility of a traditional novelistic ending is imaginable, at least from a formal perspective. But the potential turn towards excessive earthly love is counteracted at once by its negation. The encounter with Vathek as the personification of the sublime and of evil has kindled an unruly desire in Nouronihar to enjoy poisonous beauty, so that she does not cherish any other thought but escape from her prison. Vathek discovers the fugitive, and Nouronihar tells her story, referring to the "subterranean palace" where both of them are expected. Vathek suddenly returns to his evil nature, encouraged by the fact that Nouronihar too is addicted to the "terrestrial influences." Vathek again sees his goal clearly before him, though the indulgence in beauty covers his desire for a moment:

"Light of my eyes, the mystery is unravelled; we both are alive! Your father is a cheat, who, for the sake of dividing us, hath deluded us both: and the Giaour, whose design, as far as I can discover, is, that we shall proceed together, seems scarce a whit better. It shall be some time, at least, before he finds us in his palace of fire. Your lovely little person, in my estimation, is far more precious than all the treasures of the pre-adamite sultans; and I wish to possess it at pleasure, and, in open day, for many a moon, before I go to burrow underground, like a mole" (84).

Vathek shows weakness in all his perversity; he lacks consistency of action, because always he is guided by an appetite for the highest quality and quantity of satisfaction. Vathek acts on the grounds of the pleasure-pain-principle. His negativity amounts to decomposition, noble rottenness and passive lust for destruction.

Vathek's favourite, Dilara, to be revenged on Vathek's neglect, writes to Carathis that he is interrupting his journey, "and acquaint[ed] her that all things went ill" (88-9). "The eagerness of Carathis may be easily guessed at receiving the letter ... 'Is it so!' said she: 'either I will perish, or Vathek shall enter the palace of fire'" (89). Here, as in other passages of the novel, the mother takes the decisions for her son, at least in her imagination. It makes sense to assume that this mother-son relationship indicates a case of the Oedipus complex, but extended by the motherly syndrome of self-sacrifice.[26]

Carathis at once follows Vathek. Beckford cannot resist including a churchyard-scene. Carathis and her "negresses" are resting at night in such a place, in order to do homage to the ghouls—they are necrophages—by giving them the corpses of their scouts, who died from the exertion of this journey.[27]

The negresses even want to spend some tender lover's hours with the ghouls, but are forbidden to do so, because Carathis, "being chastity in abstract, and an implacable enemy to love intrigues and sloth" (92), gives immediate orders to take up the journey. When Carathis meets Vathek, she urges him to resume his journey to the "subterranean palace" and to drown Nouronihar. A compromise is found, and Nouronihar is allowed to accompany Vathek to the place of evil.

After a short stay in the vale of Rocnabad, where "[t]he season of spring was in all its vigour, and the grotesque branches of almond trees, in full blossom" (100), both enjoy earthly pleasures for the last time, before they cross a huge plain: "...from whence were discernible, on the edge of the horizon, the dark summits of the mountains of Istakar" (103). The good jinns [= genii] entreat Mahomet to save Vathek from destruction; one comes to cause fear and shame in Vathek. After a short struggle, goodness is defeated. The Caliph overcomes his anxiety and rejects the jinn's warning not to pursue his way to Eblis.

Vathek's decision in favor of evil induces most of his company to flee. The remaining royal household experiences an ecstatic expectation. The journey is continued in haste. The encounter with evil itself is reserved only to an elite. "The impetuosity of (Vathek's) blood prevented him from sleeping; nor did he encamp any more, as before. Nouronihar, whose impatience, if possible, exceeded his own, importuned him to hasten his march, and lavished on him a thousand caresses, to beguile all reflection" (106).

### THE END OR SATAN'S APOTHEOSIS

> Nemo contra deum nisi deus ipse.
>
> Goethe, *Dichtung und Wahrheit*

The end of Vathek's journey to hell is near. The landscape, which Vathek traverses with his few remaining followers, is nearly deserted. On an elevated terrace of black marble, the Giaour receives them. Deadly silence reigns. Vathek and Nouronihar, gazing wildly around, climb up the stairs of the ruined palace of Istakar with beating hearts. The text does not mention any companions. Gigantic stone animals—one is reminded of the door keepers of Chorsabad—guard the portal: "The rock yawned, and disclosed within it a staircase of polished marble, that seemed to approach the abyss" (108). Both esteem themselves as deified: "As they descended, by the effulgence of the torches, they gazed on each other with mutual admiration..." (108)

The spatial progress in Beckford's novel now comes to an end, a progress which in the final analysis cannot claim the temporal dynamic force that we very often find in highly plotted narrative texts. The sublimity of the subterranean halls cannot be described in detail. However, Beckford at the end of his novel gives literary shape to Satan's apotheosis. Vathek and Nouronihar behold groups of promenading people, of whom "...several...kept their right hands on their hearts, without once regarding any thing around them ... **They all avoided each other**" (109–10). The sight of evil in all its grandeur has to be paid for by the loss of communication and even by the loss of love.

After some time, Vathek and Nouronihar perceived a gleam brightening through the drapery, and entered a vast tabernacle hung around with the skins of leopards. An infinity of elders with streaming beards, and afrits in complete armour, had prostrated themselves before the ascent of a lofty eminence; on the top of which, upon a globe of fire, sat the formidable Eblis. His person was that of a young man, whose noble and regular features seemed to have been tarnished by malignant vapours. In his large eyes appeared both pride and despair: his flowing hair retained some resemblance to that of an angel of light. In his hand, which thunder had blasted, he swayed the iron sceptre, that causes the monster Ouranbad, the afrits, and all the powers of the abyss to tremble. At his presence, the heart of the Caliph sunk within him; and he fell prostrate on his face. Nouronihar, however, though greatly dismayed, could not help admiring the person of Eblis... (111)

Indeed, the appearance of the youthful Eblis in the beauty and depravity of the fallen angel in the fiery hell is a climax in Beckford's novel which no reader will ever forget.[28] The privilege adjudged to Vathek and Nouronihar to look at even the most precious treasures has no power to subdue their dejection. Malignity implies a form of inner revenge–in an utterly Christian mode–by the permanent consuming fire in the hearts, which in the final analysis is identical with coldness. Soliman, one of the pre-Adamite kings, was able—on his own report—to reign only for a time over the "supernatural beings." Finally the transcendental power overpowered him by annihilation: "an unrelenting fire preys on my heart" (114).

Vathek's and Nouronihar's repentence comes too late. Their hearts are also consumed by the flames. Their eventful excursion into the hellish empire has been reversed into the repetition of the eternally identical (Nietzsche's "Wiederkehr des ewig Gleichen"). Both have reached the centre of eternal malignity, but they remain in principal different from Eblis. Riches do not affect them any longer, power cannot offer any satisfaction. Cruelty lacks any glimpse of love. What remains is desire without hope. Here no ascent is possible as in Goethe's *Faust* or in Hegel's *Phenomenology of Spirit*. The wish to turn towards the evil manifests itself in *Vathek* finally as determinate "burning downwards." Without escape, Vathek remains in the power of Eblis, who represents the "acid and the descending downwards." Moreover, there is no comfort for Vathek in punishing Carathis, who urged him on his search after the evil principle. There can be no doubt about the fact that Beckford's *Vathek* proves evil can be represented in a narrative text. The principle of exclusive amorality is transformed into artistic shape. Immanuel Kant stated in his *Metaphysik der Sitten*[29] that committing of *formal malignity* is impossible: "As far as we understand, to commit such a crime of a formal (totally useless) malignity, is impossible for human beings, and yet (though a pure idea of extreme evil) it cannot be ignored within a system of moral philosophy."[30]

But the aesthetic experience of Beckford's *Vathek*, requires one to supplement Kant's statement. If it is true that the idea of extreme malignity is a conceptual construct which cannot be neglected in an ethical system, then one has to infer—especially concerning the totally uselessness of malignity—that evil as a phenomenon of uselessness must have a place within aesthetics, because there it can claim to be the subject of "pleasure without any interest" (cf. Kant's concept "interesseloses Wohlgefallen" in his *Kritik der Urteilskraft* (1799)[31]. Within aesthetics the idea of evil loses the relationship to possible (real) actions and now takes up the quality of a negative *prototypon transcendentale*. The multidimensional quality of a novel is based on the tension between ethics and aesthetics: the aesthetic level and the personal auctorial level as well as the levels of epochal objectivations and antagonisms are mixed up. Within this field between *idea* and *mundus* Beckford's *Vathek* takes the level of "romantic irony," because the Ego in its simplicity does deny all definitions, but at the same time it constructs all contents, which it claims to be valid for itself. "What is, is only through the I, and what is through myself, can also be destroyed by myself."[32]

The negativity of irony is embedded in Vathek's essence. His vanity is reflected in his ruthlessness, his inability to be satisfied with accessible pleasures. He searches after the absolute which by definition may be something or nothing.[33] Vathek's desire opts for the negative side.

The relationship between master and subject is important in Beckford's novel. Vathek's amorality is visible in the fact that he uses his subjects totally as means to ends. With his thoughtless grandiosity, he degrades them into mere objects. His boundless egotism is breathtaking in its obliviousness to his kinship with humanity. Within it human dignity has no scope or meaning.

In the romantic irony in the outcome of Beckford's tale, the fabulous powers and riches available to Vathek in the realm of Eblis become matters of indifference. Eblis's gift is identical with a negation. Satan's empire is Vathek's native place (*Heimat*); in its very

hopelessness, even human sorrow is negated. Beckford's view of hell
stands in contradictory opposition to Goethe and Hegel. *Eblis* is *Nihil*
and not "Ein Teil von jener Kraft,/Die stets das Böse will und stets das
Gute schafft."[34]

Hegel's *Dialektik* forbids us to solve the problems formulated in
Beckford's text: "The purely negative ... cannot within the ideal representation of an action be taken for the essential foundation of a necessary reaction," we read in Hegel's *Ästhetik*. "The evil ... is generally
bleak and without content, because it produces nothing else than negativity, destruction, and misery..." Beckford does not know dialectics,
but he creates the gap or the abyss. We are in his philosophy "beyond
good and evil" in a social sense as well as in a philosophical sense.[36]
Beckford with his *Vathek* is from an intellectual point of view nearer
to Nietzsche, Heidegger, and Thomas Mann (Adrian Leverkühn)[37]
than one would expect. Beckford's nothingness, however, remains
within the boundaries of the *ens rationis negative*, whereas we
encounter in Nietzsche and Heidegger the *Nihil Privativum Entis
Rationis Positive Sive Dei*.[38]

Thus one has good reasons to assume that Beckford's *Vathek*, in its
narrative structure as well as its semantic focus, gives an insight into
the dialectics of space and time, but also into the opposition between
infinity and finitude.

The escape from time cannot any longer be expressed and experienced in metaphysical terms. Gothic novels—and this is true for
*Vathek*—construct worlds as destinations for man's metaphysical
being, worlds that transcend the intellectual possibilities of metaphysics. The tension between infinity and finitude circumscribes the concept of *Paradise*, so that according to a general theory of knowledge

the aesthetic statement of man's autopoietic modelling can shift from positive to negative. The difference between a positive and a negative paradise always has to refer back to experiments to develop a theory of the modern self and concomitant world constructions. Do not all Gothic novel writers try to define the modern self, either within the context of a traditional spatial environment accompanied by the epochal value system or within a problematic field where difficulties of value production are implied in a series of paradoxes (quantity, self, sense, and meaning)? Eblis's hall constructs the meaning, which one could call "loss of bliss," a meaning, found in twentieth-century literature, certainly in James Joyce's *Ulysses*, in T.S. Eliot's *The Waste Land,* and in the works of Samuel Beckett. In Vathek's paradoxical subterranean palace, eternity is subject to time and space; though infinite, it is circumscribed by agony. In Beckford's solipsistic creativity, there is no truth unless you construct it yourself. The question of the modern self therefore is bound to basic epistemological questions. The debates on "quantity," "time," and "space" are at stake. The self is not "just there." When perceptions have something to do with a syntax of the self, then the difficulties we encounter in Beckford's text lead us to define the inner person. Therefore it is the reader who creates the inner self. The mind is the theatre, where many perceptions come together. Memory, however, makes personal identity possible by constructing unity, but not by necessary connections.[39]

University of Marburg

## REFERENCES

*This article is adapted from Jürgen Klein's *Der gotische Roman und die Ästhetik des Bösen* (Darmstadt: Wissenschaftliche Buchgesellschaft, 1975).

[1]Devendra Varma, *The Gothic Flame* (New York: Russell & Russell), p. 135.

[2]Denis Diderot, *Enzyklopädie*. Philosophische und politische Texte aus der "Enzyklopädie" (Munich 1969), pp. 308–334.

[3]William Beckford, *Vathek*, ed. Roger Lonsdale (London: Oxford University Press, 1970), pp. 2–3. All references to *Vathek* will be from this edition and will be inserted into the text.

[4]Cf. Pieter Breughel's canvas "Building of the Tower of Babel (1563, Kunsthistorisches Museum, Wien). Vathek's tower seems to be a reminiscence of Francis Bacon's tower in *New Atlantis*, which is used by the scholars of the House of Solomon for their scientific experiments and investigations.

[5]Cf. Garleff Zacharias-Langhans, *Der unheimliche Roman um 1800* Diss. phil. Bonn 1968, p. 88 *et seq.*

[6]There are parallels between Carathis and Beckford's mother, whom he called "the Begum."

[7]Sigmund Freud, "The Uncanny," *Collected Papers*, trans. Joan Riviere (New York: Basic Books, 1959), IV, 368–407.

[8]Georg Lukács, *The Theory of the Novel*, trans. Anna Bostock, (Cambridge: MIT Press, 1971) p. 71 ff.

[9]Wolf Lepenies, *Melancholie und Gesellschaft* (Frankfurt/Main, 1972), pp. 47–75.

[10]Lukács, p. 71.

[11]Here the aesthetics of the beautiful is contrasted with the aesthetics of the ugly.

[12]In Goethe's *Faust* the initiative to conclude the contract is taken up by Mephistopheles (cf. Prolog im Himmel); Faust is not forced to abjure his Christian belief, because he had lost his faith already. Beckford uses a different construction from Goethe, because he does not start from the God–Satan dualism, but from the dualism "übermensch" – "terrestrial influences": in *Vathek* a human being is striving

after absolute power, but the adversary is not God, but a counter-God. See G. Roskoff, *Geschichte des Teufels* (Leipzig, 1869) I, 84 ff.

[13]Roskoff, I, 89.

[14]See Helmut von Glasenapp, *Glaube und Ritus der Hochreligionen* (Frankfurt/ Main 1964).

[15]Mario Praz, *The Romantic Agony*, trans. Angus Davidson (New York: Meridian Books, 1956), pp. 201–202.

[16]Claude Lévi-Strauss, *Strukturale Anthropologie* (Frankfurt/Main 1969) pp. 184–185.

[17]Richard Cavendish, *Die schwarze Magie* (Frankfurt/Main 1969), esp. chapters 6 and 7. Cavendish stresses the fact that sexual abstinence intensifies psychical powers, which are necessary in a "grimoire". See pp. 269–270. Also Lévi-Strauss, *Strukturale Anthropologie* (1969), pp. 183 ff; Wilheim Reich, *Die Funktion des Orgasmus* (Wien 1926), pp. 58 ff. According to Wilhelm Reich sexual abstinence produces a neurosis, because the somatic substances cannot be removed.

[18]Note Carathis's conjuration of the fish: "... Carathis and her negresses soon arrived at the lake; where, after burning the magical drugs, with which they were always provided; *they stripped themselves naked,* and waded to their chins; Nerkes and Cafour waving torches around them, and Carathis pronouncing her barbarous incantations." [my italics] (95–96)

[19]See Freud's discussion of exhibitionism as an erotic activity in "Instincts and their Vicissitudes" in *Collected Papers*, trans. Joan Riviere (New York: Basic Books, 1959) IV, 60-83. This essay also links exhibitionism and sadism.

[20]According to Cavendish (1969), p. 282 smoke which comes from burning different substances, which is prescribed in magic practices, leads to disturbances of consciousness and to ecstatic states of mind.

[21]In her malignity she reminds us of the goddess Kali. Cf. H.W. Haussig (Ed.), *Wörterbuch der Mythologie* I. Abt. Die alten Kulturvölker, 8. Lief. (Stuttgart 1966), pp. 119 ff.

[22]Deggial is the Moslem counterpart to Antichrist.

[23]Karl Rosenkranz, *Aesthetik des Hässlichen* (Königsberg 1853), p. 4.

[24]*Ibid.*

[25]Lukács, *The Theory of the Novel*, p. 72.

[26]The figure of Carathis reminds us of a caricature of puritanism, which is inseparably connected with teleological action. The figure of Carathis possibly represents a rebellion against the strains of aristocratic culture in late 18th-century England. Beckford's creed of lust must have been judged as scandalous in England as Lord Byron's liaison with his half-sister Augusta Leigh.

[27]Ghoul = "Spirit preying on corpses in Eastern tales ..." (C.O.D. (1966), p. 515). - "Among the necrosadists, sexual murderers, who mutilate corpses, a destructive drive overgrows the sexual drive. Their sexual desire is expressed as a subdued cannibalism. The necrosadists are similar to the *oriental ghouls*, who like Al Rachid in 'The Arabian Nights' disentomb corpses in churchyards at night and consume them." (Dieter Sturm/Klaus Völker (Eds.), *Von denen Vampiren oder Menschensaugern. Dichtungen und Dokumente* (Munich 1968), Bibliotheca Dracula, p. 531.

[28]Kurt Otten, *Der englische Roman vom 16. zum 19. Jahrhundert* (Berlin 1971), p. 106.

[29](Hamburg: *Philosophische Bibliothek* vol. 42), p. 146 n.

[30]*Ibid.*

[31]Immanuel Kant, *Kritik der Urteilskraft*, ed. Karl Vorländer (Leipzig 1924), PhB 39, pp. 40 ff. "Man kann sagen, dass unter allen ... Arten des Wohlgefallens das des Geschmacks am Schönen einzig und allein das uninteressierte und freie Wohlgefallen sei; denn kein Interesse, weder das der Sinne noch der Vernunft, zwingt den Beifall ab." (Kant, *Kritik der Urteilskraft* (1924), p. 47).

[32]G.W.F. Hegel, *ästhetik*, ed. by Friedrich Bassenge, with an introduction by Georg Lukács (Frankfurt/Main n.d.), I, 72.

[33]Immanuel Kant, *Kritik der reinen Vernunft*, ed. by Raymund Schmidt (Hamburg 1956), PhB 37a, B 346. The page numbers A in Kant's first critique refer to the edition of 1781, the page numbers B refer to the second edition of 1787. The B quotation in the text refers to Schmidt's edition.

[34]Goethe, *Faust* I, Studierzimmer.

[35]Hegel, *Ästhetik*, vol. 1, p. 218.

[36]Otten (1971), p. 106.

[37]Thomas Mann, *Doktor Faustus*. Das Leben des deutschen Tonsetzers Adrian Leverkühn erzählt von einem Freunde (Frankfurt/Main, 1963).

[38]Kant, *Kritik der reinen Vernunft* (1956), B 346-B 349.

[39]For these reflections I am indebted to the "Round Table on William Beckford's *Vathek*", which was held at the VIIth International Congress on Enlightenment, Budapest 1987, organized by Kenneth W. Graham. From a theoretical point of view the paper by Giuseppe Massara (Salerno) "Beckford's Idea of Space in *Vathek*" was particularly stimulating. For constructivist aspects within literary studies, which investigate the construction of meanings by autopoietic systems, see Siegfried J. Schmidt, *Grundriss der empirischen Literaturwissenschaft* (Braunschweig/Wiesbaden 1980), Vol. 1; S.J. Schmidt, "Empirical Studies in Literature: Introductory Remarks", in: *Poetics 10* (1981): 317–336; Helmut Hauptmeier/S.J. Schmidt, *Einführung in die empirische Literaturwissenschaft* (Braunschweig/Wiesbaden 1985); Jürgen Klein, "Trends in Modern German Literary Theory", in *CLIO*, Vol. 15 No. 1 (1985): 31–45; S.J. Schmidt (ed.), *Der Diskurs des Radikalen Konstruktivismus* (Frankfurt/Main: Suhrkamp Taschenbücher Wissenschaft vol 636, 1987).

# "INCONNUE DANS LES ANNALES DE LA TERRE": BECKFORD'S BENIGN AND DEMONIC INFLUENCE ON POE*

## Kenneth W. Graham

In studies devoted to Edgar Allan Poe, discussions of the influence of William Beckford on Poe's thought and technique do not loom large. Una Pope-Hennessy acknowledges that Poe was "greatly impressed by *Vathek* and by accounts of the author's way of life,"[1] and N. B. Fagin makes a reluctant reference to Beckford on a single occasion in *The Histrionic Mr. Poe* when he dismisses Ellison's domain at Arnheim as "Kubla Khanish, Arabian Nightish, Beckfordian, Wagnerian, and Max Reinhardtish (at his lushest—and worst)."[2] But at least until recently the generality of Poe criticism has remained quite silent about Beckford.

The publication of the Mabbott edition of Poe's Collected Works encourages some re-examination of Beckford's role in Poe's writing career. The two-volume edition of Poe's *Tales and Sketches* draws attention to five specific Beckfordian references and speculates on a number of other possibilities. Indeed, Mabbott cites Beckford more frequently than other more popular writers who, common sense suggests, might have engaged Poe's imagination more readily. Walpole, Radcliffe, Lewis, Ainsworth, Maturin, Brockden Brown and E. T. A. Hoffmann are all cited less often than Beckford. The contexts of Poe's references to Beckford support Pope-Hennessy's observation: they show that Poe was impressed by the Oriental tale *Vathek* and fascinated by the taste, wealth, and imagination that could call into being such a place as Beckford's Fonthill. The least significant of the five direct references to Beckford shows Poe willing to credit a rumor that the most obscure and scholarly parts of Catherine Gore's novels were furnished by Beckford.[3] That Beckford's influence on Poe may be more extensive than the five direct references indicate is suggested in two pieces of information related to "The Domain of Arnheim," Fagin's *bête noire*. The first is Poe's comment, "This story contains more of myself and of my inherent tastes and habits of thought than anything I have written." The second is Mrs. Helen Whitman's report that she believed that Poe decided to expand "The Landscape Garden" into "The Domain of Arnheim" after having read "some account of William Beckford's famous estate at Fonthill, Wiltshire."[4] That expanded version not only contains a reference to Fonthill, but includes descriptive features that recall popular accounts of Beckford's estate. This connection between Poe's reading about Beckford and his writing a story containing so much of himself suggests an affinity between the two men that not surprisingly manifests itself in a series of Beckfordian echoes and parallels throughout Poe's work, echoes and parallels that form a pattern that calls attention two broad aspects of Poe's creative genius. On the one hand, Beckfordian references underline Poe's fascination with the benign mysteries of genius and creativity. Beckford's Fonthill is a reference point of this inclination. On the other hand, Poe's imagination is stirred when genius is touched by perversity to create visions of a demonic disorder that is sometimes fearful and sometimes ludicrous. Poe may have regarded *Vathek* as a demonic extension of Beckford's creative genius—

certainly some of its *diablerie* finds echoes in Poe's work. It should be remembered in what terms Poe specifically disclaimed the influence of German Gothic writers in his Preface to *Tales of the Grotesque and Arabesque* (1840): "If in many of my productions terror has been the thesis, I maintain that terror is not of Germany, but of the soul ..." [5] In Poe's portrayal of terrors of the soul, the influence of William Beckford may have been more extensive and pervasive than has hitherto been thought.

A good introduction to the nature of the Beckfordian influence in Poe's canon is found in "The Domain of Arnheim" and in its companion piece, "Landor's Cottage." Both contain direct references to Beckford's works and together they offer contrasting studies of the interdependence of landscape and structure in architecture, an interdependence Poe was aware that Beckford had accomplished boldly at Fonthill. The contexts of those two references to Beckford introduce the two aspects of Beckfordian creativity, the benign and the demonic, that seem to have interested and influenced Poe. Included in Beckford's benign creativity is his passion for building magnificently and recklessly, a passion echoed by Poe in "The Domain of Arnheim." The second aspect of Beckfordian creativity, the demonic, is reflected in a quotation from *Vathek* in "Landor's Cottage" that evokes a dark vision of reality. The taste for the benign and the demonic that could call into existence both Ellison's Arnheim and the House of Usher is similar to the spirit that created Fonthill and *Vathek*. It reflects an affinity between Poe and Beckford that is revealed in imaginative visions of triumphant accomplishment and inexorable decay.

Poe has Ellison create at Arnheim a domain with "a species of secret and subdued if not solemn celebrity, similar in kind, although infinitely superior in degree, to that which so long distinguished Font-hill."[6] The reference to Fonthill is specific enough; it is for Poe an effective simile for presenting the nature of Arnheim's celebrity: a celebrity resulting from the admiration of a select few rather than the acclaim of the many. That Fonthill is referred to in "The Domain of Arnheim" but not in "The Landscape Garden" supports Helen Whit-man's contention that Poe expanded his first version after having read an account of Fonthill. It is tempting to conclude that the version "that expresses so much of [Poe's] *soul*"[7] is the version that contains a refer-ence to Fonthill. So many editors have assumed that Poe preferred the second version that Mabbott quite rightly protests the neglect of the first version, pointing out that "The Landscape Garden" has much of his soul too.[8] It contains also something of Fonthill in a reference, not yet acknowledged, near to one of the sources of Poe's inspiration.

In both versions Poe justifies Ellison's extraordinary inheritance in a footnote recounting a similar incident of an heir to a hundred-year-old estate named Thelluson. His source is Prince Hermann Pückler-Muskau's *Tour of England, Ireland and France*. Commentators have generally accepted Poe's note at face value, pointing out the Ellison–Thelluson phonetic similarity, but sometimes calling attention to John Allan's partner Charles Ellis who also created a beautiful garden. Thus critical speculation has *Ellison* an ingenius conflation of Poe's two main sources, the examples of Ellis and Thelluson. So fascinating has been this play on names that no one appears to have noticed that Pückler-Muskau's chatty *Tour* contains another account in Letter 45 that may well have been more subtly but significantly influential than the story of Thelluson in Letter 22. Since it seems to be little known, it is worth quoting the passage at length:

Have you ever heard of the eccentric Beckford—a kind of Lord Byron in prose— who built the most magnificent residence in England, surrounded his park with a wall twelve feet high, and for twelve years suffered nobody to enter it? All on a sudden he sold this wondrous dwelling, Fonthill Abbey, with all its rare and costly things it contained, by auction, and went to Bath, where he lives in just as solitary a manner as before. He has built a second high tower (there was a celebrated one at Fonthill,) in the middle of a field ... The possessor is said, at one time, to have been worth three millions sterling, and is still very rich ... Mr. Beckford formerly wrote a very singular, but most powerful romance, in French: it was translated into English, and greatly admired. A high tower plays a conspicuous part in that also: the denouement is, that the Devil carries off everybody.[9]

It seems likely that Poe read Pückler-Muskau's accounts of both Thelluson and Beckford, and though his mind may have seized immediately on the example of Thelluson when he wrote "The Landscape Garden," the work is informed also by thoughts of Beckford as a Lord Byron of prose and as a poet of landscape. Certainly Poe's Ellison and Pückler-Muskau's Beckford have in common extraordinary wealth, poetic gifts and a taste for retirement. But Poe did not truly complete "The Landscape Garden" until four years later when, apparently, he was motivated to continue by a later reading of a description of Fonthill that Mrs. Whitman refers to. Yet the earlier account of Beckford's accomplishments may have lingered in his mind, since notable features of Arnheim are those emphasized in Pückler-Muskau's Fonthill—a lofty wall, a famous park and a wondrous dwelling. In both stories, early and late, Ellison has more in common with Beckford than he has with Thelluson. Pückler-Muskau's account of Beckford's passion for towers, both real and fictional, may also have quietly impressed itself on Poe's imagination.

In Poe's account of the landscape gardener as poet, one need not be surprised to find a similarity of spirit linking the designs of Arnheim and Fonthill. That spirit rejects the so-called "natural" style of landscape gardening with its concern with "nice relations of size, proportion, and colour." To quote Poe further: "That the true result of the natural style of gardening is seen rather in the absence of all defects and incongruities than in the creation of special wonders and miracles, is a proposition better suited to the grovelling apprehension of the herd than to the fervid dreams of the man of genius."[10] Consequently, Poe's Ellison combines on his estate "beauty, magnificence, and *strangeness*" [Poe's italics]. The result is an audacious blending of art and nature similar in spirit to Fonthill but greater in scope.

While Poe may well have derived some of his ideas for Arnheim from Pückler-Muskau's references to Beckford, the account of Fonthill that Mrs. Whitman reports him reading is probably more extensive than anything Pückler-Muskau provides. Poe may have been reading James Storer's *A Description of Fonthill Abbey, Wiltshire* or John Rutter's *A Description of Fonthill Abbey and Demesne*. Both works are illustrated with views of Fonthill Abbey and the huge estate surrounding the castellated structure, and both contain descriptive passages of astonishing similarity owing to Rutter's shameless plagiarizing from Storer. Rutter's account, which passed through many printings, offers a vivid view of the scope and magnificence of the Fonthill estate. It conducts the reader along the twenty-seven miles of paths leading through a variety of landscape and flora in a manner not unlike that experienced by the river-traveller in Ellison's Arnheim. Rutter's account of Fonthill emphasizes effects that Ellison achieved at Arnheim, a variety of landscape surrounding a structure of imposing

Fonthill Abbey, Beckford's Gothic mansion. View from the southwest by James Storer in <u>A Description of Fonthill</u> (1812).

majesty:

Over a long extent of ground, varied by gentle undulations, and finely broken by an intervening valley, presenting a rich assemblage of glowing and luxurious tints, appears the Abbey, forming a grand mass of embattled towers, surmounted by the lofty octagon tower which composes the centre. This enchanting scenery is backed by an elevated woodland of a sombre aspect, which by contrast heightens the striking and brilliant effect of the edifice.[11]

Poe's concluding vision in "The Domain of Arnheim" echoes a passage from Rutter. When "the whole Paradise of Arnheim bursts upon the view" and one sees "a mass of semi-Gothic, semi-Saracenic architecture sustaining itself by a miracle in mid-air," Poe is adopting a descriptive language reminiscent of that used by Rutter:

Enclosed by large forest trees the way may be pursued in a winding course to the summit of the great avenue: having attained the eminence, as we turn to the east, the Abbey bursts upon the view in solemn and imposing majesty.[12]

Beckford and Poe shared an interest in landscape architecture at a transcendent level of artistry: both were interested in creating effects that compelled attention and challenged convention. Poe saw in Beckford an artist like Ellison, wealthy and audacious enough to carry into realization the grandiose conceptions of an ardent imagination.

A second specific reference to Beckford that the Mabbott edition calls to our attention, and the only direct quotation from Beckford to be found in Poe's canon, carries us through architecture into mystery. In describing Landor's cottage, Poe misquotes slightly Beckford's French version of *Vathek*. Poe's narrator observes: " ... this house, like the infernal terrace seen by Vathek, 'était d'une architecture inconnue dans les annales de la terre'."[13] That Poe found the passage remarkable reflects his fascination with the relationship between structures and their proprietors, a fascination underlined in a multitude of his stories from "The Fall of the House of Usher" to "The Masque of the Red Death." The quotation may have recalled to Poe the arrogance of any builder, like Ellison and Beckford, who dares to create "une architecture inconnue dans les annales de la terre."

Perhaps the poignant aptness of that quotation to Beckford himself made it memorable to Poe since Beckford's life and work reflect a similar fascination with audacious architecture. In a letter of 1790, the enthusiastic Beckford has written: "I am growing rich, and mean to build Towers ... "[14] and for twenty years he built grandly and intrepidly Fonthill Abbey, a structure as large as Westminster Abbey, with a tower soaring to 276 feet. The interior of his Abbey he adorned with Persian and Aubusson carpets, tapestries and crimson damask wall coverings, rare books, paintings by Claude, Breughel, Veronese, Rembrandt, Bellini, and Raphael, and *objects d'art* carefully selected during European tours. The passage from *Vathek* that Poe quotes describes a ruin and may have recalled to his mind the fragmenting of Beckford's accomplishments at Fonthill. His Abbey was sold, his library dispersed in a series of sales, his paintings auctioned and his carefully designed grounds ultimately divided for the benefit of less pecunious purchasers. Even the soaring tower of his abbey collapsed upon its inadequate foundations. The fate of William Beckford and Fonthill Abbey could illustrate a sermon on the vanity of human wishes.

Another significance of that quotation resides in the context of *Vathek* from which Poe drew it. Perhaps Pückler-Muskau's observations about Beckford's towers, real and fictional, may have helped, but Poe was too sensitive to irony to fail to notice that the succession of structures in Vathek's Faustian quest foreshadows the collapse of Fonthill Abbey in 1825. Beckford's tale, written forty years earlier, begins in opulence as Vathek, himself an impetuous builder, decrees the construction of five palaces devoted to the gratification of each of the senses and a tower arrogantly dedicated to the search for forbidden knowledge. Vathek's quest for that knowledge carries him away from his lofty tower and nears fulfillment at the ruin to which Poe's quotation refers. That architecture unknown in the records of the earth refers to the ruined palace of another audacious builder, King Solomon. Thus grandiose structures form way stations in Vathek's earthly quest for unearthly secrets. He proceeds from splendor to ruin just as the tower of Fonthill and Beckford's adult life began in confidence and ended in collapse.

Another area of common interest may have made that passage from *Vathek* remarkable to Poe. The quotation is drawn from a context redolent of mystery, foreboding and an oppressive sense of the vanity of human accomplishment. Note the "*oiseaux nocturnes*" in the context of Poe's poem, "The Raven."

Un silence funèbre régnait dans les airs et sur la montagne. La lune réfléchissait sur la grande plate-forme l'ombre des hautes colonnes qui s'élevaient de la terrasse presque jusqu'aux nues. Ces tristes phares, dont le nombre pouvait à peine se compter, n'étaient couverts d'aucun toit; et leurs chapiteaux, d'une architecture inconnue dans les annales de la terre, servaient de retraite aux oiseaux nocturnes, qui, alarmés à l'approche de tant de monde, s'enfuirent en croassant.[15]

Its evocation of the records of the earth also calls to mind the attractions of the ancient mysteries and the unfathomable expanse of time and space. Time in *Vathek* extends to a remote and arcane past when, with the help of genii, Solomon built his fabulous palace at Istakar of an architecture "inconnue dans les annales de la terre." Space reaches beyond a sweating, breathing world to embrace a heaven and a hell, as if those metaphysical situations were closer to our conventional world than we might think. Thus the remembered quotation echoes a tintinnabulation of the uncanny that is appropriate to Solomon's palace and attractive to Poe. Istakar is a place of ruin, gloom and death whose unearthly barrenness and loneliness is echoed in Poe's "Silence—A Fable." Beckford's powerful vision of the desolation of time and space, a desert of vast eternity in the ruins of Solomon's palace, contrasts with an even more disturbing vision of desolation in the next structure encountered by Vathek in his quest. Solomon's ruin stands on the threshold of an unearthly architecture more magnificent, more mysterious and more terrible than any edifice so far encountered. Marking the end of Vathek's journey is a proximate hell, the subterraneous palace of fire of the diabolical Eblis, the evil principle in Muslim demonology.

The Hall of Eblis forms the focus of the meaning of *Vathek* and of the various structures in the tale. It offers a last powerful perception of disorder in two contrasting pictures. First is the sensual luxuriousness of the palace itself, with its ordered rows of columns and arcades sweeping to infinity, its pavement "strewed over with gold dust and saffron," its "infinity of censers" emitting the ardent perfumes of "ambergrise and the wood of aloes," its mysterious music arising from no apparent source, its tables of wines and delicacies around which supernatural creatures dance lasciviously.[16] The lavish, rich palace of Eblis promises the satisfaction of all Vathek's appetites as earlier represented in his palace and his tower, even his lust after the secrets of nature.

In contrast to this tableau of order and pleasure is a second perspective on the Hall of Eblis, a picture of disorder and pain:

In the midst of this immense hall, a vast multitude was incessantly passing; who severally kept their right hands on their hearts; without once regarding any thing around them. They had all, the livid paleness of death. Their eyes, deep sunk in their sockets, resembled those phosphoric meteors, that glimmer by night, in places of interment. Some stalked slowly on; absorbed in profound reverie: some shrieking with agony, ran furiously about like tigers, wounded with poisoned arrows; whilst others, grinding their teeth in rage, foamed along more frantic than the wildest maniac. They all avoided each other; and, though surrounded by a multitude that no one could number, each wandered at random, unheedful of the rest, as if alone on a desert where no foot had trodden.[17]

In their random wanderings, the damned are oblivious to the opulence surrounding them, so enwrapped are they in the unceasing agony that not only dominates their consciousness but will continue to do so through all eternity. The contrast of splendor and agony that informs the Hall of Eblis fulfills a pattern initiated in the splendor of Vathek's own lifetime, a splendor impervious to the pain of the people on whom it was founded.

Beckford's vision of damnation with its contrasting blend of luxury and pain seems to have had an abiding influence on Poe's imagination. Beckford's Hall of Eblis finds echoes in some of Poe's lush, perfumed interiors. In the pentagonal tower chamber of "Lygeia" the Hall of Eblis with its fearful secrets of life and death seems to have been confounded with the octagonal tower of the real Fonthill Abbey. In "The Duc de l'Omelette" Eblis's palace is recalled in the description of the infernal apartment, in its space and light, its "innumerable censers" and "voluptuous, never-dying melodies" that are associated in the Duc's mind with "the wailings and howlings of the hopeless and the damned."[18] In "The Masque of the Red Death" there is something of the Hall of Eblis in the sumptuous decor, the delirious frenzy of the revellers and the terrible sense of inevitability represented in the brazen strokes of the clock that recalls the end of Beckford's tale as Vathek awaits the pain of damnation to fall upon him.

So sensitive was Poe to Beckfordian inspiration that his mind was ready to note and retain references to Beckford even when they were offered to him indirectly. Mabbott makes the case that a reference in "The Premature Burial" to Carathis, Vathek's mother, comes directly from Horace Binney Wallace's *Stanley* (1838).[19] It may be so, but the reference was meaningful enough to Poe for him to remember it only because of the particular power that *Vathek* had over his imagination.

The Carathis reference is worth examining more closely. Poe writes,

There are moments when, even to the sober eye of Reason, the world of our sad Humanity may assume the semblance of a hell—but the imagination of man is no Carathis, to explore with impunity its every cavern. Alas! the grim legion of sepulchral terrors cannot be regarded as altogether fanciful—but ... they must be suffered to slumber, or we perish.[20]

Poe's narrator, in this important last paragraph of his story, is discussing the dangers of human curiosity in the light of his own previous obsessive terror at the idea of being buried alive. For the sake of health and sanity, he is arguing, there are certain terrifying and hellish possibilities in the range of human experience over which the imagination must not be permitted to linger. A particularly potent source of terror lies in that shadowy transitional realm where life is divided from Death. He expresses the self-imposed limiting of the imagination by the reference to Carathis.

Mabbott quotes, as a primary source, the context from *Stanley* : "... he explored, with the indomitable spirit of Carathis, every chamber and cavern of the earthly hell of bad delights." He goes on to explain that Carathis is "the wicked old witch" in *Vathek* "who, granted a day to command the treasures of Hell before her damnation, boldly enjoys them." What is unfortunate about the Mabbott explanatory note is not so much its inaccuracy (Carathis is not old and no precise stay of damnation is granted her), but its insensitivity. The trivializing phrase "wicked old witch" understates her significance in *Vathek*, and the passage from *Stanley* about exploring the delights of sin, is not particularly relevant to Poe's story. If Mabbott had sought the context of the reference in *Vathek*, he would have discovered why the reference to Carathis in *Stanley* reverberated in Poe's memory with significance not confined to Wallace's novel.

The context in *Vathek* refers to Carathis's arrival in the Hall of Eblis eager to reap the rewards of a life of viciousness, the forbidden knowledge of the mysteries of nature.

... she compelled the dives to disclose to her the most secret treasures, the most profound stores ... She passed, by rapid descents, known only to Eblis and his most favoured potentates; and thus penetrated the very entrails of the earth, where breathes the sansar, or the icy wind of death. Nothing appalled her dauntless soul... She even attempted to dethrone one of the Solimans, for the purpose of usurping his place; when a voice, proceeding from the abyss of death, proclaimed: 'All is accomplished!' Instantaneously, the haughty forehead of the intrepid princess became corrugated with agony: she uttered a tremendous yell; and fixed, no more to be withdrawn, her right hand upon her heart, which was become a receptacle of eternal fire.

In this delirium, forgetting all ambitious projects, and her thirst for that knowledge which should ever be hidden from mortals, she overturned the offerings of the genii ... [21]

The context in *Vathek* gives point to Poe's reference to Carathis. It is about the hellish agonies that the unrestrained imagination can create, particularly in the fearful shadow realm between life and death. In *Vathek* it is in this realm that the damned in the Hall of Eblis reside. Carathis's lust for forbidden knowledge carries her to the icy breath of death itself, and from death proceeds the signal for the commencement of an eternity of agony. The fate of Carathis is an appropriate illustration of the horrors provoked by an unrestrained imagination.

In those influential final pages of *Vathek* the bleak desolation of Solomon's palace at Istakar gives way to the opulent desolation of Eblis' subterraneous palace of fire. What is particularly terrible about the Hall of Eblis is the grim disharmony of its two contrasting pictures in which lavish luxury becomes an affront to a hellish intensity of burning pain. Eblis, Beckford's fallen angel, presides over his palace, yet one has the impression that he does not control it. The gorgeousness of the structure is undermined by the indiscriminate wanderings of that nondescript throng. The ironic conjunction of planned order but resultant chaos fulfills a pattern established in the body of the tale that links evil with disorder and grotesquerie. The realm of Eblis is nocturnal and bizarre; it manifests the inclination of evil to create, often in its own despite, disorder out of order.

As Poe and Beckford knew, the realm of primordial perversity is effectively presented through the use of techniques of the grotesque. It is the nature of the grotesque to disorient the observer by evoking simultaneously the contradictory responses of amusement and terror by projecting a world that is both familiar and alien. Beckford and Poe employ the grotesque as a reminder of the omnipresence of forces that can transform our conventional, law-obeying nature into a realm of mystery and disorder. The terror in Poe arises from the very unnatural-ness of the grotesque. His fictional accounts blur the division between life and death and between animal and vegetable. People die, are entombed and come to life. Others die but continue to speak. Animals, even fungi, assume a human percipience. Such conditions reflect a sin-ister blending of fantasy and reality that confers a sense of the uncanny on many of Poe's fictional works. While his employment of the grotesque ranges between the sportive in which the ludicrous pre-dominates and the terrible in which humor all but disappears,[22] the result of all these projections is an extension of the metaphysics of reality to affirm the existence of a chaos and evil capable of transform-ing the world into, in Poe's words, "a kingdom of inorganization."[23]

This vision of disorder is at the root of Beckford's *Vathek* and accounts for some of its compelling qualities. Beckford's Caliph Vathek follows his casual quest for the secrets of nature through a bizarre world inhabited by a variety of grotesques including impotent grey beards, dwarfs, squinting one-eyed servant women, and swarms of disfigured cripples. Vathek himself is at times sublimely magnifi-cent and powerful and at times a flaccid slave to his own appetites. Pausing to heap injustice and misery on his gullible subjects, Vathek pursues successfully his lackadaisical quest. He finds himself in the subterranean palace of the Evil Principle, Eblis, where the respositories of all the secrets of nature are placed at his disposal. His curiosity is quickly dissipated, however, when he learns that with access to these secrets he has won a state of eternal damnation. Vathek does not die in the course of the tale. He is simply translated from a life dominated by exquisite sensual pleasure to an eternity dominated by exquisite sensual pain, a torment unremitting as flames envelop his heart. In *Vathek* too the division between life and death is left undefined.

Poe's awareness of "the spirit of the Perverse," the "overwhelming tendency to do wrong for the wrong's sake,"[24] while central to his story "The Imp of the Perverse," is reflected in other of his stories where the protagonist feels irrationally compelled to evil or self-destructive acts. That fundamental perversity is present in "The Pit and the Pendulum," "The Fall of the House of Usher," and notably in "The Black Cat." Irrational perversity is a deeply human characteristic, yet one of its effects is to separate us from humanity. Vathek, too, with a perversity supported by his political and religious powers as caliph, separates himself from humanity and permits himself almost to forget his human limitations until he is reminded of his human susceptibility to pain in the Hall of Eblis. Eblis himself is another imposing representation of the alienation of perversity; his self-banishment from goodness damns him just as Vathek is damned for his wilful self-alienation from humanity. Beckford's description of Eblis evokes the mysterious melancholy of the tainted angel in a few deft images: "His person was that of a young man, whose noble and regular features seemed to have been tarnished by malignant vapours. In his large eyes appeared both pride and despair: his flowing hair retained some resemblance to that of an angel of light."[25] When Poe comes to describe another figure of alienation, Roderick Usher, he gives his character the sensitive features, large eyes and flowing hair of Beckford's Eblis. Usher, with self-tormenting perversity, cannot act to free Madeline who has desperately awakened from death to find herself entombed and entrapped.

A similar spirit of alienation links *Vathek* with another Poe story, "The Man of the Crowd." The narrator, convalescing after an illness, is sitting by the window of a coffee house in London observing the tide of passers-by. He describes the various classes comprising that moving mass: business men who "seemed to be thinking only of making their way through the press"; others, "restless in their movements ... flushed faces ... talking and gesticulated to themselves as if feeling in solitude on account of the very denseness of the company around."[26] The description recalls Beckford's account of the throngs of the damned in the Hall of Eblis pursuing their chaotic wanderings in anguish and despair with a similar self-absorption that prevents a crowd from becoming a community. Although a like ominousness resides in the very chaos of Poe's crowd, the significance of its disturbing disorder is not introduced until the narrator happens on a face of a particular old man that seemed to him a "pictural [incarnation] of the fiend" arousing in him "ideas of vast mental power, of caution, of penuriousness, of avarice, of coolness, of malice, of blood-thirstiness, of triumph, of merriment, of excessive terror, of intense—of supreme despair."[27] Here is an echo of the pride and despair that Beckford associates with evil. Poe's terrible old man reminds us of Vathek and his mother both wilfully separating themselves from humanity in the vicious means they employ and the evil ends they seek, a power and knowledge that is superhuman, that will forever separate them from humanity. It is ironic that Poe's old man "refuses to be alone" yet his alienation has already been well established by his life of evil. A similar irony pervades the end of *Vathek*. Vathek and his mother have scorned morality, the ethical bonds that create community, and chosen alienation. Appropriately when they are damned it is not to a splendid isolation but to an eternity "plunged ... into the accursed multitude."[28]

The spirit of perversity may be manifested also in lighter forms of the grotesque. Poe and Beckford demonstrate an attraction to what Ruskin calls the sportive grotesque,[29] a slightly fearful vision of life in which a sense of the ludicrous is dominant. More important, they choose similar methods and motifs to present the sportive grotesque. A method that both employ is to create a ludicrous disparity between tone and content by presenting absurdities or *bizarreries* in a serious and earnest narrative tone. The technique is apparent in "The Predicament" when the fussy, self-important narrator describes her own slow decapitation by the minute hand of a clock. Beckford employs a similar technique in *Vathek* by having his unidentified narrator recording with reluctance and restraint some of Vathek's more extreme behaviors, particularly a series of exaggerated reactions to the appearance of the Giaour.

The Giaour enters the tale as a merchant of magical wares, "abominably hideous," who sells to Vathek a pair of sabres, their sides engraven in an unknown language. He refuses to answer Vathek's questions about his extraordinary merchandise but merely rubs his paunch and laughs hideously, discovering "his long amber-colored teeth, bestreaked with green."[30] A sage is found to decypher the language on the sabres, but when he dons his green spectacles to read the sabres a second time, he discovers a different message, the characters of the sabres having changed. The grotesquerie surrounding the Giaour reaches its climax when, still unable to draw an answer from him, Vathek aims a kick at the Giaour who rolls away like a soccer ball compelling all who see him to attempt a few kicks until the whole populace of Vathek's capital city, the women indelicately foregoing veil and harem, are clattering in sweat and dust after the rolling Giaour.

The scene is predominantly ludicrous, yet the slightly ominous implications of the breakdown of custom and restraint that the Giaour's influence encourages gains significance as the tale develops and the Giaour emerges as a servant of evil.

If, in its blend of the ludicrous and the ominous, this episode of *Vathek* has in manner its echoes in Poe's canon, in terms of matter it offers striking resemblances to Poe's story "Bon-Bon." There the green spectacles worn by the devil, his discomfiting laughter accompanied by a wicked display of extraordinary teeth, his book with its changing title, all suggest the episode of the Giaour and the sabres with their changing messages. The earlier version of "Bon-Bon," "The Bargain Lost," makes reference to "the Ptolemaiad of the Rabbi Vathek,"[31] a title and author invented by Poe for the occasion. The mention of the name of Beckford's hero has no significance to the story; it is made, however, in the context of metaphysical speculations, intense curiosity and a visit from the devil. It is significant that such circumstances encouraged Poe to employ the name *Vathek*.

Mallarmé wrote to Mrs. Whitman to ask a perceptive question that no one else seems to have asked her: had Poe ever read *Vathek*? "Ce livre," he exclaimed, "eût pu le séduire."[32] Surely what prompted the question is a recognition of kinship, a kinship too frequently ignored. Poe may not have been seduced by *Vathek*, but as should now be apparent, his mind had frequent recourse to Beckfordian examples.

Poe and Beckford are linked by an imaginative audacity that moves easily from reality to dream, that can carry their visions to the metaphysical extremes of the sublime and the grotesque. In Poe's transforming imagination the idea of Beckford's Fonthill could be expanded to the domain of Arnheim or distorted to the House of Usher with its uncanny sentience and its "vacant eye-like" windows, a house that shared a fall with the impossibly lofty tower of Fonthill Abbey. Poe's isolated structures reflect the alienation of their proprietors: the creative individualism of an Ellison with his contempt for the taste of the mob, or the debilitated alienation of a Roderick Usher, declining into the exquisite agony of a sensibility so acute that he might, indeed "die of a rose in aromatic pain." That passage from *Vathek* that came so readily to Poe's mind, "unknown in the records of the earth," may point to a vision of sublime order that he shared with Beckford, the grandiose vision of Fonthill or Arnheim. But the passage reflects also a contrasting vision of disorder communicated in the employment of the grotesque that reflects an awareness of a nocturnal world presided over by a "spirit of the Perverse" in which dreams of grandeur fragment and disintegrate into nightmares of horror or perceptions of absurdity. If one is looking for a precursor for Poe's peculiar vision, one will find similarities in Beckford's. Poe dismissed the German Gothic as an influence in his writings, but he knew Beckford's *Vathek* and had read of Beckford's Fonthill, two creations of the same unique imagination. One can conclude that there are evident affinities between the sensibilities of the two writers. Both are capable of offering a comforting vision of moral order that indeed may rise to apocalyptic sublimity. But neither limits himself to that vision. Each perceives within the natural world and the individual the perverse force of disorder that gives to our world and our behavior a mysterious and grotesque dimension. Both share the ability to look coolly and directly at a dark reality haunted by the inexplicable and fraught with unremitting despair.

University of Guelph

REFERENCES

* A version of this essay was published in *Sphinx* #16, vol. 4, no. 4 (1985) by the University of Regina.

¹Una Pope-Hennessy, *Edgar Allan Poe 1809–1849: A Critical Biography* (1934; rpt. New York: Haskell House, 1971), p. 171.

²N. B. Fagin, *The Histrionic Mr. Poe* (Baltimore: The John Hopkins Press, 1949), p. 180.

³E. A. Poe, "Thou Art the Man," *Collected Works of Edgar Allan Poe: Tales and Sketches*, ed. Thomas Ollive Mabbott. 3 vols. (Cambridge, Massachusetts: The Belknap Press of Harvard University Press, 1979), III, 1051. Subsequent references to Poe's works will be to this edition. Poe alludes to a story told more fully by H. B. Gotlieb in *William Beckford of Fonthill* (New Haven: Yale University Press, 1960), p. 51.

⁴Both citations are supplied in the Mabbott edition, III, 1266.

⁵Poe, Preface to *Tales of the Grotesque and Arabesque*, II, 473.

⁶Poe, "The Domain of Arnheim," III, 1278.

⁷*Ibid.* III, 1266.

⁸Mabbott's introduction, II, 701.

⁹[Hermann Pückler-Muskau], *Tour in England, Ireland, and France in the years 1828 and 1829* (Philadelphia: Carey & Lea, 1833), p. 534.

[10]Poe, "The Domain of Arnheim," III, 1274. 1275.

[11]John Rutter, *A Description of Fonthill Abbey and Demesne* (London: John Rutter, 1822), p. 21.

[12]Rutter, *Description of Fonthill*, p. 14. The same passage is in James Storer, *A Description of Fonthill Abbey, Wiltshire* (London: W. Clarke, 1812), p. 3.

[13]Poe, "Landor's Cottage," III, 1335.

[14]Boyd Alexander, *England's Wealthiest Son* (London: Centaur Press, 1962), p. 157.

[15]William Beckford, *Vathek* (Londres: Chez Clarke, 1815), pp. 182–3.

[16]William Beckford, *Vathek*, ed. Roger Lonsdale (London: Oxford University Press, 1970), p. 109. All references to the English version of *Vathek* will be from this edition.

[17]Beckford, *Vathek*, 109–110.

[18]Poe, "The Duc de l'Omelette," II, 35–6.

[19]Mabbott, Note to "The Premature Burial," II, 971–2.

[20]Poe, "The Premature Burial," II, 969.

[21]Beckford, *Vathek*, 118–9.

[22]Kenneth W. Graham, "Implications of the Grotesque: Beckford's *Vathek* and the Boundaries of Fictional Reality", *Tennessee Studies in Literature* 23 (1978), 64–65.

[23]Poe, "The Fall of the House of Usher", II, 408.

[24]Poe, "The Imp of the Perverse", III, 1223, 1221.

[25]Beckford, *Vathek*, 111.

[26]Poe, "The Man of the Crowd", II, 508.

[27]*Ibid.*, II, 511.

[28]Beckford, *Vathek*, 119–120.

[29]John Ruskin, *The Stones of Venice*, in E. J. Cook and Alexander Wedderburn, eds., *The Works of John Ruskin* (London: G. Allen, 1904), XI, 151.

[30]Beckford, *Vathek*, 6.

[31]Poe, "The Bargain Lost", II, 89.

[32]Stephane Mallarmé, *Correspondance*, eds. Henri Mondor and L. J. Austin (Paris: Éditions Gallimard, 1965), II, 144.

# *VATHEK* AND PORTUGAL

Maria Laura Bettencourt Pires

According to Umberto Eco[1] a work of art gains its aesthetic validity in proportion to the number of different perspectives from which it can be viewed and understood. That is certainly one of the reasons why the multitude of studies and interpretations of *Vathek* still increases. Indeed the number of valuable works that have been devoted to *Vathek* is so great that one could now think it would be difficult to take an original approach. In their doctoral theses André Parreaux[2] and Kenneth W. Graham[3] have each thoroughly investigated and solved most of the puzzling problems set by this "literary rarity."[4] Boyd Alexander and Parreaux, among others, have written about the travel books and the time Beckford spent in Portugal. But no one has tried yet to investigate the reception *Vathek* had in the country Beckford referred to as "this fair realm of Portugal."[5] The purpose of this essay is to relate *Vathek* to Portugal: to investigate how well *Vathek* was known in Portugal, to study the impact of the work on Portuguese readers, and to determine when and how it was translated.

Curiously, the references to *Vathek* and to its first readers in Portugal were made by Beckford himself. In *Journal of William Beckford in Portugal and Spain, 1787–88,* [6] written during his first stay that lasted from March to December 1787, we can see his preoccupation with *Vathek*. His *Journal* of 20 July reflects his interest in the reviews it was receiving in the monthly periodicals:

... Manique, the Intendent of Police, would not deliver up some cases of books, etc. that are arrived for me at the Custom House ... I am extremely impatient to rummage the contents of the cases in question. They contain I believe some very valuable prints and the last monthly reviews in which I expect to read a critique on Vathek.[7]

Some days later, on Monday 6 August, Beckford referred to the French edition that had been edited that year by Louis-Sebastian Mercier:[8] "I have received a letter from Mrs. Hervey by land conveyance and I read to my great joy that Mercier's edition of my *Vathek* is at length published."[9] When he is relating his visit to the Palace and the Convent of Mafra, in the company of the Grand-Prior and Dr. Verdeil, he tells us how they were followed wherever they went by a strange medley of inquisitive monks and country beaux. In the entry of the *Journal* that must have been written either on the spur of the moment or when he returned home, he says that the scene reminded him of *Vathek*:

The Marquis was quite sick at being trotted after in this tumultuous manner and tried several times to leave the crowd behind him; but it kept close to our heels and increased to such a degree that we seemed to have swept the whole convent and village of its inhabitants and to draw them after us like the rolling Giaour in my story of Vathek.[10]

It is not surprising that Beckford should have thought so often of *Vathek* at the time of his first stay in the country about which he later said "o poor beloved Portugal, my own true country,"[11] for there was much in common in the world of the Caliph and in the Portugal of the last years of the eighteenth century. There was the same "un-British immoderation,"[12] the same gratification of pleasure and excess. Much in Portugal reminded him of *Vathek*. When Beckford describes the pantagruelian appetite of the Marquis of Marialva[13] or the magnificent repast of "sixty dishes at least, eight smoking roasts, and every ragout, French, English, and Portuguese"[14] that Street Arriaga served him, we could be in the palace of "The Eternal or unsatiating Banquet"[15] where tables were continuously "covered with the most exquisite dainties"[16] and where the Caliph, having lost his appetite, tasted only thirty-two of the "three hundred dishes that were daily placed before him."[17]

In the *Journal* Beckford referred to those who must have been the first Portuguese readers of *Vathek*. There may, of course, have been others to whom he read or spoke of his work, such as his best friends, the Marialvas, or the Penalva family that he admired so much,[18] but he mentions that D. José de Mateus, Bezerra and the old Abade Xavier have read and discussed it as well as the *Episodes*. On Friday 1 June 1787 Beckford wrote in his *Journal*:

D. José de Mateus and Bezerra came in with the tea. Bezerra who posted home from Sintra at two o'clock in the morning with his black hair frizzling over his ears and his eyes like coals of fire, bounces about like a cracker. He is a most squibbish being and I could really blow him into the air at anytime with some of my desperate Arabian stories. I must not give him a sight of Barkiarokh lest he should go quite mad. Vathek has more than half done his business. D. José— though much his friend—laughs in his sleeve at such extravagancies. These two men form a perfect contrast and yet they are continually together.[19]

Research into these two Portuguese, who remained good friends of Beckford for the rest of their lives, explains why they should have enjoyed reading *Vathek*. As a matter of fact, they are quite different from the type of empty-headed and full-bellied Portuguese *fidalgos* most Beckfordians seem to think were the only ones Beckford ever met in Portugal.

D. José de Mateus, whose full name was D. José de Sousa Botelho (1758–1825), had a family estate in the north of the country in the province of Trás-os-Montes, from which he had the official title of *Morgado de Mateus*. As we can see in the *Journal* he wanted Beckford to visit his country-seat.[20] He was a man of great knowledge and culture, who later became one of the members of the Royal Academy of Sciences of Lisbon and a *Comendador* of the Order of Christ. He was ambassador of Portugal in St. Petersburg, Stockholm, Copenhagen, London, and Paris. He spoke French fluently and was married to a French woman, who was a writer. After his retirement he remained in Paris.

Beckford met him in 1787 and must have been conscious of the great interest this young Portuguese had in literature when he gave him *Vathek* to read. D. José de Mateus proved to be well worthy of Beckford's trust and friendship. His cultural interests and profound literary knowledge led him in 1818 to publish in Paris what became one of the most famous editions of *Os Lusíadas*; the epic poem of Camoens. To illustrate this magnificent work, a model of typographical perfection, *Morgado* de Mateus had the collaboration of the most distinguished engravers and painters, like Gérard and Fragonard. In what could be classified as a Beckfordian attitude, he decided that not one single volume of this luxurious edition was to be sold. They were all given as presents to every monarch and library in Europe. We know that William Beckford was one of the *connoisseurs* to whom his friend sent a volume.[21]

The friendship, which started in 1787, when D. José read *Vathek*, together with Bezerra, is certainly one of the reasons why another work by D. José de Mateus was amongst Beckford's books that were sold in 1882. I am referring to the translation into Portuguese of *Lettres Portugaises* by Mariana Alcoforado. Mateus published it in Paris in 1824. It is to be regretted that the library of Fonthill should have been sold and dispersed by Beckford's grandson. It would have been quite interesting for a Portuguese Beckfordian to see if, as was his custom, Beckford had written any *marginalia* either in this edition of *Os Lusíadas* or in the love letters of the seventeenth-century nun.

João Paulo Bezerra de Seixas (1756–1817) was another Portuguese reader of *Vathek* who became a close friend of Beckford's. He even visited him at Fonthill Abbey. He was married to an English lady of the Factory (one of the Miss Sills),[22] who in 1819 became *Viscondessa Tagoahi*. Bezerra can be considered a typical Portuguese gentleman whose culture and spirit are representative of the last years of the *Ancien Régime*. Like Mateus, he also became a diplomat. He was sent as ambassador of Portugal to the U.S.A., the Batavian Republic, and Russia. In 1801 he was Secretary of State and Chancellor of the Exchequer and later acted as Prime Minister in Brazil.

In 1810, when Bezerra visited him, Beckford seemed to enjoy his company and appreciate his qualities as much as when he first read *Vathek*. He wrote about his old friend to his Portuguese secretary, Franchi: "Bezerra is full of taste and intelligence; he sees and understands everything with an incomparable fervour of spirit."[23] In 1817, some days before Bezerra's death, Beckford was worried about him and wrote: "Poor Bezerra in the midst of so much glory, so much solid power. I doubt whether he is still alive ... "[24] Beckford was such a close friend of Bezerra's that, besides *Vathek*, he even allowed him to read his private *Journal*, as we may see in the entry for 18 October: "Bezerra was also here. After dinner I lighted up his imagination into a fervent blaze by reading him part of this scrawl of a journal."[25]

During the time he spent in Portugal in 1787 Beckford's best friend was the old *Abade* Xavier, the foster-father of the Marialvas. Although he was ninety-two, the *Abbé* (as Beckford used to call him) was a man of vast culture and interests. The author of *Vathek* was certainly aware of that and he appreciated him so much that he even gave him the *Episodes* to read. We can conclude that he had already enjoyed reading the adventures of the Caliph. It is easy to visualise the scene Beckford, in his pictorial style, describes on 28 September: "We found the Abade as usual seated in a snug corner of the saloon ramming his nose with snuff and fancying himself very busy in reading my Arabian Stories."[26] *Abade* Xavier was already dead when Beckford came back to Portugal in 1793. But thanks to his devotion, and to the friendship of so many Portuguese who shared Beckford's interests and appreciated him, the author of *Vathek* became a legend in Portugal.

Beckford's way of living, his way of furnishing and decorating his houses in Lisbon and Sintra, and the improvements and landscape gardening he did in Monserrate stayed in the memory of the Portuguese. Beckford's literary references to writers and poets, like Bocage and Camoens, and his accurate descriptions of life in court and of the customs of the common people were very often quoted and referred to in Portugal long after he had left the country and even after his death. The name of the author of *Vathek* appeared in the most important periodicals.[27] The works he devoted to Portugal were obviously the most quoted even by historians,[28] but *Vathek* also was well known and read by many writers.

It is not hard to understand that a work such as *Vathek* should make a deep impression in a country where the Arabs had been for five hundred years and in whose literature there are many oriental *topoi*, as, for instance, a hidden Princess who lives at the bottom of a well or heroines that, like Nouronihar, have eyes of an indefinite color. As almost everywhere in Europe, there was a revival of interest in things oriental at the beginning of the nineteenth century in Portugal. There are several buildings one could easily believe had been inspired by the architectural descriptions in *Vathek*. Curiously enough one of the most impressive houses that were built in the oriental style has replaced the Gothic castle where Beckford used to live in Monserrate.

Besides an obvious interest in the Orient in architecture, that led people to build fountains in their gardens and decorate buildings in *mudejar* art,[29] many writers also continued a long tradition that came from the time of the Discoveries, and wrote about eastern themes. *Vathek* represents the real Orient that the Portuguese knew and in a way it is a travel book, so it was to be expected that it should be appreciated at this time in Portugal. The fact that there was a French version and that it was discussed in literary periodicals in France[30] must also have contributed to its popularity in Portugal.

Among other novelists and playwrights who have been inspired by Beckford, is Francisco Rocha Martins (1879–1952), who deserves a special reference because he was particularly interested in *Vathek*. Like many others, he devoted several articles and essays to Beckford.[31] In 1904 he wrote *Conto Oriental* apparently under the influence of *Vathek*. This oriental tale, that tells the story of a Caliph, was one of a series of *Chrónicas*. In these chronicles, which were published weekly in a well-known periodical,[32] Rocha Martins even tried to imitate Beckford's style and often chose the same subjects as the author of *Vathek*.[33]

Several other novelists have written about Beckford's visits to Portugal. The title of the work of one of them *Lágrimas e Tesouros* (Tears and Treasures) could easily have been inspired by Beckford's life. This novel by Luís Augusto Rebelo da Silva appeared first as a serial in a periodical and was later, in 1863, printed in book form.[34] In it, and in innumerable articles in periodicals[35] and references in literary works, we find much more information about the man and his life than about the writer and his work. He is nevertheless often referred to as the author of *Vathek* and his oriental tale was already mentioned in 1879 by Manuel Bernardes Branco in his work *Portugal e os Estrangeiros*.[36]

Most Portuguese writers, perhaps unconsciously trying to do him justice, call him "Lord Beckford"[37] and ascribe to him a secret diplomatic mission in their country. They seem to see Beckford through his own eyes and to know that he should have had both the title and the mission, as he probably would have had but for the scandal of Powderham.

Besides Rebelo da Silva, who not only used Beckford's *Italy* and *Recollections of an Excursion to Alcobaça and Batalha* as a source for his historical novel but also wrote fantastic tales[38] like the author of *Vathek*, we must also mention the playwright Marcelino Mesquita (1856–1915). Mesquita sought inspiration for the historical play *Peraltas e Sécias* that he wrote in 1899, in a description of an evening visit that Beckford and his Portuguese noble friends paid to an old country-seat outside Lisbon.[39] There is no reference to *Vathek* in this play, but it is worth noticing that its author was thus mentioned not only in articles, essays and novels, but also in the theatre.

Carlos Malheiro Dias (1875–1941) seems to be the first Portuguese writer who was more conscious of the darker sides of Beckford's personality. In his works "Lord Beckford" is a kind of secret agent and is suspected of belonging to the Freemasons. Malheiro Dias wrote a novel based on Beckford's meeting with Cagliostro in Lisbon. In 1905 he adapted this novel[40] into a play[41] to which he also gave the title *O Grande Cagliostro*. This play was quite popular and it contributed to the fame of the author of *Vathek* in Portugal. It is one of those bourgeois tragedies that were typical of the first years of the twentieth century with much adventure, romantic violence, and exact historical details. Malheiro Dias, who has been called "the last great romantic writer in Portugal,"[42] could speak English and lived for some time in London. Although no volume of *Vathek* was found in his library (that has been carefully kept by his family), there is much of Eblis in the satanic character of Cagliostro.

Dias tells us that even "Lord" Beckford feared him[43] and that Machiavelli's blood was running in his veins.[44] According to him Cagliostro had a double personality, was an alchemist, a wizard full of mysteries, knowing even the secrets of state, an adventurer with the science of a philosopher and the arrogance of a prince.[45] It is, of course, difficult to say with any certainty if all these characteristics came specifically from *Vathek* or if they belong to the common literary stock of Europe at the time. There is, however, a trait of Cagliostro for which Malheiro Dias must have sought inspiration in *Vathek*: his eyes, like the one of the Caliph "became so terrible that no person could bear to behold"[46] them. Malheiro Dias referred repeatedly to the

fire in Cagliostro's eyes saying: "olhar chamejante," "olhar fulgu-
rante," "aquele olhar que o penetrava até ao cérebro e parecia desafiá-
lo com um magnético poder de adivinhação."[47] One of the most
impressive scenes of the novel is the one in which Cagliostro meets
Beckford and succeeds in withering a bunch of roses the English
"Lord" was holding in his hand just by looking at them intently from a
distance.

As had already happened with *Lágrimas e Tesouros*, *O Grande
Cagliostro* was also published as a serial in one of the most popular
and widely read periodicals, *A Ilustração Portuguesa*.[48] In this way,
Portuguese readers throughout the country became familiar with the
character of the English Lord who was interested in necromancy and
had met a mysterious visitor who seemed to come from the underworld. Though completely different from *Vathek*, Dias' "romantic
novel"[49] made the Portuguese who didn't know Beckford's work curious about it. When Malheiro Dias changed his novel into what has
been classified as "one of the most charming comedies of the Portuguese literature"[50] he contributed even more to the popularity of the
author of *Vathek* in Portugal.

But *Vathek* itself was going to inspire yet another work of art that
Portugal continues to be very proud of. Curiously enough it was in the
world of music—a world which so much impressed Beckford when he
visited Portugal—that *Vathek* was going to have a most remarkable
influence in that country. In 1913, a well known Portuguese musician,
Luís de Freitas Branco (1890–1955), composed what he called a symphonic poem; his source was Beckford's work and he adopted the
same title.

Luís de Freitas Branco, who as a child had an English private tutor, could speak fluent English and lived for some time in London. He was the first Portuguese musician to compose "symphonic poems" that were based on literary motifs. He composed *Manfred,* inspired by Byron's poem, and in 1910 *Paraísos Artificiais,* based on De Quincey's *Confessions of an Opium Eater. Vathek* is one of his most renowned works. In it, Freitas Branco used a real Arabic theme that was recorded in *The History of Music* by Ambros. This theme is introduced by a bassoon solo.

There are several variations, one for each palace. The first, corresponding to *The Eternal or Unsatiating Banquet,* is called *Festim Eterno* in Freitas Branco's composition. To the second palace, which Beckford named *The Temple of Melody or Nectar of the Soul,* corresponds *Templo da Melodia;* the third *The Delight of the Eyes or the Support of Memory* is called *Delicías dos Olhos* in the symphonic poem and it is the most modernist and historically important of all the variations. It is a fugato. To the fourth Freitas Branco gave the title *Aguilhão dos Sentidos,* while in Beckford's *Vathek* it is *The Palace of Perfumes or the Incentive of Pleasure.* Finally the fifth, *The Retreat of Mirth, or the Dangerous,* which evokes sensual pleasure, is *O Reduto da Felicidade.*

The critics consider Freitas Branco "the most important personality in his generation and one of the most remarkable in Portuguese music"[51] and "the founder of modernism in our country."[52] It is certainly due to its original and daring characteristics that *Vathek* was only played in public for the first time in 1950[53] and without the famous third variation. In 1961[54] it was finally played in its complete form as well as in 1974[55] and in 1975[56] to commemorate the 20th anniversary of its author's death. With *Vathek* and his other impressionistic works in which he used atonal techniques, Freitas Branco contributed to the evolution of Portuguese music at the beginning of the twentieth century and succeeded in bringing it to the same level music was reaching in the rest of Europe.

Besides being known in Portugal for his original personality and enormous fortune, Beckford has also been famous for his literary work. The Portuguese are familiar with the travel books he wrote about Portugal but, as has been made evident, they are also interested in *Vathek*. We know that it was thanks to Beckford's own copies and manuscripts that *Dreams, Waking Thoughts and Incidents*,[57] *Vathek*, the *Episodes* and even the *Journal* (which he never intended to publish) were read in the original by some of his Portuguese friends. But it must have been after his work was translated that its popularity increased.

It must be mentioned that the first translations of *Italy*[58] and of *Recollections*[59] that appeared in a Portuguese periodical were in French. They were published in *A Abelha*[60] in 1836 and in 1840. The translations were done by the director of this bilingual periodical, Mme. C. d'Andrade.[61] She also wrote a long article on Fonthill Abbey in which she mentioned that Beckford had offered four magnificent gold filigree candle holders for the Queen's (D. Maria I) private chapel.[62] The first Portuguese translation of *Italy* was published over a period of three years in *O Panorama*.[63] It must have been quite appreciated as it was later repeated in another popular periodical *A Leitura—Magazine Litteraris*[64] in 1895 and in book form (although incomplete) in 1901 with the title *A Corte de D. Maria I— Correspondência de William Beckford—1787*.

Although *Vathek* had all the characteristics that would make it a popular work in Portugal, it has been translated only quite recently. The fact that there was a French version written by Beckford himself and that the Portuguese can easily read French, may, of course, have contributed to delaying the translation of *Vathek*. The first Portuguese *Vathek* was published by *Amigos do Livro*. This is a kind of club which sells books only to its members and consequently has a reduced public. In the same volume, besides *Vathek*, there are also the translations of two other tales, one by Chamisso and one by Achim von Arnim. Although it is not clearly expressed, the translation was done from a French edition, probably the Paris edition of 1787, as it is the only one that has the same title. This early edition is the likely source, since the number of stairs to the tower is still eleven thousand. Beckford reduced them to fifteen hundred in the London edition of 1815. The translation, by Pedro Reis, is careless and the whole edition has been deservedly neglected. When we compare it to the original text we can only conclude that Beckford has been betrayed.

Beckford was doubly betrayed by the introduction that is signed with the initials A.D.[65] It says, in faulty Portuguese, that Beckford built two castles (one in Fonthill and one in Sintra) and that he had two sons![66] The author of this introduction also informs us that due to Beckford's ignorance and insufficient documentation about the East he was forced to use his fantasy instead of giving us correct information. "Kitty" is mentioned not as William Courtenay but as a female cousin who addressed Beckford as "my infernal lover"; he means obviously Louisa Beckford. We also learn (!) that Beckford, while in Europe, seduced some Arab peasant girls (where that could have happened is not mentioned); that after Nelson's visit he decided to build a tower out of which he never emerged again, and that he died on a mountain opposite Longdown Hill [sic] ...

After this private edition, there was another one in 1978.[67] It is entitled *Vathek* and was translated by Manuel João Gomes. It is a small booklet with notes and an introduction written by the translator. In it there are again incredible blunders. It says that Louisa was Courtenay's wife and that *Vathek* is more like a chapter of the *Koran* than like a story of the *Arabian Nights*! The notes, although scholarly, seem to have as their main object to show Beckford's negative side as a man and as a writer. According to M. J. Gomes the descriptions were copied from the *Arabian Nights*, Beckford was a drug addict and he did not quote the Bible correctly. Gomes concludes by saying that anachronisms are one of Beckford's talents.

The most recent Portuguese edition of *Vathek* dates from 1982. According to the title *História do Califa Vathek*[68] and to the fact that it is illustrated, it seems to be intended for a younger audience. Yet some of the illustrations, done by Manuela Bacelar, seem to be meant for pornographic comics. It is a much more noticeable and thicker volume. It includes the translation of Henley's notes and a preface by Michael Gordon Lloyd.

As this seems to be what could become the edition that will introduce *Vathek* to a wider and younger generation of Portuguese, it deserves a more detailed treatment than the previous ones. The preface, although full of information, still contains some inaccuracies. Lloyd says that the part of *Italy* devoted to Portugal was translated for the first time by Rebelo da Silva in 1895. We know that it had already been translated in 1836 in *A Abelha* and in 1855 in *O Panorama* and that the translator was Meira (Rebelo da Silva only revised part of it). We also read in the preface that Beckford had started his studies of

Oriental literature with the Arab Zemir in 1781. It is known that, before that, his interest for the East had already been awakened by Alexander Cozens and possibly by Sir William Chambers.

The translation by Mário Claudio deserves some comment. We are not informed which edition of the original was chosen, but comparing the texts, one can conclude that it was neither the French nor the English editions of 1815 and 1816. There are in this Portuguese translation sentences (and sometimes whole paragraphs) that Beckford omitted and changed in those revised editions. Claudio must have used either the English or the Lausanne editions of 1786. On the other hand there are expressions in this English text that have not been translated into Portuguese like "confound," "Whilst the naturalist on his part" (p. 4)[69] and "as well as he could" (p. 9). There are also sentences in Claudio's translation that have no correspondence in the English original like "que juncavam o chão" (p. 23) or "Em vez disso" (p. 24). Some words and expressions are wrongly translated or at least the meaning of the original is altered, such as "support" (p. 4), "entire" (p. 4) and "intelligence" (p. 10) which appear in Claudio's translation as "colina" (p. 14), "perene" (p. 14) and "Alvíssaras" (p. 24). "What is beneath you to learn" (p. 9) is turned into "nem está em tuas mãos entender" (p. 24) which means "you are unable to learn"; "whose vicars the caliphs are" (p. 5) becomes in the Portuguese text "a quem os Califas prestam culto como sacerdotes" (p. 16) (to whom the Caliphs worship as priests).

More important than these slight imperfections—which occur in so many translations—there is another aspect that, from my point of view, must be strongly criticized. Claudio often chooses a different, lower register or level of language that gives to his text a general impression of vulgarity and coarseness that is not to be found in *Vathek*. In a way it seems he is trying to make Beckford's text fit the uncouth illustrations chosen for this edition. I include some examples to prove my point but this is the kind of language subtlety that is much more evident to a native speaker than to a foreigner.

Claudio translates "crowd" (p. 9) by "malta" (p. 25) which is a slang word for mob; "smell" (p. 10) becomes "fedor" (p. 26) which is stink; "quaffed large bumpers" (p. 14) that almost evokes a classical text, is turned into "despejava grandes copadas" (p. 32) which would be used by roughly spoken people; "would be more to his taste" (p. 15) is translated with a very familiar expression "lhe dariam no goto" (p. 33) which means, more or less, would take his fancy.

The necessarily restricted dimensions of this essay do not allow me to include here a more detailed analysis of these translations and of their comparison with the original. I must regretfully acknowledge the damage to the plasticity of the images and to the irony in all of them and to what seems a deliberate lowering of the level of language in Claudio's text. When we read the different introductions written for the translations we can only conclude that Beckford is no longer the cherished English traveller whose life everyone in Portugal seemed to know in every detail till the first half of the twentieth century. On the other hand, a Portuguese Beckfordian cannot but rejoice that three versions of *Vathek* should have been published in Portugal since 1970. It is only to be regretted that none of them should be a scholarly edition.

This rejoicing is better understood when one knows that in Portugal, the part of *Italy* devoted to my country has been as often published in French as in Portuguese. The only Portuguese translation dates from the nineteenth century and is now out of print. Such is also the case with the 1914 incomplete version of *Recollections,*[70] which has never been translated as a whole in Portuguese.

The reading of *Vathek* has been restricted to a kind of cultural elite, like Beckford's intimate friends in the eighteenth century, to writers and novelists, like Rebelo da Silva and Malheiro Dias in the nineteenth, and to *avant garde* musicians, like Freitas Branco in the first years of the twentieth. With these new translations, *Vathek* has become more popular in Portugal. This change in attitude shows that if for Beckford the memories of Portugal were always the ones nearest to his heart,[71] the Portuguese can also say that they will never forget their famous English friend even if, over the years, his image has changed from the wealthy "Lord Beckford" who lived in Sintra, to the enigmatic author of a version of *Vathek*, that may not entirely correspond to what he considered "the proudest feather in my cap."[72]

Universidade Nova de Lisboa

## REFERENCES

[1]Umberto Eco, *The Role of the Reader—Explorations in the Semiotics of Texts* (London: Hutchinson, 1981) p. 49 et passim.

[2]André Parreaux, *William Beckford Auteur de Vathek*, Paris, A. G. Nizet, 1960.

[3]Kenneth Graham, "William Beckford's Vathek: A Critical Edition," Diss. University of London, 1971.

[4]Kenneth Graham, "Vathek in English and French," *Studies in Bibliography*, 28, (1975), p. 158.

[5]William Beckford, *Recollections of an Excursion to the Monasteries of Alcobaça and Batalha* (London: Centaur Press, 1972) p. 128.

[6]Boyd Alexander, ed. *Journal of William Beckford in Portugal and Spain, 1787–88* (London: Rupert Hart Davis, 1954).

[7]Alexander, *Journal*, p. 139.

[8]L. S. Mercier (1740–1814) author of *Tableau de Paris*, a work of social criticism that made him famous. He had also written a curious anticipatory fantasy called *L'An 2240*.

[9]Alexander, *Journal*, p. 151.

[10]Alexander, *Journal*, p. 180.

[11]Boyd Alexander, ed. *Life at Fonthill 1807–1822 with Interludes in Paris and London* (London: Rupert Hart-Davies, 1957) p. 65.

[12]Robert Kiely, *The Romantic Novel in England* (Cambridge: Harvard University Press, 1973) pp. 43–64.

[13]William Beckford, *Italy, with Sketches of Portugal and Spain* (Paris: Baudry's European Library, 1834) p. 188.

[14]Beckford, *Italy*, p. 192.

[15]Roger Lonsdale, ed. *Vathek,* (London: Oxford University Press, 1970) p. 2.

[16]Lonsdale, *Vathek*, pp. 1–2.

[17]Lonsdale, *Vathek*, p. 7.

[18]Beckford, *Italy*, p. 213.

[19]Alexander, *Journal*, p. 56.

[20]Alexander, *Journal*, pp. 198, 208, 251.

[21]Mateus' edition is mentioned in the *Sale Catalogue of the Hamilton Palace Library—The 1st Portion of the Beckford Library* (London 1882–83) as lot 1527, L. de Camoens, *Os Lusíadas*, Nova Edição Correcta e Dada a Luz por Dom J. M. de Sousa Botelho (Paris, F. Didot, 1817).

[22]Alexander, *Journal*, p. 41.

[23]Alexander, *Life at Fonthill*, p. 91.

[24]Alexander, *Life at Fonthill*, p. 238.

[25]Alexander, *Journal*, p. 235.

[26]Alexander, *Journal*, pp. 212–213.

[27]Some of the periodicals where Beckford's name appeared are (up to 1950): *Gazeta de Lisboa* (1796); *A Abelha* (1836,1840–43); *A Distracção Instrutiva* (1842); *O Panorama* (1855–57); *Revista Literária e Dramática* (1863); *Archivo Pittoresco* (1866); *Artes e Letras* (1872); *A Illustração Portuguesa* (1885–87,1904,1906); *A Leitura* (1895); *O Século* (1898); *Brazil e Portugal* (1906); *Boletim da Classe de Letras* (1922); *O Diário de Notícias* (1927); *O Primeiro de Janeiro* (1932–36); *Diário da Manhá* (1938,46); *Portucale* (1930); *The Anglo-Portuguese News* (1943–45).

[28]J. M. Latino Coelho, *História Política e Militar de Portugal desde os Fins do XVIII Século até 1814* (Lisboa: Imprensa Nacional, 1874) pp. 201, 233, 240, 248, 281.

[29]Palácio da Pena (Sintra) built in 1841 by Prince Consort Ferdinand Saxe-Coburg.

[30]Valery Larbaud, Lucien Lavault and André Gide, *Nouvelle Revue Française—Revue Mensuelle de Littérature et de Critique* (Paris, 1913) Nos. 143, 687, 868, 1044. Daily papers, such as *Figaro* (14.5.1932), *Le Temps* (19.1.1934) and *Le Courrier Litteraire* often referred to Beckford.

[31]Francisco Rocha Martins, *Lisboa de Ontem e de Hoje* (Lisboa: Empresa Nacional de Publicidade, 1915) pp. 149, 159, 213, 243; "Bocage e Lord Beckford" *Vultos e Sombras* 17.7.1932; "Um Visita de Beckford a Laveiras" *Lisboa de Ontem e de Hoje* 11.7.1946.

[32]Francisco Rocha Martins, "Chronicas", *A Illustração Portuguesa—Revista Semanal dos Acontecimentos da Vida Portuguesa* Nos. 38, 25.7.1904, 594.

[33]Francisco Rocha Martins, *Santo de Casa* (St. Anthony) No. 32, 13.6.1904, 498; *Os Círios* (The Processions) No. 44, 29.8.1904, 674.

[34]Luís A. Rebelo da Silva, *Lágrimas e Tesouros—Fragmentos de Uma História Inédita* (Porto: Typ. do Comércio, 1863).

[35]Luís A. Rebelo da Silva, *Viagens de Beckford a Portugal,* (translation of *Italy*), *O Panorama,* Vol. XIII (1855) 266–268.

[36]Manoel Bernardes Branco, *Portugal e os Estrangeiros* (Lisboa: Academia Real de Sciências, 1879) p. 76. B. Branco refers to *Recollections, Italy* and to Rebelo da Silva's article. He includes the translation of *Italy* published in *O Panorama.*

[37]Teófilo Braga, *História da Litteratura Portuguesa,* (Porto: Imprensa Portuguesa, 1870) pp. 27, 109, 116, 122; Carlos Malheiro Dias, *Cartas de Lisboa* (Lisboa: Editora Teixeira, 1905) pp. 131, 299; *O Grande Cagliostro* (Porto: Editorial Porto, 1905) pp. 50, 66, 99; Agostinho de Campos, *Camões Lírico* (Lisboa: Livraria Bertrand, 1926) p. 5.

[38]Rebelo da Silva, *Contos e Lendas* (Lisboa: Livraria Editora Matos Moreira, 1873).

[39]Marquez de Resende, *Pintura de um Outeiro Nocturno* (Lisboa: Typographia da Academia Real das Sciências, 1868).

[40]Malheiro Dias, *O Grande Cagliostro—Novela Romântica* (Lisboa: Livraria Bertrand, 1904).

[41]Malheiro Dias, *O Grande Cagliostro* comédia em cinco actos (Porto, Magalhães e Moniz, 1905). This comedy was played for the first time on October 30, 1905 in the theatre D. Amélia.

[42]Victor Sousa Garcia, "'*A Exortacao à Mocidade*' de Malheiro Dias "(Lisboa, 1950). Conference held on 18 February 1954 in the Centro de Cultura Popular.

[43]Dias, *O Grande Cagliostro*, p. 115.

[44]Dias, *O Grande Cagliostro*, p. 60.

[45]Dias, *O Grande Cagliostro*, p. 198.

[46]Beckford, *Vathek*, p. 1.

[47]Dias, *O Grande Cagliostro*, pp. 17, 21.

[48]M. Dias, "O Grande Cagliostro", *A Ilustração Portuguesa* No. 43, 29.8.1904, p. 686.

[49]This subtitle was chosen by Dias himself.

[50]Júlio Dantas, preface to *O Grande Cagliostro*, p. 4.

[51]Humberto Ávila, Jacket notes. *Paraísos Artificiais* by Luís de Freitas Branco: Secretaria do Estado da Cultura.

[52]Nuno Barreiros, *Notas à Margem do Programa*. Concertos Sinfónicos da Emissora Nacional, Teatro Nacional de S. Carlos Outubro–Novembro de 1974.

[53]Freitas Branco, *Vathek*, Symphonic poem, Cond. Joly Braga Santos, Estufa Fria do Parque Eduardo VII, Lisbon, 1950.

[54]Branco, *Vathek*, Cond. Álvaro Cassuto, Symphonic Orchestra, 1961.

[55]Branco, *Vathek*, Cond. Silva Pereira, Symphonic Orchestra, 1974.

[56]Branco, *Vathek,* Cond. Silva Pereira, 1975.

[57]Alexander, *Journal*, p. 88.

[58]The French translation of *Italy* published in *A Abelha* was entitled *Lettres sur le Portugal*. The first "Lettre" appeared in April 1836, No. 1, 135.

[59]The title of the French translation of *Recollections* was *Souvenirs d'un Voyage à Alcobaça. A Abelha* started its publication in 1840, 2o anno, 309 and it lasted until 1843, No. 51, p. 414.

[60] *A Abelha—Jornal de Utilidade, Instrução e Recreio em Portuguez e Francez* (Lisboa: Imprensa de C. A. Silva Carvalho). There is a second edition totally in French with the title *L'Abeille Française, Journal Encyclopédique*.

[61]Bernardes Branco, *Portugal*, p. 558, attributes the Portuguese translation of *Italy* to Mme. Andrade but it was done by Meira and revised by Rebelo da Silva.

[62]C. d'Andrade, "L'Abbaye de Fonthill", *L'Abeille* 2 (1840) p. 250.

[63]"Viagens de Beckford a Portugal", *O Panorama—Jornal Litterário e Instrutivo* Vols. XII (1855); XIII (1856); XIV (1857).

[64]Portugal in 1787, *A Leitura—Magazine Literário* Nos. 42-46 (1895).

[65]The name of the author who wrote the introduction is Albert Demazière and the date of the edition is 1973.

246          *VATHEK*: ESCAPE FROM TIME

[66]Pedro Reis, trans. *Vathek—Conto Arabe* (Lisboa: Amigos do Livro, n.d.) pp. 117–120.

[67]Manuel João Gomes, trans. *Vathek* (Lisboa: Editorial Estampa, 1978).

[68]*História do Califa Vathek* (Porto: Edições Afrontamento, 1982).

[69]All subsequent page references to the English text are from *The History of the Caliph Vathek; and European Travels* (London: The Minerva Library of Famous Books, 1891)that reproduces the first edition of *Vathek*.

[70]J. Lobo and M. Natividade, *Alcobaça e Batalha* (Recordações de uma Excursão) (Alcobaça: Officina de A. M. d'Oliveira, 1914).

[71]Beckford, "Letter to Franchi 2 July 1812," in Boyd Alexander, *Life at Fonthill*, p. 125. [MS in Italian in Beckford Papers].

[72]Alfred Morrison, *Collection of Autograph Letters and Historical Documents*, Second Series, 1882–93 (London: Printed for Private Circulation, 1893), I, p. 196.

# A CHECKLIST OF VATHEK CRITICISM

Frederick S. Frank

The following compilation of *Vathek* criticism is a bibliographical summation of important critical writing about the novel which
has appeared in the twentieth century. It is designed to serve as a com-
plement to the essays in the present collection. The volume of critical
study on the novel corresponds with the increased research interest in
*Vathek*'s connections with Gothic literature. Because Gothic fiction in
general has become the object of intense analysis since the mid-
1950's, studies of *Vathek* have often followed this trend and their
number has thus risen proportionately.

The checklist contains references to writings about *Vathek* to be
found in essay collections, histories of the novel, monographs on
Beckford and his life, journal articles, and doctoral dissertations.
Introductions to the numerous editions of *Vathek* published in the
twentieth century are also included as a vital segment of this critical
canon. Not cited are passing allusions to *Vathek* in the historical sur-
veys of the Gothic novel by Dorothy Scarborough (*The Supernatural
in Modern English Fiction*, 1917), H.P. Lovecraft (*Supernatural
Horror in Literature*, 1927), Eino Railo (*The Haunted Castle: A Study
of the Elements of English Romanticism*, 1927), Montague Summers
(*The Gothic Quest: A History of the Gothic Novel,* 1938), and Maurice
Lévy, (*Le Roman 'gothique' anglais*, 1968). The user of the bibliogra-

phy needs to be aware that *Vathek* is also briefly mentioned in a Gothic context in the following recent investigations of Gothic literature: G.R. Thompson (*The Gothic Imagination: Essays in Dark Romanticism*, 1974), Coral Ann Howells (*Love, Mystery, and Misery: Feeling in Gothic Fiction*, 1979), Elizabeth Mac Andrew (*The Gothic Tradition in Fiction*, 1979), Robert I. LeTellier (*An Intensifying Vision of Evil: The Gothic Novel (1764–1820) as a Self-Contained Literary Cycle*, 1980), David Punter (*The Literature of Terror: A History of Gothic Fiction from 1765 to the Present Day*, 1980), Linda Bayer-Berenbaum (*The Gothic Imagination: Expansion in Gothic Literature and Art*, 1982), Patrick Day (*In the Circles of Fear and Desire: A Study in Gothic Fantasy*, 1985), Elizabeth R. Napier (*The Failure of the Gothic: Problems of Disjunction in an Eighteenth-Century Literary Form*, 1986), Margaret L. Carter (*Specter or Delusion? The Supernatural in Gothic Fiction*, 1987), and S.L. Varnado (*Haunted Presence: The Numinous in Gothic Fiction*, 1987).

The genre, symbolic qualities, variegated tone, and philosophical outlook of Beckford's *Vathek* all remain areas of vigorous inquiry and debate. *Vathek* criticism shows no signs of abatement some two hundred years after Beckford first erected his infernal tower on the literary landscape.

ALEXANDER, Boyd. "William Beckford, Man of Taste," *History Today*, 10 (1960): 686–694.

_____. "The Decay of Beckford's Genius," in *William Beckford of Fonthill, 1760–1844. Bicentenary Essays*, ed. Fatma Moussa

Mahmoud. Cairo, Egypt: C. Tsoumas, 1960; Rpt. Port Washington, NY: Kennikat Press, 1972, pp. 17–29.

_____. "William Beckford of Fonthill," *Yale University Library Gazette*, 35 (1961): 161–169.

_____. "The Origins of *Vathek*, 1780–1781" and "*Vathek* and its Episodes," in *England's Wealthiest Son: A Study of William Beckford*. London: Centaur Press, 1962, pp. 79–102.

ANDERSON, Jorgen. "Giant Dreams: Piranesi's Influence in England," *English Miscellany*, 3 (1952): 49–59.

ARMOUR, Richard W. "The Caliph of Fonthill," *Reading and Collecting*, 1 (1937): 9–10.

B., G.F.R. "Vathek," *Notes & Queries*, 7 (February 20, 1886): 154.

BABB, James T. "William Beckford of Fonthill," *Yale University Library Gazette*, 41 (1966): 60–69.

BAKER, Ernest. "The Oriental Story from *Rasselas* to *Vathek*," *The History of the English Novel*. New York: Barnes & Noble, 1924–39, V, 55–76.

BELL, C.F. "William Beckford," *Times Literary Supplement*, May 13, 1944, p. 235.

BELLOC, Hilaire. "On Vathek," in *A Conversation with an Angel and Other Essays*. New York: Harper, 1929.

BIRKHEAD, Edith. "The Oriental Tale of Terror: Beckford," in *The Tale of Terror: A Study of the Gothic Romance*. London: Constable, 1921; Rpt. New York: Russell & Russell, 1963, pp. 94–99.

BLEILER, E.F. Introduction to *Vathek* by William Beckford, in *Three Gothic Novels*. New York: Dover Publications, 1966, pp. xix–xxx.

BLOOM, Margaret. "William Beckford's Vathek," *University of California Chronicle*, 33 (1931): 424–431.

BORGES, Jorge Luis. "About William Beckford's *Vathek*," in *Other Inquisitions, 1937–1952*, trans. Ruth L.C. Sims. Austin, TX: Texas UP, 1964.

BROCKMAN, Harold A.N. *The Caliph of Fonthill*, intro. Nicholas Pevsner. London: Werner Laurie, 1956.

BROWN, Wallace Cable. "Prose Fiction and the English Interest in the Near East, 1775–1825," *Publications of the Modern Language Association*, 53 (1938): 827–836.

BRULÉ, A. "Une Visite à Fonthill en 1792," *Revue Anglo-Américaine*, 10 (1933): 33–42.

BRUNEAU, Jean. "Madame Genlis, William Beckford et *Vathek*,"

*Nineteenth Century French Studies*, 5 (1977): 34–38.

BUCKLEY, W.E. "Beckford's *Vathek*," *Notes & Queries*, 7 (February 20, 1886): 154.

CANNON, Peter. "The Influence of *Vathek* on H.P. Lovecraft's *The Dream Quest of Unknown Kadath*," in *H.P. Lovecraft: Four Decades of Criticism*, ed. J.T. Joshi. Athens, OH: Athens UP, 1980, pp. 153–157.

CARNERO, Guillermo. "William Beckford (1760–1844) o el Erotismo de Fina Estampa," *Insula*, 24 (Oct.–Nov., 1969): 18–19.

CARTER, John. "Beckford and Vathek: Ged and Stereotype," *Library*, 18 (1963): 308–309.

CARTER, Lin. Introduction to *The History of the Caliph Vathek, including "The Episodes of Vathek"* by William Beckford. New York: Ballantine Books, 1971.

CHADOURNE, Marc. "L'Incroyable William Beckford," *Revue de Paris*, 69 (1962): 43–58.

_____. *Eblis, ou L'Enfer de William Beckford: L'Homme et l'oeuvre*. Paris: Jean-Jacques Pauvert, 1967.

CHAPMAN, Guy. Introduction to *Vathek, with the Episodes of Vathek* by William Beckford. Cambridge: Constable, 1929.

_____. "The Nonesuch Vathek," *Times Literary Supplement*, January 2, 1930, p. 12.

_____. "Beckford the Caliph: A Traveller of Two Worlds, Passion and Fantasy," *Times Literary Supplement*, May 6, 1944, pp. 222.

_____. "William Beckford," *Times Literary Supplement*, May 20, 1944, p. 247.

_____. *Beckford*. London: Rupert Hart-Davis, 1952.

CHAPMAN, Guy and John Hodgkin. *A Bibliography of William Beckford of Fonthill*. London: Constable, 1930.

CHURCH, Richard. "Undergrowth," in *The Growth of the English Novel*. New York: Barnes & Noble, 1957, pp. 88–89.

CONANT, Martha Pike. *The Oriental Tale in England in the Eighteenth Century*. New York: Columbia University Studies in Comparative Literature Number 9; Columbia UP, 1908; Rpt. New York: Octagon Books, 1966.

CRAIG, Randall. "Beckford's Inversion of Romance in *Vathek*," *Orbis Litterarum*, 39 (1984): 95–106.

DE GRAAF, D.A. "Potgieter en *Vathek*," *Revue des Langues Vivantes*, 24 (1958): 469–475.

DE MEESTER, Marie E. "*Vathek* and its Influence," in *Oriental Influences in English Literature of the Nineteenth Century*. Heidelberg, Germany: Winters, 1915.

DIDIER, Béatrice. "L'Exotisme et la mise en question du système familial et moral dans le roman à la fin du XVIIIe siècle: Beckford, Sade, Potocki," in *Transactions of the Fourth International Congress of the Enlightenment*. Oxford: Voltaire Foundation, 1976, pp. 571–586.

FAIRCLOUGH, Peter and Mario Praz. Introduction to *Vathek* by William Beckford, in *Three Gothic Novels*. Baltimore, MD: Penguin Books, 1968, pp. 7–34.

FARRELL, John T. "A Reinterpretation of the Major Literary Works of William Beckford," *Dissertation Abstracts International*, 45 (1984): 1758A (University of Delaware).

FOLSOM, James K. "Beckford's Vathek and the Tradition of Oriental Satire," *Criticism*, 6 (1964): 53–69.

FOTHERGILL, Brian. "William Beckford, Prince of Amateurs," *Essays by Divers Hands*, 38 (1975): 33–47.

_____. *Beckford of Fonthill*. London: Faber & Faber, 1979.

FRANK, Frederick S. "The Gothic Romance: 1762–1820," in *Horror Literature: A Core Collection and Reference Guide*, ed. Marshall

B. Tymn. New York: R.R. Bowker, 1981, pp. 3–175.

_____. "William Beckford's *Vathek: An Arabian Tale*," in *Survey of Modern Fantasy Literature*, ed. Frank Magill. Englewood Cliffs, NJ: Salem Press, 1983, pp. 2023–2027.

_____. "William Beckford," in *Guide to the Gothic: An Annotated Bibliography of Criticism*. Metuchen, NJ: Scarecrow Press, 1984, pp. 50–65.

_____. *The First Gothics: A Critical Guide to the English Gothic Novel*. New York: Garland Publishing, 1987, pp. 23–27.

_____. "William Beckford," in *Gothic Fiction: A Master List of Twentieth Century Criticism and Research*. Westport, CT: Meckler Publishing Corporation, 1988, pp. 18–25.

GARBER, Frederick. "Beckford, Delacroix, and Byronic Orientalism," *Comparative Literature Studies*, 18 (1981): 321–332.

GARNETT, Richard. "Beckford's Vathek," in *Essays of an Ex-Librarian*. London: William Heinemann, 1901; Rpt. Freeport, NY: Books for Libraries, 1970.

_____. Introduction to *Vathek* by William Beckford. London: William Glaisher, 1924.

GEMMETT, Robert J. "William Beckford and the Picturesque: A Study of Fonthill," *Dissertation Abstracts*, 28 (1967): 1740A–1741A (Syracuse University).

_____. "An Annotated Checklist of the Works of William Beckford," *Papers of the Bibliographical Society of America*, 61 (1967): 243–258.

_____. "William Beckford: Bibliographical Addenda," *Bulletin of Bibliography*, 25 (1967): 62–64.

_____. "The Caliph Vathek from England and the Continent to America," *American Book Collector*, 18 (1968): 12–19.

_____. "The Critical Reception of William Beckford's Fonthill," *English Miscellany*, 19 (1968): 133–151.

_____. Introduction to *Vathek* by William Beckford. Delmar, NY: Scholar's Facsimiles and Reprints, 1972.

_____. *William Beckford*. Boston: Twayne English Authors Series Number 204; Twayne, 1977.

GIDDEY, Ernest. Introduction to *Vathek et les Episodes* by William Beckford. Lausanne, Switzerland: Rencontre, 1962.

_____. "Beckford and Byron," *Byron Journal*, 6 (1978): 36–47.

GIDE, André, Lucien Lavault, Lewis Melville, Valery Larbaud. "Le Dossier *Vathek*," *Nouvelle Revue Française*, 54 (1913): 1044–1050.

GIFFORD, Stephanie. "Genesis of a Caliph, *John O'London's*, 5 (August 24, 1961): 221.

GOTLIEB, Howard B. *William Beckford of Fonthill, Writer, Traveller, Collector, Caliph, 1760–1844: A Brief Narrative and Catalogue of an Exhibition to Mark the Two Hundreth Anniversary of Beckford's Birth*, ed. Boyd Alexander. New Haven, CT: Yale UP, 1960.

GRAHAM, Kenneth W. "Beckford's *Vathek*: A Study in Ironic Dissonance," *Criticism*, 14 (1972): 243–252.

_____. "Who Revised the 1823 *Vathek*?" *Papers of the Bibliographical Society of America*, 67 (1973): 315–322.

_____. "Beckford's Adaptation of the Oriental Tale in *Vathek*," *Enlightenment Essays*, 5, number 1 (1974): 24–33.

_____. "*Vathek* in English and French," *Studies in Bibliography*, 28 (1975): 153–166.

_____. "Implications of the Grotesque: Beckford's *Vathek* and the Boundaries of Fictional Reality," *Tennessee Studies in Literature*, 23 (1978): 61–74.

_____. "'Inconnue dans les Annales de la Terre': Beckford's Benign and Demonic Influence on Poe," *Sphinx: A Magazine of Literature and Society*, 4, number 4 (1985): 226–240.

GREEN, Andrew J. "Essays in Miniature: *Vathek*," *College English*, 3 (1942): 723–724.

GRIMM, Reinhold. "*Vathek* in Deutschland: Zwei Zwischenfälle Ohne Folgen?" *Revue de Littérature Comparée*, 38 (1964): 127–135.

GRIMSDITCH, Herbert B. Introduction to *Vathek* by William Beckford, illustrated with lithographs by Edward Bawden. Bloomsbury: Nonesuch Press, 1929; Rpt. London: Folio Press, 1958.

GUERRA, Olive. "Sintra e Lord Beckford," *Coloquio*, 46 (1967): 14–16.

HAGGERTY, George E. "Literature and Homosexuality in the Late Eighteenth Century: Walpole, Beckford, and Lewis," *Studies in the Novel*, 18 (1986): 341–352.

HANNAFORD, Justin. Introduction to *Vathek* by William Beckford. New York: Brentano's, 1921.

HEARN, Lafcadio. "William Beckford," in *Some Strange Literary Figures of the Eighteenth and Nineteenth Centuries*, ed. R. Tanabe.

Freeport, NY: Books for Libraries, 1965.

HENDERSON, Philip. Introduction to *Vathek* by William Beckford, in *Shorter Novels of the Eighteenth Century*. New York: E.P. Dutton, 1958.

HENNESSY, Brendan. "William Beckford: Vathek," in *British Writers*, ed. Ian Scott-Kilvert. New York: Charles Scribner's, 1980, III, 327–329.

HEPPENSTALL, Rayner. "The Palace of Subterranean Fire," in *The Fourfold Tradition, Notes on the French and English Literatures, With Some Ethnological and Historical Asides*. London: Barrie & Rockliff, 1961.

HERRICK, George H. "Fabulous Fonthill," *College Art Journal*, 12 (1953): 128–131.

HODGKIN, John. "*Vathek*: The Henley Letters," *Athenaeum*, December 25, 1909, pp. 789–790.

_____. "The Nonesuch *Vathek*," *Times Literary Supplement*, December 26, 1929, p. 1097.

HOLLINGSWORTH, Keith. "*Vathek* and 'The Ode to a Nightin-gale,'" *Times Literary Supplement*, October 27, 1961, p. 771.

HUNTER, A.O. "Le *Vathek* de William Beckford: Historique des

Éditions Françaises," *Revue de Littérature Comparée*, 15 (1935): 119–126.

HUSSAIN, Imdad. "Beckford, Wainewright, De Quincey, and Oriental Exoticism," *Venture*, 1 (1960): 234–248.

HYLAND, Peter. "*Vathek*, Heaven and Hell," *Research Studies*, 50 (1982): 99–105.

JANTZEN, Hermann. "Source of 'The Hall of Eblis' by B. Cornwall," *Archiv für das Studium der Neuren Sprachen und Literaturen*, 107 (1902): 318–323.

JEAN-AUBRY, G. "Autour de *Vathek* de William Beckford," *Revue de Littérature Comparée*, 16 (1936): 549–562.

JOHNSON, R. Brimley. Introduction to *Vathek* by William Beckford. London: Chapman and Dodd, 1922; Boston: Abbey Classics; Small, Maynard, 1922.

KIELY, Robert. "Vathek," in *The Romantic Novel in England*. Cambridge, MA: Harvard UP, 1972.

KLEIN, Jürgen. *Der gotische Roman und die Ästhetik des Bösen*. Darmstadt: Wissenschaftliche Buchgesellschaft, 1975.

KNIPP, Charles C. "Types of Orientalism in Eighteenth-Century England," *Dissertation Abstracts International*, 35 (1974): 2944A–

2945A (University of California at Berkeley).

LANE-POOLE, Stanley. "The Author of *Vathek*," *Quarterly Review*, 213 (October, 1910): 377–401.

LANGE, Bernd-Peter. "Orientierungsarbeit: Radikale Fantasie in William Beckfords *Vathek*," *Zeitshrift für Anglistik und Amerikanistik*, 33 (1985): 33–43.

LEES-MILNE, James. *William Beckford*. Tisbury, England: Compton Russell, 1976; Rpt. Montclair, NJ: Allanheld and Schram, 1979.

LE YAOUANC, Collette. "Le Thème Sexuel dans *Vathek*," in *Liguistique, Civilisation, Littérature*, ed. André Bordeaux. Paris: Didier, 1980, pp. 257–264.

LIU, Alan. "Toward a Theory of Common Sense: Beckford's *Vathek* and Johnson's *Rasselas*," *Texas Studies in Literature and Language*, 26 (1984): 183–217.

LOCKHART, John Gibson. Introduction to *Vathek* by William Beckford. London: Philip Allan, 1923.

LONSDALE, Roger. Introduction to *Vathek* by William Beckford. London: Oxford UP, 1970, pp. vii–xxxi.

MAGNIER, Mireille. "*Vathek* Hommage à Voltaire ou Avatar de Faust?" *Mythes, Croyances et Religions dans le Monde Anglo-*

*Saxon*, 4 (1986): 98–108.

MAHMOUD, Fatma Moussa. "Beckford, *Vathek*, and the Oriental Tale," in *William Beckford of Fonthill, 1760–1844. Bicentenary Essays*, ed. Fatma Moussa Mahmoud. Cairo, Egypt: C. Tsoumas, 1960; Rpt. Port Washington, NY: Kennikat Press, 1972, pp. 63–121.

_____. "*Rasselas* and *Vathek*," in *Bicentenary Essays on Rasselas*, ed. Magdi Wahba. Cairo, Egypt: Studies in English, 1960.

_____. "A Monument to the Author of *Vathek*," *Études Anglaises*, 25 (1962): 138–147.

MANZALAOUI, Mahmoud. "Pseudo-Orientalism in Transition: The Age of *Vathek*," in *William Beckford of Fonthill, 1760–1844. Bicentenary Essays*, ed. Fatma Moussa Mahmoud. Cairo, Egypt: C. Tsoumas, 1960; Rpt. Port Washington, NY: Kennikat Press, 1972, pp. 123–150.

MARLOW, Harriet. "Beckford's *Vathek*, 'Londres 1791,'" *Book Collector*, 11 (1962): 211.

MARSHALL, Julian. "Beckford's *Vathek*," *Notes & Queries*, 7 (January 23, 1886): 69.

_____. "Beckford's *Vathek*," *Notes & Queries*, 7 (April 20, 1889): 312–313.

MAY, Marcel. *La Jeunesse de William Beckford et la Genèse de son "Vathek".* Paris: Presses Universitaires de France, 1928.

MAYNARD, Temple. "Depictions of Persepolis in William Beckford's Istaker," *Eighteenth Century Life,* 3 (1977): 119–122.

_____. "The Landscape of *Vathek*," *Transactions of the Samuel Johnson Society of the Northwest,* 7 (1974): 79–98.

MAYOUX, Jean-Jacques. "La Damnation de Beckford," *English Miscellany,* 12 (1961): 41–77.

MCNUTT, Dan J. "William Beckford (1760–1844)," in *The Eighteenth Century Gothic Novel: An Annotated Bibliography of Criticism and Selected Texts.* New York: Garland Publishing, 1975, pp. 265–310.

MELVILLE, Lewis. "Vathek," *Athenaeum,* November 27, 1909, p. 658.

_____. "William Beckford, of Fonthill Abbey," *Fortnightly Review,* December 1, 1909, pp. 1011–1023.

_____. "Vathek," *Athenaeum,* December 4, 1909, p. 696.

_____. *The Life and Letters of William Beckford of Fonthill (Author of "Vathek").* London: William Heinemann, 1910.

_____. Introduction to *The Episodes of Vathek* by William Beckford, trans. Sir Frank T. Marzials. London: Stephen Swift, 1912.

MOCHI, Giovanna. "L'Inferno rassicurante di *Vathek*," *Paragone*, 350 (1979): 64–102.

MORE, Paul Elmer. "William Beckford," in *The Drift of Romanticism*. Boston: Houghton, Mifflin, 1913, pp. 1–36.

MOURET, François J.L. "Le *Vathek* de William Beckford et le 'Voyage d'Urien' d'André Gide," *Modern Language Review*, 64 (1969): 774–776.

NOCHIMSON, Martha. "Gothic Novel," in *Critical Survey of Long Fiction*, ed. Frank Magill. Englewood Cliffs, NJ: Salem Press, 1983, VIII, pp. 3121–3131.

OLIVER, John W. *The Life of William Beckford*. London: Oxford UP, 1932.

PARREAUX, André. "Beckford and Byron," *Études Anglaises*, 8 (1955): 11–31, 113–132.

_____. "Un *Vathek* Ignoré," *Bulletin de Bibliophile et du Bibliothécaire*, 5 (1957): 176–179.

_____. "Beckford's Vathek, 'Londres 1791,'" *Book Collector*, 7

(1958): 297–299.

_____. "Beckford en Italie: Rêve et voyage in XVIIIe siècle," *Revue de Littérature Comparée*, 33 (1959): 321–347.

_____. *William Beckford auteur de "Vathek" (1760–1844): Étude de la Création Littéraire*. Paris: Nizet, 1960.

_____. "The Caliph and the Swinish Multitude," in *William Beckford of Fonthill, 1760–1844. Bicentenary Essays*, ed. Matma Moussa Mahmoud. Cairo, Egypt: C. Tsoumas, 1960; Rpt. Port Washington, NY: Kennikat Press, 1972, pp. 1–15.

_____. "Beckford: Bibliographie sélective et critique," *Bulletin de la Société d'Études Anglo-Américaines des XVIIIe*, 3 (1976): 45–55.

PIRES, Maria Laura Bettencourt. *William Beckford e Portugal*. Lisbon: Edições 70, 1987.

PRAZ, Mario. "Il Califfo Beckford," in *Studi e Svaghi Inglesi* by Mario Praz. Firenzi, Italy: Sansoni, 1937.

_____. "Swift, Johnson, Beckford: Tre Inglesi Pazzi," *Tempo*, February 9, 1977, p. 3.

PRITCHETT, V.S. "Vile Body," *New Statesman*, February 23, 1962, pp. 265–266.

PRYCE-JONES, Alan. "William Beckford, Dilletante," *New York Times Book Review*, February 16, 1969, pp. 2, 40.

REDMAN, Ben Ray. Introduction to *Vathek* by William Beckford, illustrated by Mahlon Blaine. New York: John Day, 1928.

REILLY, Donald T. "The Interplay of Natural and Unnatural: A Definition of Gothic Romance," *Dissertation Abstracts International*, 31 (1970): 2353A (University of Pittsburgh).

REVAUGER, Marie-Cécile. "L'Unique et le multiple dans le *Vathek* de William Beckford: Folie du mimétisme," in *Folie, Folies, Folly dans le Monde Anglo-Américain aux XVIIIe Siècles*. Aix-en-Provence, France: PU de Provence, 1984, pp. 71–80.

RIEGER, James H. "*Au Pied de la Lettre*: Stylistic Uncertainty in *Vathek*," *Criticism*, 4 (1962): 302–312.

SAGE, Lorna. "Violet Cream," *New Statesman*, August 19, 1977, pp. 250–251.

SENA, John F. "Drawing from Blots: The Landscapes of *Vathek* and the Paintings of Alexander Cozens," *Etudes Anglaises*, 26 (1973): 210–215.

SITWELL, Sacheverell. *Beckford and Beckfordism*. London: Duckworth, 1930.

SOLOMON, Stanley J. "Subverting Propriety as a Pattern of Irony in Three Eighteenth-Century Novels: *The Castle of Otranto*, *Vathek*, and *Fanny Hill*," *Erasmus Review*, 1 (1971): 107–116.

SPECTOR, Robert D. "Schauer-Romantik: Matthew Gregory Lewis and William Beckford," in *The English Gothic: A Bibliographical Guide to Writers from Horace Walpole to Mary Shelley*. Westport, CT: Greenwood Press, 1984, pp. 153–203.

STEEVES, Harrison R. "Oriental Romance: Johnson and Beckford," in *Before Jane Austen: The Shaping of the Eighteenth Century*. New York: Holt, Rinehart, 1965, pp. 226–242.

STOCK, R.D. "Spiritual Horror in the Novel: Richardson, Radcliffe, Beckford, Lewis," in *The Holy and the Daemonic from Sir Thomas Browne to William Blake*. Princeton, NJ: Princeton UP, 1982, pp. 259–313.

SUMMERS, Montague. "Beckford, William Thomas of Fonthill (1760–1844)," in *A Gothic Bibliography*. London: Fortune Press, 1941; Rpt. New York: Russell & Russell, 1964, pp. 8–9.

_____. "The Abbot of Fonthill," *Everybody's Weekly*, November 23, 1946, p. 13.

THOMPSON, Karl F. "Henley's Share in Beckford's *Vathek*," *Philological Quarterly*, 31 (1952): 75–80.

_____. "Beckford, Byron, and Henley," *Etudes Anglaises*, 14 (1961): 225–228.

TRACY, Ann B. "William Beckford," in *The Gothic Novel 1790–1830: Plot Summaries and Index to Motifs*. Lexington, KY: UP of Kentucky, 1981, pp. 18–19.

VARMA, Devendra P. "The Schauer-Romantik: or Chambers of Horror," in *The Gothic Flame*. London: A. Barker, 1957; Rpt. New York: Russell & Russell, 1966, pp. 132–172.

_____. "William Beckford," in *Supernatural Fiction Writers*, ed. E.F. Bleiler. New York: Charles Scribner's, 1985, I, pp. 139–144.

VIGIL, Julian Josue. "A Nightmare in Literary Criticism," *New Mexico Highlands University Journal*, 1 (1979): 48–50.

WAGENKNECHT, Edward. "*Vathek* and the Oriental Tale," in *Cavalcade of the English Novel*. New York: Henry Holt, 1954, pp. 130–131.

WEITZMAN, Arthur J. "The Oriental Tale in the Eighteenth Century: A Reconsideration," *Studies in Voltaire and the Eighteenth Century*, 58 (1967): 1839–1855.

WHIBLY, Charles. "The Caliph of Fonthill," in *The Pageantry of Life*. New York: Harper, 1900, pp. 81–96.

"William Beckford and Islam," *Connoisseur*, 191 (1976): 250–253.

WILSON, Edmund. "Firbank and Beckford," in *The Shores of Light: A Literary Chronicle of the Twenties and Thirties*. New York: Farrar, Straus, and Young, 1952, pp. 264–266.

ZEIDLER, Karl. "Beckford, Hope und Morier als Vertreter des Orientalischen Romans," Unpublished Doctoral Dissertation, University of Leipzig, 1908.

# INDEX

Note: Characters from *Vathek* and *The Episodes* are in block capitals.